INTERCOUNTRY
ADOPTION
FROM CHINA

INTERCOUNTRY ADOPTION FROM CHINA

Examining Cultural Heritage and Other Postadoption Issues

Jay W. Rojewski and Jacy L. Rojewski

BERGIN & GARVEY
Westport, Connecticut · London

Library of Congress Cataloging-in-Publication Data

Rojewski, Jay W., 1959–
 Intercountry adoption from China : examining cultural heritage and other postadoption issues / Jay W. Rojewski and Jacy L. Rojewski.
  p. cm.
 Includes bibliographical references and index.
 ISBN 0–89789–754–4 (alk. paper)—0–89789–812–5 (pbk. : alk. paper)
 1. Intercountry adoption—China. 2. Intercountry adoption—United States. 3. Adoptive parents—Attitudes. 4. Ethnicity in children. 5. Multiculturalism I. Rojewski, Jacy L. II. Title.
 HV875.5.R64 2001
 362.73′4′0951—dc21   2001025176

British Library Cataloguing in Publication Data is available.

Library of Congress Catalog Card Number: 2001025176
ISBN: 0–89789–754–4
  0–89789–812–5 (pbk.)

First published in 2001

Bergin & Garvey, 88 Post Road West, Westport, CT 06881
An imprint of Greenwood Publishing Group, Inc.
www.greenwood.com

Printed in the United States of America

The paper used in this book complies with the Permanent Paper Standard issued by the National Information Standards Organization (Z39.48–1984).

10 9 8 7 6 5 4 3 2 1

Copyright Acknowledgments

The authors and publisher gratefully acknowledge permission for use of the following material:

Excerpts, reprinted with permission of The Free Press, a Division of Simon & Schuster, Inc., from *Are Those Kids Yours? American Families With Children From Other Countries* by Cheri Register. Copyright © 1991 by Cheri Register.

Excerpts from *Raising Adopted Children: Practical Reassuring Advice for Every Adoptive Parent* (Rev. ed.) by LOIS RUSKAI MELINA. Copyright © 1998 by Lois Ruskai Melina. Reprinted by permission of HarperCollins Publishers, Inc.

To our daughters
Emily
Who has brought us untold joy
And baby Claire
Who represents a new beginning for us all

Contents

Appendixes

Figures and Tables

Preface

"Don't you think you're overdoing it a bit on this Chinese thing?"
This question looms large for many parents with children adopted
from China. How do parents decide whether to introduce and nurture an appreciation for Chinese cultural values, traditions, and
heritage in their adopted children? What do adoptive parents do, if
anything, to instill a sense of cultural pride and ethnic identity in
their adopted child(ren)?

As parents ourselves of a four-year-old daughter adopted from
China and another on the way, we wonder how to best incorporate
Chinese culture, customs, and tradition into our daily lives. We
also think ahead on occasion and anticipate our daughters' experiences as adolescents and adults, their trials and tribulations, their
joys and triumphs. While a good deal of information has become
available in recent years on preadoption issues related to intercountry adoption in general, and adoption from China in particular, information concerning postadoption issues remains relatively
limited. While notable exceptions exist—for example, Tessler,
Gamache, and Liu (1999), Register (1991), Bartholet (1993a), and
Web sites such as *Families with Children from China, About Adoption,* and *Our Chinese Daughters Foundation*—most available in-

formation is fragmented throughout the professional and popular literature, on the World Wide Web, and through anecdotal reports.

The limited availability of information and resources does not, however, reflect a lack of parental interest or concern. In fact, a cursory review of e-mail messages posted to the post-adopt-china list on any given day quickly reveals the broad spectrum of issues and concerns important to adoptive parents.[1] Amid the more routine parenting questions and answers about toilet training, selection of day care, or reaching any one of a dozen different developmental milestones, other types of questions are posed that focus on cultural heritage, physical differences between parent and child, ways to handle negative racial comments, and concerns for the future of children who for all practical purposes are American but will always look and often be treated as Asian. Indeed, at the core of many questions about intercountry adoption is a concern about what it means to raise a child born in another country to a birth mother who made difficult decisions that are next to impossible for us to understand about her future and that of her newborn child.

We are interested in a host of questions that sometimes seem to multiply faster than we can understand them, let alone answer them. Consider some of these questions common to many parents who have adopted a child from China and professionals interested in supporting this process. What contexts exist that contribute to the availability of children, mostly girls, from the People's Republic of China? How do parents and professionals view these contexts? How do parents resolve the disparities that exist between themselves and their child's birth parents? How do parents address their views about race–ethnicity and the likelihood that they or their child will experience discrimination or prejudice? Can parents who for the most part represent the cultural majority adequately prepare their child(ren) to successfully cope with the likelihood of experiencing racial bias and discrimination?

In addition to these more general questions regarding parenting, specific questions about parents' views and practices are also important. Are developmental or adjustment issues like attachment or identity development problematic for adoptees? What is bicultural socialization? How do adoptive parents determine the right amount of Chinese culture and heritage to introduce into their family's lives? What types of activities or resources do parents use to expose their children to Chinese culture? Are some methods more effective than others? How do parents and other family members react to and cope with the demands placed on a bicultural or multicultural family? These questions are not by any means an exhaustive list of parental issues and concerns about the role of culture, heritage, race, and ethnicity in raising children adopted from China. They are, however, concerns adoptive parents often struggle to resolve.

The more we searched for relevant information to guide our own parenting decisions, the more convinced we became of the need to address these types of postadoption issues in a cohesive and systematic way. Gradually, the idea for an empirical investigation of how parents acknowledge the cultural heritage issues of children adopted from China emerged. We developed and administered a survey on the World Wide Web in the latter months of 1999 and the first few months of 2000. Several dozen in-depth interviews, via both e-mail and telephone, were also conducted with selected survey respondents and adoption professionals to elicit greater understanding and perspective. Portions of this book detail the results of our investigation and reflect, in part, the collective responses of over 300 families living across the United States and Canada with children adopted from China.

We also synthesize much of the current literature on intercountry adoption, taking a multidisciplined approach by drawing on findings from anthropology, sociology, psychology, and education. When appropriate, we include information obtained from reliable Internet Web sites. And when literature is lacking, particularly information about Chinese adoptees entering adolescence and adulthood, we use research on the status of domestic and other intercountry adoptee groups (e.g., Korean children adopted from the 1950s to the 1970s who are now themselves parents). Finally, while we occasionally rely on our personal experiences to frame questions or illustrate important points, this book is not about our personal adoption and parenting experiences, per se. Rather, we focus on issues related to acknowledging Chinese cultural heritage and on related adoption issues in families with children from China.

Up front, we acknowledge that answers to some of the questions we pose in this book are complex, incomplete, and at times contradictory. To complicate matters further, there are probably as many "right" answers to some of our queries about acknowledging Chinese cultural heritage to children adopted from China as there are adoptive families. Therefore, throughout the book we try to clarify the issues and provide alternative points of view. We hope that this approach will allow readers—including adoptive parents and professionals involved in aspects of intercountry adoption—to gain insight about the context that surrounds intercountry adoption from China, identify relevant questions and formulate answers about acknowledging Chinese cultural heritage, and take stock of issues that may influence the future personal development of child(ren) adopted from China.

We are indebted to many people who graciously provided us with their time and professional expertise in this endeavor. Nancy "Sass" Stanfield, the site guide for adoption at About.com, was one of the first people to contact us after we initiated the survey in November 1999. Her early interest in and support of our project, as well as her willingness to actively promote the existence of the survey, is truly appreciated. The Board of Directors of the Families with Children from China (FCC) Web site, particularly Charles Bouldin and Jim Weaver, responded promptly and positively to our request for assistance. This project would have enjoyed far less success without their support and promotion of our Web site survey. Individuals representing several regional FCC chapters also promoted the survey through chapter newsletter advertisements or Web site links, including Terry Fry and Amy Klatzkin (FCC–San Francisco), Ken and Carol Nelson (FCC–Chicago), Julie Michaels (FCC–New England), and Marlee Groening (FCC–British Columbia and Northwest Washington). Crystal Chaya and Betsy Gooch are consummate professionals who work tirelessly on behalf of children from China and their adoptive families. Their insights into various aspects of intercountry adoption were both reinforcing and enlightening.

Thoughtful insight and reaction to earlier drafts of our work were provided by H. David Kirk, Kay Johnson, Howard Altstein, Bill Feigelman, and Elizabeth Bartholet. We have great respect for these professionals and are grateful for the time they took from their own busy schedules to share their understanding of and experience with adoption-related issues. Finally, the assistance of Ms. Heeja Kim, a doctoral student at the University of Georgia, with background research, data entry, and analysis was invaluable. While this final product reflects the contributions of all the people mentioned, we are quick to note that any omissions or errors in this work are, ultimately, our responsibility.

We have valued the interest and support received from representatives of the Greenwood Publishing Group and their imprint, Bergin & Garvey. Special thanks to our acquisitions editor, Lynn Taylor, for her willingness to advance our project and see the potential that our initial proposal had to make a contribution to the literature on intercountry adoption.

We are especially thankful for the parents who responded to the Chinese adoption survey. Throughout the period of data collection, we were continually impressed with their degree of candor, depth of insight, and willingness to share information about their lives. They have entrusted us with their stories and perspectives in the hope that adoptive parents now and in the future may benefit. We are continually reminded of that collective act of trust and have worked hard to justify respondents' faith in us. We hope that through all of our efforts children adopted from China may grow up to be more successful, better adjusted, and happier in their adult lives.

To our family and friends we extend our love and appreciation. Like most, our parenting styles are modeled and shaped by the parenting we experienced as children. We thank our parents, Jim and Jan Rojewski and John and Wyllie Lessig, for teaching us well. We also want to acknowledge the place our siblings—Joy Henn, Jon Rojewski, Jed Rojewski, Jeff Godel, and John (Jay) Lessig— have in our hearts and daily lives. While distance separates us, we think of you all often. We also thank our close friends for their contributions to our adoption journey. On a warm fall evening several years ago, we told friends John and Barb Schell about our decision to adopt a child from China. Being the first people we told, their enthusiastic, warm embrace of our decision meant a great deal and sustained us in the early months of the adoption process. We treasure the friendship and support George and Susan Dougherty and their family have given us. Few have championed our parental and professional journeys more than George and Susan. We thank them for "adopting" us and allowing us to share their loving, caring family. The support and friendship of Jeff and Susan Maher have been a constant throughout the course of completing this book. In sharing our parenting experiences with one another we have gained better insight into the meaning of parenthood and friendship.

Finally, for our daughters Emily and Claire, we extend our deepest love and acknowledge the role they have played in our decision to pursue this project. We find ourselves marveling at their accomplishments and savor the moments we share with them on their paths to adulthood.

NOTE

1. For more information about or to subscribe to the post-adopt-china e-mail list, go to http://www.egroups.com/community/post-adopt-china.

Chapter 1

Background and Context of Intercountry Adoption and Research Study

> We are an internationally adoptive family. This is the heritage
> that we truly have "given" our children. Filling it out and giv-
> ing it meaning is a shared family endeavor, which we must
> undertake with deliberate care and sensitivity.
>
> Register, 1991, p. 182

In the early 1990s intercountry adoption from China was practically nonexistent. A decade or so later more than 23,000 Chinese
children have been adopted by people, single and married, living in
the United States and Canada, with many more adopted by families in Western European countries. What has caused thousands to
choose China as an avenue for adoption over other available options? And just who are these families? "The parents, in their 40s
and 50s, are obviously Caucasian, and their very young children
are obviously Chinese" (Tessler, Gamache, & Liu, 1999). Many questions can be posed when considering adoption from China, ranging
from parental concerns about child health or potential behavior
problems to the international debate about the underlying motives
for or outcomes of intercountry adoption. The questions raised are
more than mere curiosity. For despite the heightened interest in

and attention placed on the adoption of children—mostly young girls—from China, empirical and clinical investigations are relatively few and far between.

Available research on Chinese adoptees and others (e.g., Korean adoptees in the 1970s, Vietnamese and Columbian children in the 1980s, and Russian and Romanian children in the 1990s) has tended to focus on the initial and long-term physical and emotional adjustment of adopted children and families. While most empirical and clinical investigations on Chinese adoptees describe generally positive outcomes, results of studies on some important issues like family acknowledgment or rejection of differences, bonding and attachment, and identity development of intercountry adoptees are either nonexistent or inconclusive (Wilkinson, 1995). Relatively little is known about the scientific, psychological, or social issues surrounding children adopted from China and their parents (Kim, 1995).

As a result, we initiated an investigation of intercountry adoption from China, focusing specifically on postadoption issues like how adoptive parents acknowledge their child's Chinese cultural heritage. Was the issue important to them? If so, how did they acknowledge Chinese cultural heritage to their adopted child(ren) and other family members? What reasons did they give to explain their decisions? This book presents the results of our inquiry. In this first chapter we describe the historical context of intercountry adoption and then take a closer look at adoption from China. We also detail the quantitative and qualitative research design and methods we employed in conducting our Internet-based survey. Finally, we describe the adoptive parents who participated in our study and whose responses form a substantial portion of this book.

HISTORICAL CONTEXT

Increasingly, most people in the United States and other industrialized countries view adoption as an acceptable solution to infertility and a viable alternative for building a family, although it hasn't always been this way. In fact, the negative stigma surrounding adoption only diminished after the end of World War II (Kim, Hong, & Kim, 1979). At that time the intercountry adoption of European children orphaned by the war was essentially seen as a North American humanitarian gesture.[1] In the middle to late 1950s extensive humanitarian efforts were again initiated to bring children orphaned and abandoned as a result of the Korean War to the United States. Similar efforts also occurred in the early 1970s, when large numbers of children orphaned or abandoned during the Vietnam

War, as well as the offspring of American soldiers, were adopted by U.S. parents (Serbin, 1997; Tizard, 1991; Wilkinson, 1995).

The renewed interest in intercountry adoption that began in the early 1980s and continues to this day is quite different from these earlier, mostly humanitarian, efforts. Howard Altstein and Rita Simon (1991), noted adoption researchers, explained the differences this way: "In the mid-1940s, Western countries were interested in ICA [intercountry adoption] as a solution to the problem of parentless children. By the 1980s, their interest was sparked primarily by the needs of childless couples" (p. 1). In fact, the demand for babies to adopt has continued to increase in recent years, while the availability of adoptable babies and young children in the United States, Canada, and other industrialized countries has decreased. Studies cite a number of factors that contribute to fewer children available for adoption: lower fertility rates (and higher infertility rates) in Western industrialized countries, access to legalized abortion and birth control, decisions to delay marriage and starting families, increased independence for women, and a growing acceptance of single parenthood. As a result of some combination of these factors, many adoptive singles and couples have looked to other countries and cultures for adoptable children (Kim, 1995).

Regardless of adoptive parents' motives, intercountry adoption has steadily increased over the past decade to where the practice is now a permanent part of American culture (Deacon, 1997; Riley, 1997; Tizard, 1991). In 1989 a total of 7,948 intercountry adoptions were recorded by the U.S. Immigration and Naturalization Service (INS, 1999). This figure almost doubled to 15,774 in 1998. Annually, intercountry adoptions account for approximately 12 to 13 percent of all nonrelative adoptions in the United States.[2] While many countries are represented, a majority of intercountry adoptees come from Asia, Central America, and South America.

One country where international adoption has received increased attention over the past several years has been the People's Republic of China (PRC). Intercountry adoption from China by U.S. families has grown from 201 children in 1992 to 5,053 children in 2000 (FCC, 2000; see Figure 1.1). Currently, adoption from China accounts for 3.5 percent of all adoptions in the United States. Using INS immigration visas as a tally, from 1985 through 2000, 23,093 Chinese children, mostly girls, were adopted by U.S. parents (FCC, 2001). A comparable number of children were adopted by Canadian and Western European—primarily British, Scandinavian, Spanish, and Dutch—parents (Klatzkin, 1999).

Why the dramatic rise in intercountry adoptions from China? As with most other things connected to intercountry adoption, the

Figure 1.1
Intercountry Adoption of Children from China to the United States, 1985–1999

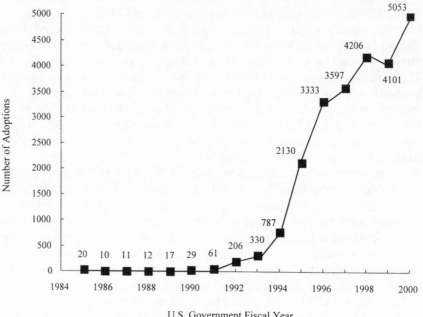

U.S. Government Fiscal Year

answer is complex and encompasses personal, historical, cultural, and political concerns. As we have tried to understand and describe the myriad factors that influence the adoption of children from China, we have been mindful that most Chinese do not condone child abandonment. However, they do understand and empathize with parents who experience constraints imposed by the government, the momentum of tradition and culture, personal needs and desires that may conflict with government policy, and the children that are born into the confluence of these pressures.

Child abandonment is not sanctioned by the Chinese government either, and is, in fact, subject to severe penalties. However, parents who abandon a child are rarely identified, prosecuted, or penalized. Conservative estimates place the number of children abandoned in China between 100,000 and 160,000 annually, although these figures are disputed by the Chinese government. Johnson, Huang, and Wang (1998) posited, "No one, including the Chinese government, truly knows how many children are abandoned each year" (p. 471). In an effort to relieve the heavy demands placed on state-run orphanages to provide for the care and well-being of abandoned children, Chinese adoption laws were enacted in 1991 that, in part, eased previously restrictive requirements for international adoption (Riley, 1997).[3]

The reasons for the increase in abandoned infants in China are complex, but include some combination of political, cultural, and social structures. Among these reasons are the role of family in Chinese society, the importance of sons, ideology and tradition regarding motherhood and women's roles in Chinese society, gender inequalities, and government fertility restrictions. Child abandonment increased substantially in the late 1980s and early 1990s, coinciding with the implementation of a somewhat more lenient birth policy—one son/two child—in rural areas and a more strict enforcement of existing one-child policies in urban areas. We take a closer look at two issues that have been identified as crucial: China's one-child policy, implemented in the late 1970s–early 1980s to control burgeoning Chinese population growth, and a preference in China's patriarchal society for sons over daughters.

The one-child policy, instituted by the People's Republic of China in 1979, was a response by the Chinese government to the country's exploding population growth. Dire consequences were predicted if population growth rates were left unchecked. Government officials justified their regulation of Chinese citizens' reproductive rights and the strictness of the policy as being in the best interest of China's social and economic development. Government-subsidized incentives are given to couples who abide by the policy, including financial, educational, and health allowances. A variety of methods are available to enforce birth policies, ranging from the monitoring of individuals' reproductive behavior to more coercive measures such as forced sterilization and abortion. Various penalties, including 5- to 20-percent cuts in annual income, also exist for those not abiding by the policies (Vonk, Simms, & Nackerud, 1999).

Far from simple, the one-child policy does not merely reduce to "one child, one family." Rather, the policy is vigorously enforced for families living in urban and densely populated areas, while rural Chinese families, which constitute roughly 70 to 75 percent of the population, are likely to adhere to a one son/two child policy. In these circumstances, if the firstborn child is a boy then no more children are allowed, but if it is a girl then couples are allowed to try again after a set waiting period (Johnson et al., 1998; Klatzkin, 1999). While the one son/two child policy was expected to lower the rate of child abandonment, rates actually increased. In fact, Johnson (1996; Johnson et al., 1998) reported that the efforts of the Chinese to establish, implement, and enforce birth-planning policies has been directly related to the incidence of child abandonment.

What little is known about the abandonment of Chinese children, including the parents of these children, is gleaned from the work of Johnson and colleagues (1998). Despite the threat of being discovered and severely punished, Johnson and her colleagues were able to locate and interview 237 Chinese parents who had abandoned a child. Information they provided gave us a tantalizing glimpse into their lives and thoughts. All but three of the participants were married. A majority lived in rural areas, with approximately one-third listing agriculture as their primary occupation. On the whole, abandoning parents held average educational and income levels for their areas of residence. At the time of abandonment, parents' ages ranged from the mid-twenties through late thirties.

Birth fathers were the ones who decided to abandon a child, almost always a daughter, in about half of the cases studied by Johnson and colleagues (1998). Both birth parents mutually arrived at an abandonment decision another 40 percent of the time. The primary reasons for deciding to abandon a birth child were gender, birth order, and the gender of other siblings. One of Johnson and colleagues' most interesting findings was that 87 percent of abandoned girls in their investigation had no brothers, but two-thirds had one (35%) or two biological sisters (32%). Only 5.5 percent of abandoned children were first daughters without siblings. In fact, Kay Johnson's (1996; Johnson et al., 1998) groundbreaking research revealed that firstborn girls in China are often kept in the family.[4] However, if the second (or third or fourth) child is also a girl, she is likely to be abandoned in the hope of giving birth to a male child. Thus, the typical profile of an abandoned child is a healthy newborn girl with one or more older sisters and no brothers. Birth parents often expressed a reluctance to abandon their daughter but felt they had no choice given China's birth-control policies.

For a host of historical and cultural reasons, a preference exists in Chinese society for sons over daughters. In a patriarchal society like China, sons are valued because they will carry on the family name. Equally important, sons are expected to care for parents in their old age. Conversely, girls will marry, become part of their husband's family, and be expected to help with the support of their in-laws.[5] Securing care from one's children in old age is important, especially "in economically underdeveloped rural areas of China where there are no equivalents of social security or pension programs" (Tessler et al., 1999, p. 85). Major social changes also contribute to the abandonment of baby girls in China, including migration from rural to urban areas, changes in government, and unprecedented economic development.

Several conditions in the United States have also contributed to the rise in intercountry adoption from China. For many childless individuals and couples, the adoption process in the United States is simply too difficult. The scarcity of babies available for adoption in the United States typically results in lengthy waiting periods of up to seven years or more for even a chance at adoption. In contrast, the availability of infants in most countries where intercountry adoptions occur, including China, where infants from six to nine months of age and older can be adopted, make foreign adoption especially attractive for some parents (Stolley, 1993). Bureaucracy and uncertain legal issues associated with domestic adoptions are also cited as reasons for turning to intercountry adoption. Sensationalized stories of birth parents attempting to regain custody of their relinquished children are in sharp contrast to most intercountry adoptions, where birth parents have no knowledge about the future whereabouts or condition of their abandoned children. Some prospective parents view the requirements associated with open adoption as too demanding from emotional, financial, and practical perspectives. The need for parents to advertise themselves to potential birth mothers and the selection of an adoptive couple by the birth mother are viewed as too competitive and uncertain (Alperson, 1997).

THE CHINESE ADOPTION STUDY

Design

Much of this book describes and discusses results from the Chinese Adoption Study we conducted from November 1, 1999 to April 30, 2000. During this time we administered an Internet-based survey that asked a series of questions related to the practices and beliefs of adoptive parents about acknowledging intercountry adoption and Chinese cultural heritage to children adopted from China.

Sampling

Our decision to use the Internet for data collection is relatively unique and not without limitations. Despite use of the World Wide Web (WWW) for literally thousands of informal surveys, marketing queries, and polls, surprisingly limited scholarly literature is available on the use of this technology to conduct empirical investigations. Even so, researchers have generally been quite enthusiastic about the unprecedented possibilities represented by the Internet

(Coomber, 1997; Jaisingani & Jain, 1998). The potential benefits of using the WWW include ready access to a large and dispersed population, and savings of both time and money for conducting survey research. Coomber examined the relative merits of WWW-based questionnaires and concluded that "the Internet can be a valuable source of *indicative* as opposed to easily *generalized* data" (emphasis added).

Despite the potential benefits represented by the Internet, limitations have also been identified. Coomber (1997) observed that the methodological issues raised by Web-based surveys are not new to survey research. However, one difficulty unique to WWW surveys is that the population of interest must have access to the Internet and be savvy enough to use it (Smith, 1997). Access to the WWW is also part of a larger issue—the method of sampling.

Most Internet-based surveys employ a form of nonprobability convenience sampling based on self-selection (volunteering) that relies on user awareness of the survey for participation. Bradley (n.d.) considered this feature to be unique to WWW-based surveys, and it is, perhaps, the most critical problem encountered when Internet-based surveys are used. Fisher, Margolis, and Resnik (1996) flatly declared that getting a representative sample from the Internet was a virtual impossibility and that no comprehensive solutions exist. It is likely our study includes some degree of coverage error (i.e., a failure to survey certain portions of an eligible population; Schmidt, 1997). As a result, our ability to generalize to all families of children adopted from China is reduced, since individuals who were not aware of or chose not to participate in the survey may differ from parents who completed the survey (GVU's WWW Surveying Team, n.d.). To minimize concerns of coverage error, we compare the demographic information of our respondents with our knowledge of the population of adoptive parents and their children from China as a whole to establish the representativeness of our sample.

To address the problem of survey visibility or exposure, we chose several of the recruitment methods described by Schmidt (1997) to advertise the existence of our questionnaire. First, we registered our Web site with ten major Internet search engines (e.g., Alta Vista, Yahoo, HotBot, AOL, etc.). Second, we advertised our Web site on several large, "high-traffic" adoption-related Internet sites, including the adoption site at About.com and Families with Children from China. Several regional FCC chapters—San Francisco, Chicago, New England, British Columbia, and Northwest Washington—also promoted the survey through chapter newsletter advertisements or Web-site links. Finally, we made three separate announcements at six-week intervals on two e-mail lists that focus on pre- and post-adoption issues for families with children from China: a-parents-china and post-adopt-china.

Coomber (1997) asserted that "while it is proper, indeed essential, to point out the problems with data derived from restricted sampling, it is also worth remembering that such data can also lead research in new and exciting directions." In addition to our hope of finding "new and exciting directions," we chose to use the Internet for data collection because of several factors. One of our primary concerns was not having easy access to a national population of parents with children adopted from China. We felt the Internet provided the best alternative strategy to reach adoptive parents from across the country who would, in all likelihood, have contracted with a host of different adoption agencies and hold varying perspectives on intercountry adoption and parenting. Internet surveys are especially well suited for accessing a group of individuals who share interest in a narrow topic domain, and provide a way to access these individuals based on the content of their interest. Other considerations in our decision were the relatively low cost and time effectiveness of WWW-based surveys, the quick turnaround times for data collection, an ability to span geographic boundaries, receipt of responses that are not bound by time but guided by user convenience, and the notion that the anonymity of the WWW may provide more candid responses (Jaisingani & Jain, 1998; Smith, 1997).

Web Site

The adoption study Web site (http://www.negia.net/~jwrjlr) consisted of seven separate Web pages that described the purpose of the study, explained informed consent and confidentiality, posed the survey questions, provided opportunities for contact with us, and thanked respondents for their participation. We felt that two issues—confidentiality and informed consent—were important issues given the nature of our investigation. Preliminary information stressed that personal identities and answers would remain confidential, meaning that responses would not be individually identified or distributed, unless required by law. A five-digit code provided by respondents was used for tracking purposes. We also reminded visitors to the Web site that they were under no obligation to complete the survey (i.e., participation in the research project was entirely voluntary).

Participating Families and Children

Participating Families and Households

During the six months we collected data, our Web site received in excess of 3,400 "hits" that resulted in 339 completed and useable surveys from parents (households) with children adopted from China. To avoid potential problems—missing data, receiving data from only one spouse, nonparticipation, inability to generalize to families in survey—we collected data from only one parent per household. While spouses do not necessarily agree on all aspects of child rearing, we assumed that survey responses would reflect prevailing views and practices for the entire family. Our assumption is based on an expectation that more women were likely to respond to our survey, reflecting an "acceptance of traditional gender roles in which mothers take more responsibility for children" (Tessler et al., 1999, p. 71).

As expected, an overwhelming number of respondents to our survey were female (n = 289, 85.3%), Caucasian (n = 310, 91.5%)—3.8 percent were Asian American—and married (n = 234, 69.0%). Eighty-two respondents (24.2%) reported being single parents. Slightly more than one-third (n = 117) of responding families had additional children in the household, 51.7 percent by birth and 48.3 percent adopted. Respondents were geographically dispersed throughout North America: Forty-five states, the District of Columbia, and Canada were represented. The largest groups of responses came from the northeastern (n = 98) and western United States (n = 81). Individual states with the largest representation included California (n = 32), Pennsylvania and Texas (n = 16 per state), and New York and Washington (n = 15 per state). Cumulatively, these five states accounted for one-quarter (27.7%) of all survey respondents.[6]

The age of survey participants ranged from a low of 25 to a high of 56 years old. The mean age was 42.7 years old (sd = 5.0 years), with two-thirds of the sample between 37 and 48 years of age. Respondents were highly educated. Almost one-half of the sample (n = 164) had obtained some level of graduate education, with an additional 38.1 percent (n = 129) reporting the completion of a college degree.

Information about spouses, mostly male and Caucasian, was also requested when appropriate. The age of spouses ranged from 25 to 67 years old (M = 43.9, sd = 7.5), with two-thirds between 37 and 51 years of age. Spouses were also highly educated, although at a slightly lower level than respondents. Of 234 spouses, over 45 percent (n = 108) held a graduate-level degree, while an additional one-third had a college degree (n = 77). Forty-six spouses (19.7%) had received some postsecondary technical school training or a community college degree.

Chinese Adoptees

Three hundred thirty-nine Chinese adoptees, almost exclusively female (n = 323), were represented by those completing the survey. The age of adopted children at the time of survey completion ranged from a low of two months to a high of 13.3 years, with a median age of 3.1 years (M = 3.3 years, sd = 2.1 years). Almost half of the adoptees (n = 160) were 3 years of age or younger. Children were placed in their adoptive families, on average, at thirteen months of age (sd = 10.7 months). Slightly over half of all children were placed between eight and fourteen months of age.

Most parents know very little about the circumstances surrounding the abandonment of their children. Two-thirds of parents (n = 230) had some knowledge of their child's abandonment, although information was almost exclusively based on Chinese police or orphanage reports. Based on available information, 79.7 percent of all adoptees were found abandoned and placed in a Chinese orphanage within the first four weeks of their lives. The greatest proportion of children, 40.1 percent, were found abandoned at one week of age or less, while an additional 9.4 percent were abandoned at two weeks of age. Approximately two-thirds of adoptees (n = 222) spent twelve months or less in an orphanage before adoption, with times ranging from as little as two months to as long as 9.25 years.[7]

Since we relied on a nonprobability sampling strategy to secure respondents, our ability to account for possible threats to external validity—self-selection bias, nonrepresentative sample, lack of generalization—is unknown. We sought to reduce these threats by determining the possible distinctiveness or similarity of our sample to other research samples of parents involved in intercountry adoption. Two questions were pursued: What information is available in the empirical literature about the type of people who pursue intercountry adoption from China? Who are the children adopted from China and what are their preadoption experiences?

Unfortunately, there is no comprehensive information currently available on the particular characteristics of parents with children adopted from China (or any other country), nor the children who are adopted (Bartholet, 1993b; National Adoption Information Clearinghouse, 1999c; Riley, 1997). However, the literature does provide some clues as to the general demographic composition of adoptive parents and Chinese adoptees.

As a general profile, parents who adopt foreign-born children are likely to be white, in their late thirties to early forties, college educated, live in the suburbs, have higher levels of income, be childless, and turn to intercountry adoption as a result of infertility (Register, 1991). Table 1.1 provides a summary of the demographic composition of our parent sample, as well as that of parents from three recent studies that investigated Chinese adoption. The similarity of parent demographic profiles in these four studies is an apparent indication that these samples each represent the same general population of intercountry adoptive parents, although not necessarily the population of all families with children adopted from China.

What do we know about the demographic composition of intercountry adoptees from China? Although not broken out by nationality, information from the National Adoption Information Clearinghouse (1999b) indicates that of all intercountry adoptions that occurred in fiscal year 1997, 73.5 percent were female. Almost half of all intercountry adoptees (47%) were under one year of age at the time of adoption, while 41 percent were between the ages of one and four. We did not interview or collect data directly from adopted children, given their young age and our interest in parenting issues. However, we did ask parents for some demographic information about their adopted children to establish a profile. The bottom half of Table 1.1 displays descriptive information obtained from our study and the three other studies. Descriptions of adoptees included in these past investigations are similar in many respects, both to each other and to the data collected from our sample.

Again, while not conclusive evidence of the representativeness of our sample, we did find a common profile shared by the adoptees in our sample and in other studies on intercountry (Chinese) adoption. We have no way, however, to determine if differences exist between parents who completed our survey and those who did not respond. It is likely that parents who responded are more positive about their adoptive experiences and more actively involved in issues related to adoption, child rearing, and Chinese culture and heritage.[8] Kirk (1984) noticed a positive bias of parents who responded to an adoption-related mail questionnaire, concluding that "we can now feel confident that the response rate is an index of the degree of involvement in the adoptive parental role" (p. 80). Interestingly, two of our respondents also commented on the possibilities for sample bias. One father commented, "I imagine that you realize that you have a non-random biased sample. There are adoptive parents who don't give a damn about China or its culture, but

Table 1.1
Demographic Composition of Parents and Chinese Adoptees from Selected Studies on Intercountry Adoption

Demographic Characteristics	Chinese Adoption Study (2000)		Tessler, Gamache, & Liu (1999)		Rojewski, Shapiro, & Shapiro (2000)		Trolley, Wallin, & Hansen (1995)	
PARENTS	n = 339		n = 526		n = 44		n = 34	
Gender	Female	85.3%	Female	68.0%	Not available		Not available	
	Male	12.4%	Male	32.0%				
Marital status	Married	69.0%	Married	81.0%	Not available		Married	100.0%
	Single	24.2%	Single	19.0%				
Age	M = 42.7 yrs		Mdn = 42.7 yrs		Range: 35–50 yrs		M = 38.9 yrs	
	Mdn = 43.0 yrs						Range: 31–45 yrs	
	Range: 25–56 yrs							
Race-ethnicity	White	91.5%	White	96.0%	White	100.0%	White	100.0%
Education level	College	38.1%	College	35.0%	Not available		College	55.8%
	Postgraduate	48.4%	Postgraduate	65.0%			Postgraduate	44.0%
ADOPTEES	n = 339		n = 391[a]		n = 45		n = 47	
Gender	Female	95.3%	Female	97.4%	Female	86.7%	Female	56.3%
	Male	2.1%	Male	2.6%	Male	13.3%	Male	43.7%
Age at adoption	M = 13.0 mos		Not available		Mdn = 15.0 mos		M = 4.26 yrs	
	Mdn = 10.3 mos				Range: 1 mo–7 yrs		Range: infant–10 yrs	
	Range: 1 mo–5.5 yrs							
Current age	M = 3.3 yrs		M = 2.1 yrs		Mdn = 43 mos		M = 6.02 yrs	
	Mdn = 3.1 yrs		Range: 6 mos–7 yrs		Range: 22 mos–9 yrs		Range: 8 mos–15 yrs	
	Range: 2 mos–13.3 yrs							
Race-ethnicity	Chinese	100.0%	Chinese	76.4%	Chinese	100.0%	Asian	54.5%
			USA	2.7%			Latin American	17.5%
			Korea, Peru, or				White	15.0%
			Thailand	1.2%				
			Biological	19.7%				
Residence[b]	Northeast	28.9%	Massachusetts	27.0%	Not available		Not available	
	West	23.9%	Midwest	22.0%				
	Midwest	18.9%	Northeast	19.0%				
	Southeast	14.8%	California	11.0%				

[a] A total of 512 children in 316 households were included in Tessler and colleagues' (1999) final survey results. Only 391 were discussed in the bulk of their text.

[b] Candian respondents totaled 7.8 percent of the final data pool.

these people are not likely to log on." Another respondent observed that "people who are willing to do this [complete the survey] do have strong ties to their child's Chinese heritage, those that are not into the Chinese culture probably would not take the time to respond as things like this are not important to them." We agree.

Data Collection

Survey

The survey instrument we used consisted of four parts: (1) general information about adoptees, (2) parent (family) demographic data, (3) questions about parents' attitudes toward adoption, and (4) a cultural attitude survey.

The first part of the questionnaire asked for information about the adoptee's abandonment, institutional life in China, and a series of questions about initial and current development in language, learning, social-emotional, eye-hand coordination, and physical skills. Part two of the survey asked for information about the respondent and, if applicable, his or her spouse. Demographic information such as gender, race, age, educational levels, and presence of other children in the family were recorded.

Several previously developed questionnaires were selected as a starting point for developing sections three and four of the survey. Part of a questionnaire developed by sociologist H. David Kirk (1988), "Attitudes Toward Adoption" (ATA), was adapted to assess parent's acknowledgement of adoption. The ATA contains questions that pertain to the disclosure and discussion of adoption with grandparents and children, the celebration of anniversaries or other special events related to adoption, and parents' reactions to racial (physical) differences between parents and adoptees. Kirk reported acceptable validity and reliability measures for this instrument, which he used in his seminal adoption research. We decided to add several questions that asked parents (1) why they decided to adopt a child in general, and from China in particular, and (2) if they had experienced any discrimination, bias, or prejudice as a result of their decision.

A second series of questions, adapted from *The Culture Form* (Trolley, Wallin, & Hansen, 1995), provided the basis for assessing if and how parents acknowledged Chinese culture in their households and daily lives. Culture questions focused on two primary issues: (1) parents' perceptions of the relevance and importance of acknowledging China as their children's birth country, and (2) the methods and frequency used to introduce aspects of Chinese culture and heritage to their adopted children.

Questionnaire items in the third and fourth sections of the survey included space to allow written feedback. We encouraged feedback and treated all written responses as qualitative data. Comments were often quite useful in explaining difficult answers or emphasizing points of concern for respondents.

Qualitative Data: Focused Interviews

In addition to our Web survey, we interviewed several dozen families with children adopted from China, as well as others associated with intercountry adoption—adoption agency liaisons, social workers, and so forth—in order to probe certain areas of interest. We selected most interviewees from those responding to our adoption survey using several qualitative sampling techniques. We looked for both "typical" and "extreme" cases, usually through open-ended written responses, to obtain multiple perspectives about the postadoption issues we studied (Creswell, 1998). We used a constant comparative method to examine interviews. New information was compared to emerging categories in a continual cycle of comparison and revision. While this method is typically used with categories linked together by theory, it is applicable when developing purely descriptive categories as well (Gall, Borg, & Gall, 1996). We discontinued our interviews when it appeared that we had saturated our categories of interest. In all cases, when we report qualitative information, pseudonyms are used to protect parents' confidentiality.

REMAINDER OF THE BOOK

The next two chapters provide additional context and focus on the philosophical differences expressed by various parties connected to intercountry adoption (Chapter 2), and the process of completing intercountry adoption (Chapter 3). In both chapters we are concerned primarily with preadoption issues and in describing how parents react to these issues.

In the second part of the book we synthesize the available research literature on Chinese adoptees and use the results of our investigation to examine selected postadoption issues. Chapter 4 describes our current understanding of the short- and long-term adjustment of intercountry adoptees. Issues of parent–child attachment and physical and mental development in adopted children are examined in depth. Chapter 5 takes a look at how parents acknowledge their children's adoption and recognize Chinese cultural heritage in their families. The implications of being a multicultural family are important concerns that are presented and discussed. We look specifically at experiences of discrimination or prejudice and the reactions of other people in Chapter 6. One area that we did not originally set out to examine but clearly emerged as an important issue during data analysis was the perspective of traditional versus preferential adopters (Feigelman & Silverman, 1983).

Preferential adoptions are those that are completed for reasons other than infertility, including families with other children—either birth or adopted—in the home, and single parents who adopt. Chapter 7 synthesizes our findings for these two groups of preferential adopters and lends their "voices" to aid in our understanding of the reasons and challenges they encounter.

The challenges that parents and their children from China may encounter as they enter adolescence, such as racial identity development and the long-term consequences of living in a multicultural family, are examined in Chapter 8. Although most Chinese adoptees are relatively young, the literature on other groups of intercountry adoptees, particularly from Korea, is reviewed in an effort to anticipate the possible psychological and social impact of a foreign-born child adopted by an American family. In the final chapter we reflect briefly on our major findings, consider the current state of the field of intercountry adoption from China, and look ahead by suggesting several lines of inquiry and major issues that should be considered in future studies.

NOTES

1. Adoption can be broken down into three categories: domestic (also referred to as in-country or national), intercountry, and international. Domestic adoption involves a child and adoptive parents of the same nationality and the same country of residence. Intercounty adoption involves a change in the child's country of residence (birth country), regardless of adoptive parents' nationality. International adoption involves parents whose nationality differs from the adopted child, regardless of the parents' country of residence (UNICEF International Child Development Centre, 1999). Using these definitions, a Chinese girl adopted by a couple living in the United States would reflect an intercountry but not necessarily international adoption. If the girl was adopted by U.S. citizens with permanent residence in China, the adoption would be considered international. The adoption could be considered both intercountry and international if the girl was adopted by U.S. citizens living in the United States. We focus primarily on Chinese children adopted by U.S. and Canadian citizens residing in the United States or Canada.

2. No current public or private attempts exist to collect comprehensive national data on adoption (National Adoption Information Clearinghouse, 1999c; Stolley, 1993). We based our estimates on the number of orphan visas issued for intercountry adoption in fiscal year 1998 (15,774 total; 4,206 from China), and a figure of approximately 120,000 completed adoptions per year in the United States.

3. Domestic and international adoptions in China were allowed prior to 1991 under various provincial regulations that reflected common governmental guidelines, although foreign adoptive parents were subject to

the same requirements as those stipulated for native Chinese. Foreign adopters also had to be of Chinese ancestry or considered "special friends of China," meaning that a long relationship or involvement in China was evident. In December 1991 the 23rd Session of the Seventh National Plenum Conference Standing Committee established China's first national adoption laws. Soon after, "Measures on the Adoption of Children by Aliens in the People's Republic of China" was issued. The 1991 law did away with any mention of special stipulations on foreign adopters and signaled a clear change in the PRC's approach to international adoption (personal communication, Kay Johnson, 2000). In November 1998 the National Plenum Conference passed "Decision on the Amendment of the Adoption Law of the People's Republic of China," which was implemented April 1, 1999. The amendments made three alterations to Chinese adoption law: (1) stipulations for eligibility to adopt were eased, (2) the process of adoption was unified throughout China and enhanced, and (3) the purpose of Chinese adoption law was clearly stated to facilitate rational and legitimate adoption (Wei, 1999).

4. Dr. Kay Johnson (1996; Johnson et al., 1998) provides several excellent references that systematically detail the political, social, and personal aspects of child abandonment and adoption in China. We highly recommend Johnson's works for those interested in a closer look at these issues.

5. Pearl S. Buck's (1972) *The Good Earth*, a novel written in 1931 about a Chinese farmer and his family, does a reasonable job at providing readers with a sense of the prevailing attitudes held toward women in traditional Chinese society. Buck's portrayal of women has drawn criticism, however, from some scholars. In addition, socialization patterns in modern Communist Chinese society lessen the accuracy of her portrayals. Incidentally, Buck was a determined advocate for homeless children in China and other Asian countries. She was committed to advancing adoption-related issues as well. Not only was she the founder of *Welcome House*, the first international transracial adoption agency in the United States, but seven of her eight children were adopted (K. Evans, 2000): "The fact that American parents now regularly travel to China and other countries in Asia and return with a child can be traced in part to her battle against the barriers to transracial adoption. She argued pervasively that race should not be a factor in finding homes for children" (p. 136).

6. According to the Immigration and Naturalization Service (cited by National Adoption Information Clearinghouse, 1999b), individual states with the highest number of intercountry adoptions (all countries combined) included New York ($n = 1,232$), California ($n = 1,102$), Pennsylvania ($n = 916$), Illinois ($n = 662$), and New Jersey ($n = 662$) for fiscal year (FY) 1998; and New York ($n = 1,134$), California ($n = 919$), Illinois ($n = 698$), Pennsylvania ($n = 694$), and New Jersey ($n = 652$) for FY1997.

7. Recent data (Stirling, 2000) indicates that the length of time required by the Chinese Center for Adoptive Affairs (CCAA) to process a completed dossier (from the date an application is sent to the CCAA until adoptive parents receive a referral) averages 217 days. Adoptive parents wait, on average, 58 days from referral to their actual travel to China. The

average age of children at the time of referral is nine months. These figures have been compiled from data volunteered by prospective adoptive parents subscribed to the APC e-mail list. Since list members represent only a small subset of all parents adopting from China, it is not possible to determine the representativeness of this data to the entire population of adoptive parents. However, Stirling estimates that his data represents approximately 16.3 percent of the total number of entry visas issued by the U.S. State Department for Chinese adoptees during FY1999 and 16.4 percent of all Chinese adoptions during FY1998.

8. Serbin (1997) points out that adoptive parents' (1) experiences during and after the adoption process and (2) perceptions of motives or premises behind the research project "are likely to influence both their willingness to participate in research and the way they respond" (p. 87).

Chapter 2

Philosophical Issues and Concerns Surrounding Intercountry Adoption

"Made in China"—the imprint indicating that a product's origin was China can be seen everywhere, on the bottom of a coffee mug, the side of a plastic toy, the tag of a new blouse. But does the label also reflect the practice of intercountry adoption? Is the label indicative of a practice that is associated with the "export" of children from poorer or less-developed countries to affluent and powerful ones, where children are traded like commodities? Adopting across racial, economic, cultural, and national boundaries can raise complex questions. In this chapter we examine some of the issues that frame the dialogue of those that support or oppose intercountry adoption, and look at what the empirical evidence has found about these concerns.

Views toward intercountry adoption can influence the pre- and postadoption experiences for the children, parents, and countries involved. Take, for example, the situation in South Korea. From the 1950s through the 1970s South Korea was the main provider of infants and small children to the United States and Western Europe. In 1986 alone, 6,510 Korean children were adopted by parents living in the United States (Kane, 1993). However, the situation changed dramatically in the late 1980s. The South Korean government became increasingly sensitive to outside pressures and criticism by other countries, especially North Korea, of their wholesale involvement in intercountry adoption. In 1988 the tension in South Korea associated with intercountry adoption reached a critical point when the practice was scrutinized on the world stage by newspaper and television media covering the Olympic games in Seoul. Reporters characterized the practice as shameful, resulting in substantial embarrassment to the South Korean government. Shortly after this incident, international adoption was sharply curtailed. Now, over ten years later, less than 2,000 Korean children are adopted annually by U.S. citizens (National Adoption Information Clearinghouse, 1999b).[1] From an historical perspective, the situation in South Korea is unusual for the intensity of criticism levied and the worldwide scope of attention placed on its intercountry adoption practices.

Many of the arguments used to challenge South Korean intercountry adoption are still used today to support or oppose the practice. Too often, however, perspectives about intercountry adoption are presented in overly simplified, dichotomous, and absolute terms. Proponents are characterized as basing their support for intercountry adoption on the singular humanitarian concern for abandoned children and the "right" of children to a loving, caring family. Detractors, on the other hand, are said to oppose the practice because it reflects an attempt to legitimize a profitable market for selling babies, the human capital of less-developed countries, to people in the industrialized powers of the West (Simon & Altstein, 1991). Who's right? Where do parents fit into this scenario? Perhaps more important, how can parents resolve the possible conflicts this issue raises?

The debate over intercountry adoption is made more difficult, at least to the uninitiated, because of the highly politicized and sometimes emotional nature of the arguments advanced by individuals and groups connected by the practice. Saclier (1999) warned that "the passions the topic unleashes, in both countries of origin and receiving countries, distort information, confuse people's thinking and make action difficult and risky" (p. 12). The misinformation and confusion that can exist is particularly evident when viewing television or newspaper reports on international adoption.

Media reports can never give the full picture. And they have a devastating effect on the children here, who may be whispered about by adults who've seen inaccurate programs, and on the children overseas, who may never be adopted because of misplaced fears of prospective parents. They can also cause countries to close their doors to placing their children in intercountry adoption, due to embarrassment or anger about media reports. Ultimately, many of these reports . . . do more harm than good. (Evans, 1997, p. 4)

SUPPORT FOR AND OPPOSITION TO INTERCOUNTRY ADOPTION

The intensity of political arguments concerning intercountry adoption have waxed and waned over the past several decades. Throughout this time, however, one fact has remained constant. The empirical literature on intercountry (and transracial) adoption has consistently discounted all claims of intellectual, social, or emotional harm to adoptees as a result of the practice.[2] Simply, there is no factual basis for the arguments used to oppose intercountry adoption. They are without merit. However, political arguments remain intact, fueled by erroneous beliefs about the relationship of race, racial and cultural affiliation, and national identity to individual well-being. In summarizing their thirty-plus-year longitudinal study of transracial adoption (including intercountry adoptees), Simon and Altstein (2000) concluded,

The conviction that race is the overpowering predictor in a person's life dies hard. Despite all the positive experiences described by adult transracial adoptees of growing up in White families, which were reported in the professional literature of several disciplines, despite very strongly worded federal legislation prohibiting the use of race in adoption and foster care . . . organizations continue to support the use of race as vital to a child's best interests. Political correctness, it seems, keeps some organizations behind the curve of empirical evidence, social attitudes, and federal statutes. (pp. 144–145)

Similarly, Triseliotis, Shireman, and Hundleby (1997) concluded that "in spite of methodological and definition problems [identified in some investigations on intercountry adoption], and despite a number of contradictions in the research findings, there is an interesting degree of consensus, suggesting on the whole favorable outcomes" (p. 187). Yet despite an ever-increasing body of scholarly work that supports intercountry and transracial adoption, detractors are still vocal about their opposition.

One argument against intercountry adoption reflects a critical perspective, a view of the world where reality is constructed on the basis of political and economic power. In the aftermath of World War II the primary problems encountered with intercountry adoption were related to adjusting the different legal systems found in sending (birth) and receiving (adopted) countries. Today, global concerns focus less on procedural incompatibility and more on charges that the practice exploits women and children from economically undeveloped and underdeveloped countries (UNICEF International Child Development Centre, 1999). Much of the opposition to intercountry adoption stems from rising political pressures and nationalism in the Third World, where it is argued that "the practice is a new form of colonialism, with wealthy Westerners robbing poor countries of their children, and thus their resources" (Tizard, 1991, p. 746).

Bartholet (1993a), for one, voiced a strong reaction to the accusation that intercountry adoption promoted the exploitation of less-powerful countries and people. The discourse over intercountry adoption, she said, has little to do with the treatment of and concern for individuals. Rather, it "has to do with how national communities perceive their *group* interests. Children are the innocent victims, symbolic pawns sacrificed to notions of group pride and honor. . . . Poor countries feel pressure to hold on to what they term 'their precious resources'" (pp. 159–160, emphasis added).

Critics charge that intercountry adoption draws public attention and limited resources away from necessary government reforms in sending countries, thus making it more difficult to provide services for the children that remain behind. Bartholet (1993a) argued that just the opposite is true. She posited that intercountry adoption can bring attention to the plight of abandoned and homeless children. Increased awareness in the United States and elsewhere about the situation faced by children in other countries is likely to "create a climate that is more sympathetic to wide-ranging forms of support for children everywhere" (p. 152).

Some argue that separating children from their birth culture and heritage is devastating and can result in long-term, perhaps lifetime, difficulties with adjustment and identity development. A number of potential problems have been identified, such as genealogical bewilderment, problems with the parent–child relationship, loss of affiliation with racial or ethnic group(s), and a loss of heritage sometimes referred to as "genealogical genocide" (Serbin, 1997; Trolley, 1995). The resolution of these problems is purported to be complicated and intense for intercountry (and transracial) adoptees. To date, however, there is no empirical evidence available to establish the validity to these claims (Bartholet, 1993a, 1993b; Fieweger, 1991; Friendlander, 1999; Westhues & Cohen, 1998a).

Another argument concerns the increased exposure to racial discrimination and prejudice intercountry adoptees face because they are taken from their birth countries. Critics charge that adoptive parents—mostly white, older, and middle or upper class—may be quite sincere and willing to support their adopted child but are ill-equipped to handle the issues of discrimination and racism that their adopted children will undoubtedly experience.

It would be wrong to suggest that intercountry adoptees will not face discrimination and other forms of bias in their adoptive country because of their racial or ethnic minority status. Most likely, they will. However, Bartholet (1993a) found no evidence to suggest that the experiences of intercountry adoptees are somehow worse than for others who experience racism and discrimination. The false romanticization of culture or ethnic heritage and national identity, and the subsequent dangers to children who lose this group identity, implies that these problems would not exist if children remained in their birth country. In fact, orphaned and abandoned children are often exposed to the most severe forms of discrimination in their own countries because of their homeless status. Even when presented with available evidence that clearly shows "overwhelming positive adjustment" for the majority of intercountry adopted children, critics have challenged "whether the so-called good adjustment [is] accomplished at the cost of . . . [losing one's] unique ethnocultural heritage and identity, partially reinforced by parents who may be innocent and caring, but inept in their expectations" (Kim, 1995, p. 152).

On the whole, then, the benefits of intercountry adoption have been clearly established by multiple studies conducted over many years by many different investigators (e.g., Dalen & Saetersdal, 1987; Feigelman & Silverman, 1983; Simon & Altstein, 1991, 2000; Tizard, 1991):

The evidence provides no support for the critics of international adoption. The research shows that these children and their families function well and compare well on various measures of emotional adjustment with other adoptive families as well as with biologic families. These are rather striking findings, since the vast majority of international adoptees have had problematic preadoptive histories which could be expected to cause difficulties in adjustment. The studies show that adoption has for the most part been extraordinarily successful in enabling even those children who have suffered extremely severe forms of deprivation and abuse in their early lives to recover and flourish. (Bartholet, 1993a, p. 158)

Unfortunately, it appears that the political, national, and personal interests of adults often serve as the motivating factor behind expressed concerns for the welfare of abandoned and orphaned children. Until or unless this changes it is unlikely that opposition to intercountry (or transracial) adoption will be silenced anytime in the near future.

INTERNATIONAL INITIATIVES
ON INTERCOUNTRY ADOPTION

In recent years the international community has addressed the potential for abuse and perceived problems with intercountry adoption, most notably through the 1993 Convention on Protection of Children and Cooperation in Respect of Intercountry Adoption. The convention is a multilateral treaty prepared by the international organization known as the Hague Convention on Private International Law, and is being considered for ratification by countries around the world. While a detailed discussion of this initiative is beyond the scope of our text, a brief summary of the major points contained in the 1993 Hague Convention initiative may provide a broader context for understanding opposing views, major issues, and the dynamics involved in intercountry adoption.

Intercountry adoption has often been viewed as a last resort for abandoned children (Serbin, 1997). Pfund (1996) notes that language used in the U.N. Convention on the Rights of the Child might actually have served to fuel the negative perceptions held by some countries and international organizations that intercountry adoption exploits a national resource of poorer developing countries. In contrast, the convention promotes the philosophy that all children deserve to survive and to have a family, even if this means adoption by a family from a different country, culture, or racial and ethnic background. The convention also establishes a set of uniform international policies and practices for intercountry adoption. In addition, a central agency or authority must be established in each ratifying country to supervise intercountry adoptions and protect the rights of all involved: children, birth parents, and adoptive parents (Carstens & Julia, 1995; Serbin 1997). Specific provisions of the convention include the following:

- It constitutes a first formal intergovernmental stamp of approval for the process of intercountry adoption when the process conforms to minimum norms set by the Convention. The Preamble of the 1993 Convention starts by recognizing that the child, for the full and harmonious development of its personality, should grow up in a family environment, in an atmosphere of happiness, love and understanding. After recalling that every State should take appropriate measures to enable the child to remain in the care of its family of origin, the third provision of the Preamble recognizes 'that intercountry adoption may offer the advantage of a permanent family to a child for whom a suitable family cannot be found in his or her State of origin.' The Preamble thereby suggests that intercountry adoption, providing the child a permanent family, should be placed ahead of foster or institutional care in the child's country of origin—a very welcome and important endorsement of intercountry adoptions if they meet the internationally agreed minimum requirements set out in the Hague Convention.

- By providing for national Central Authorities to be established in every party country, the Convention ensures that there is a single authoritative source of information about the laws and procedures for intercountry adoptions in every such country.
- The Convention establishes a minimum set of core norms and procedures that will be uniform for every party country and every adoption involving two party countries. Safeguards include [1] mandated homestudy for adoptive parents, [2] prohibitions on inducements to birth parents, and [3] prior approval for children to emigrate to their new countries before adoptions are finalized. (Pfund, 1996, pp. 1–2)

In the United States, ratification of the Hague Convention will shift regulatory responsibility from individual states to the federal government.[3] While a central authority with oversight and troubleshooting responsibilities for intercountry adoptions must be created, the bulk of decision making and actual authority will, in all likelihood, be placed with individual states. The goals of the central authority are to remove barriers that delay or inhibit intercountry adoption, advocate and protect children without permanent families, prevent improper financial gain and fraudulent practices, and collect and disseminate data about intercountry adoption (Evans, 1997; Freivalds, 2000).

WHAT DO PARENTS THINK
ABOUT INTERCOUNTRY ADOPTION?

Although we did not directly question all adoptive parents about their views on intercountry adoption, we did ask several questions that give us some indication of their views. First, we asked for the primary reason that led parents to a decision to adopt and provided six options: infertility, to help a child in need, concern for population growth, promotion of racial tolerance, not sure, and other reasons not identified. In contrast to Tessler, Gamache, and Liu's study (1999)—they asked for a four-point Likert-type response (1 = not at all important, 4 = very important) to sixteen separate reasons for adopting—we asked parents to select only the primary reason for their decision to adopt. Despite different data-collection methods, our findings are similar to Tessler et al.'s in that being childless was a significant motivating factor in the decision to adopt a child. Almost half our respondents ($n = 161$) cited infertility as the primary reason for adopting. Forty-seven parents (13.9%) cited a humanitarian concern for helping a child in need of a home. Given the complexity of adoption, it is not surprising that one-third of our participants ($n = 111$) indicated that reasons other than those we listed on the survey were behind their adoption decision. One mother's comments are indicative of many who responded: "When we decided to adopt, it was because we felt we could give a child a good upbringing [and] if we couldn't have biological children then we would adopt."

Why do parents decide to adopt a child from China? Tessler and colleagues (1999) reported that "eligibility, health status of prospective children, and cultural and personal interests may all be involved, among other factors, in leading one to adopt in China" (pp. 79–80). Like Tessler and colleagues, we found a wide variety of reasons being cited as primary influences (see Table 2.1). Just under one-fourth of parents in our study ($n = 79$) cited a humanitarian reason for deciding on China: the large number of orphaned and abandoned children needing homes. Other reasons, such as problems with U.S. adoption laws (e.g., length of time, uncertainty with open adoption), a desire for a girl, no possibility of parental claim after finalization of adoption, and a respect for Chinese culture were all selected by a fairly equal number of respondents.[4]

Written comments we received to this question were also informative. Several parents cited the good chance of receiving a healthy child and the speed and dependability of the Chinese adoption process as main considerations in their choice of China. Others had difficulty identifying a single reason and explained that a combination of factors contributed to their decision. One parent noted that her reason for choosing to adopt from China "was a combination of reasons with no one reason more important than another."

When asked for their views on interracial and transcultural adoption, parents often advocated for the right or entitlement of children to a safe, permanent home with a loving family regardless of racial or cultural background. The following responses are illustrative of the many we received:

- "If you can place [abandoned children] in their own country . . . that is great, but it is often not possible."
- "I believe that the first choice would be for children to be placed in families [in] their own [country], but if this is not possible, all children should have loving families of their own."
- "Children need a permanent loving home, safe warm shelter, the right not to be hungry, and an education. . . . I believe that the most important thing to a child is to have loving parents."
- "A child is a child, a family is a family. Yes . . . some complexities [exist], but it's still making a home for a child who needs one."

Parents were well aware of the racial differences between themselves and their adopted children, many expressing concern that their children would experience discrimination or prejudice. How-

Table 2.1
Primary Reasons for Parents' Decision to Adopt from China

Reasons	n	%
Number of children needing homes	79	23.3
U.S. adoption laws	43	12.7
Wanted a girl	41	12.1
No possibility of parent claims on child in future	33	9.7
Respect/admiration for Chinese culture	32	9.4
Not sure	7	2.1
Other	93	27.4

Note: Missing data, $n = 11$. Total does not equal 100 percent because of missing data and rounding errors.

ever, the concerns of a majority of parents are represented by these thoughts offered by one adoptive father: "Families are created in myriad ways, transcultural–transracial adoption is simply one of them. I hope that we have and are taking the appropriate measures to educate ourselves and our daughter in this area. We have open eyes, minds, and hearts but we also know we cannot shield her from all of the unkindness the world has to offer someone who doesn't have a Caucasian face."

One of our respondents summed up the general reactions of many parents to the negative aspects of intercountry adoption (e.g., the notion that intercountry adoption exploits less-developed countries). "Remaining with parents of one's own culture is preferable but not to the exclusion of other factors affecting a child's wellbeing. We sometimes feel like we are wealthy Westerners who 'bought a baby' but we know that our child will have a much better life with us than in an orphanage."

SUMMARY

The dialogue about intercountry adoption is complex and reflects very different views. Politically, criticism of the practice tends to reflect the inherent dangers associated with the loss of group affiliation. However, arguments about the need to maintain cultural, racial, or ethnic origins ignore the empirical evidence, which is overwhelmingly supportive of intercountry adoption and the outcomes achieved by adopted children and families alike. Given the emotional investment and sensitive nature of intercountry adoption, it is unlikely that critics will concede their position, despite strong evidence to the contrary.

NOTES

1. While intercountry adoptions from South Korea have been drastically reduced during the past decade, the practice still continues, primarily involving relinquishment cases (unmarried and teenage pregnancies) and special cases for married birth parents. Acknowledging Korea's long and complex history with intercountry adoption, Sarri, Baik, and Bombyk (1998) observed, "Given the lack of development of alternatives for parentless or abandoned children under the present Korean Child Welfare Policy and the resources that adoption placements are for private agencies, the practice has continued for forty years, and is likely to continue indefinitely" (p. 87). Sarri and colleagues argue that the persistence of the practice resulted from goal displacement: "The original goal of attempting to solve the social problem of orphaned and abandoned multiracial children was gradually displaced by continuance of the practice long after the original problem no longer existed because it relieved the South Korean government of having to establish domestic programs" (p. 89). Similar criticisms have been levied against the practice of intercountry adoption from the People's Republic of China.

2. Like public debate, empirical investigations of transracial and intercountry adoption have been conducted primarily from a negative perspective (i.e., these types of adoption relationships are viewed as exceptions to accepted placement practice). Thus, questions are formulated to determine whether or not anticipated problems have materialized. An alternative perspective would be to design studies to assess the potential positive aspects of intercountry and transracial adoption (Bartholet, 1993a).

3. Bills allowing for the ratification of the Hague Convention were introduced in both houses of the U.S. Congress (House Bill 2909 on March 22, 1999, and Senate Bill 682 on September 22, 1999). Since the U.S. Senate is charged with providing advice and consent on international treaties, the Hague Convention was also considered by the Senate Foreign Relations Committee. After months of negotiation between House and Senate committees, a compromise bill—the Gilman Geidenson Substitute to HR 2909—was introduced to the House International Relations Committee on March 22, 2000. The Gilman Geidenson amendment was voted out of the committee by a unanimous vote of 28 to 0. In September 2000 both the House and Senate finally passed legislation enabling the United States to ratify and implement the Hague Convention. President Bill Clinton signed the Intercountry Adoption Act of 2000, which establishes the authorization for and sets up the plan for complying with the Hague Convention. As of January 2001, forty-one countries have adopted the convention (M. Evans, 2000; Freivalds, 2000; Joint Council on International Children's Services, 2000; Rivera, 2000).

4. The literature does not help to explain the apparent contradiction in the responses we received to the questions about the decision to adopt (general) and the decision to adopt from China (specific). It is possible that some parents viewed the two decisions separately. For example, a couple may have made their initial decision to adopt a child because of infertility and then chose to adopt from China because of humanitarian concerns or perceived problems with U.S. adoption laws.

Chapter 3

The Process of Intercountry Adoption from China

Once the decision to adopt has been made, many prospective parents face a seemingly insurmountable task: how to successfully maneuver through the maze of bureaucracies and legal requirements in the United States and China that are inherent in the process. Intercountry adoption can present numerous challenges and hurdles, and potential heartache for those who pursue this path to parenthood. The process is complex and socially constructed. It is, in essence, an arrangement that is defined and shaped by the political values and social contexts of the countries involved to meet identified needs of parents and children (Hartman & Laird, 1990). Because of its complexity and socially constructed nature, this chapter overviews major aspects of the process to provide context for understanding intercountry adoption from China and some of the topics addressed in this book.

There are a number of ways to review intercountry adoption, although dividing the process into three distinct phases—assembling the paperwork that goes to China, waiting for a referral, and traveling to China to adopt a child (FCC, 1999a)—is a common approach and one we employ in this chapter. Specific aspects of the process will be mentioned, including the role of U.S. and Chinese government agencies, eligibility requirements for adoptive parents, home-study approval, necessary documents and their proper legal recognition, costs and fees, receiving a child and finalizing the adoption in China, and returning to the United States. Despite its complexity, the U.S. Department of State (1999) recently observed that "adoption of Chinese children by U.S. citizens in accordance with Chinese law and regulations and . . . in accordance with U.S. immigration laws is operating successfully with minimal difficulty" (p. 2).

INITIATING THE PROCESS

One of the first actions prospective parents must take is the selection of an adoption agency to facilitate the entire adoption process. Chinese adoption law stipulates that all adoption applications must be submitted through an agency that is approved by both the Chinese and U.S. governments. In fact, individual or privately sponsored adoptions are illegal in the People's Republic of China. One exception to this rule is that couples (or single individuals) who have lived and worked in China for one or more years can apply directly to the Chinese Center for Adoption Affairs, the central authority for conducting and finalizing all intercountry adoption in China (U.S. Department of State, 1999). In the United States, adoption agencies must be licensed by the state in which they operate and are approved by the CCAA only after a formal application is submitted that contains, among other things, copies of the agency's license(s) and corporate documents (e.g., articles of incorporation, list of corporate officers, etc.).[1]

Determining the eligibility of prospective parents to adopt a child from China is a preliminary task of adoption agencies. Eligibility requirements—amended by the Chinese government in April 1999—for adopting an abandoned or orphaned child stipulate that applicants, whether married or single, must be at least thirty years of age.[2] While married couples or single women who were between thirty to forty-five years of age and childless were once preferred, parents no longer need to be childless to adopt a healthy abandoned child. Single men adopting a female child from China must still be at least forty years older than the child. At present, no upper age limit has been imposed by Chinese officials. While no written documentation exists to confirm the practice, it appears that CCAA officials prefer that parents over the age of forty-five take a slightly older child (over twelve months)—for example, older applicants are likely to be referred an older child. Applicants must have a sufficient level of income to support the child and be in reasonably good health (Cecere, 1999; FCC, 1999a).

Intercountry adoption can be expensive. Fees, depending on the parents' state of residence and adoption agency, can vary considerably, and range from $12,000 to $30,000, although most adoptions generally fall in the $15,000 to $20,000 range. The costs of foreign adoption represent several general categories of activity, including agency processing and placement fees, foreign government and attorney fees, and travel costs. Agency fees, usually the smallest portion of the total cost, can include a number of specific services, including initial processing of an application, authentication, and translation of required documents, serving as a liaison with Chinese and U.S. officials, and accompanying parents when they travel to China. A required home study, conducted by a state-licensed social worker, might be completed by agency personnel or can be contracted with a third party.

Approximately half of the total cost incurred for Chinese adoption is for travel to China and the orphanage and legal fees that are paid there. The Chinese government requires that a donation (approximately $3,000) be paid directly to the orphanage that cared for the adopted child. The money is used to recover the living expenses of the child while in the orphanage's care, as well as to improve living conditions for remaining children. Legal fees typically cover the various services provided by central and local Chinese governments (e.g., processing the adoption petition, adoption registration and approval by the Civil Affairs Bureau, and document notarization). Miscellaneous expenses are also incurred throughout the adoption process and represent a variety of products and services: official copies of necessary U.S. legal documents such as birth or marriage certificates; fingerprinting; local criminal background checks; notarizing, certifying, and authenticating required documents; filing U.S. Immigration and Naturalization Service (INS) forms to classify an orphan as an immediate relative; issuance of a Chinese passport and U.S. visa for travel to the United States; and postplacement visits by a licensed social worker (FCC, 1999a; Holt International, 2000; National Adoption Information Clearinghouse, 1998; U.S. Department of State, 1999).

DOSSIER PREPARATION

Preparation of the document dossier, the formal application to adopt a child from China, includes the home study, a collection of necessary documents, and a petition to the INS for approval to adopt a child out of country. The dossier describes the applicants wanting to adopt and demonstrates their capability to be adequate parents. Completion of the dossier and all that it entails can take from several weeks to several months or longer, depending on a number of factors, such as parents' motivation, the agency selected to facilitate the adoption, and the time required by others to complete necessary steps. In fact, a great deal of the waiting is dictated by how long various U.S. (local, state, and federal levels) and Chinese government agencies take to process all of the documents (FCC, 1999a).

Home Study

All adoption applicants must undergo a home study, an extended evaluation of prospective adoptive parents conducted by a licensed social worker. The purpose of the home study is to gather information about applicants' capabilities, preparedness, and general fitness (physically, financially, emotionally) to be parents of an adopted child: "The home study itself is a written report of the findings of the social worker who has met with applicants on several occasions, both individually and together, usually at the social worker's office. At least one meeting will occur in the applicant's home. . . . On average the home study process takes from 3 to 6 months to complete" (National Adoption Information Clearinghouse, 1999a).

While many prospective parents initially express apprehension about the home study, most indicate that the process is far easier and more stress-free than expected (Cecere, 1999). Even so, the home study is a reminder to many adoptive parents that the government asserts the right to determine who is and who is not allowed to become parents through adoption. In stark contrast, no such provisions exist for biological parents. The right to reproduce is seen as a God-given right (Bartholet, 1993a).

The exact procedures for conducting a home study, time required, and specific information contained in final reports vary from state to state. However, the following information is generally included:

Personal and family background including upbringing, siblings, key events and what was learned from them; significant people in the lives of the applicants; marriage and family relationships; motivation to adopt; expectations for the child; feelings about infertility (if this is an issue); parenting and integration of the child into the family; family environment; physical and health history of the applicants; education, employment and finances including insurance coverage and child care plans if needed; references and criminal background clearances; summary and social worker's recommendation. (National Adoption Information Clearinghouse, 1999a)

Document Retrieval and Authentication

Chinese law—the Adoption Law of the People's Republic of China and the Implementation Measures on the Adoption of Children by

Foreigners in the People's Republic of China—contains a number of provisions that guide the application and adoption processes, including the number and types of documents required. The specific documents required by the CCAA of all foreign adoption applicants are as follows (U.S. Department of State, 1999):

1. Adoption application (petition to the Chinese government to be allowed to adopt a child).

2. Birth, marriage (if applicable), divorce (if applicable) certificates.

A personal letter of application must state reasons for wanting to adopt and include a statement of intent to not abandon or abuse the adopted child, and to raise and educate the child to grow healthy.

3. Verification of employment, income, and property.

A certificate (letter) of employment must be issued by prospective parents' employer(s) that states position held, length of employment, and annual salary. A specific form is also required that details family assets and liabilities.

4. Health examination certificates.

A "General Physician Examination for Adoption Applicant" form must be completed for each family member that attests to the reasonable health of applicants.

5. Documentation showing criminal record or no criminal record.

6. Home study report.

Certificates issued and signed by authorized representatives of the local police station must indicate whether the applicant has any criminal record.

7. Certificate of China adoption approval.

INS Form I-171H, which states that INS Form I-600A—Application for Advance Processing of Orphan Petition—has been processed and approval has been granted for travel to China for child adoption.

All documents included as part of an applicant's dossier must be authenticated by a Chinese consulate prior to their submission to the CCAA. Authentication involves a series of steps that provide official assurance to Chinese representatives that documents are, in fact, correct and legal. Generally, U.S. civil records such as birth or marriage certificates must bear the seal of the issuing office, then be certified by the secretary of state from the issuing state, then by the U.S. Department of State Authentication Office, and finally by the Chinese embassy or consulate in the United States. Some required documents (e.g., personal tax returns, medical reports, and police clearances) must also be authenticated in a fashion similar to the procedure used for civil records (i.e., state, federal, and Chinese authentication). In addition, authentication for these types of documents starts with the seal of a U.S. notary public, which is then certified by the country clerk where the notary is licensed before being submitted to the other levels of authentication (U.S. Department of State, 1999).

Securing INS Approval

In all intercountry adoptions, U.S. government approval is required before a foreign child can be issued an entrance visa and legally immigrate to the United States. The first step in this process is filing Form I-600A, "Application for Advance Processing of an Orphan Petition," with the U.S. Immigration and Naturalization Service. Submission of this form initiates an investigation to ensure that the applicants (prospective parents) meet certain requirements. The INS conducts the investigation prior to the actual adoption in order to avoid long delays later in the process. A number of documents, many of the same ones submitted to the CCAA, are required in support of the I-600A, including complete sets of fingerprints, which are forwarded to the U.S. Federal Bureau of Investigation (FBI) for a criminal background check; a copy of the completed home study; birth and, if applicable, marriage and divorce certificates; proof of U.S. citizenship; and proof of applicants' ages.

When the required INS investigation has been completed and approval given, Form I-171H, "Notice of Favorable Determination Concerning Application for Advance Processing of an Orphan Petition," is issued to the applicant. This particular form serves as legal notice that the applicant has successfully satisfied all legal requirements to adopt a foreign child. For Chinese adoptions, the INS also forwards one copy of the approved I-600A and other related materials, collectively known as VISAS 37, to the U.S. consulate in Guangzhou, China. In turn, the U.S. consulate sends the applicant a packet of materials to be used in China when completing the adoption process, including "Petition to Classify Orphan as Immediate Relative" (Form I-600), "Application for Immigrant Visa and Alien Registration" (Form 230), "Affidavit of Support Under Section 213A" (Form I-864), a medical exam form (OF-157), and "Request for and Report on Overseas Orphan Investigation" (Form I-604). At this point the approval process has been completed and, once the dossier has been submitted to the CCAA, the waiting period begins.

WAITING FOR A REFERRAL

After INS approval is obtained and a completed dossier has been submitted to Chinese authorities, the process of actually identifying a child, arranging for travel to China, and then traveling to China to complete the adoption process can take from eight to twelve months or longer.[3] The entire application and approval process is defined by three major steps. Once received by the CCAA, an applicant's dossier is reviewed and translated into Mandarin Chinese or the existing translation is verified for accuracy. A registration form is used to condense the most relevant information from a bulky dossier into an easily readable form. Depending on the volume of dossiers, the first phase can take from two to four months. From here, the dossier is transferred to Department 1, where the family's qualifications and documents are checked. Another two to four months may be required to complete this phase of the process before transferring the documents to Department 2. Here, the family is matched with a particular child. Chinese officials "match the application with a child whose paperwork has been forwarded to the CCAA by a provincial Civil Affairs Bureau" (U.S. Department of State, 1999). The medical report and a small visa photo, collectively known as the referral, are forwarded to the applicants' agency, which, in turn, relays this information to the prospective parents:

After getting all of the information, the prospective parents have a limited amount of time, usually a week, to decide whether to accept that specific child into their family. . . . The intent is for the family to review the information and accept in writing the referral and return this approval to the CCAA. Once received, the information is shared with provincial [Chinese] officials. The mailing alone can take 2 weeks. Then, the Invitation to Travel letter is generated, and is personally signed (with a special red chop) by one of the two Vice Directors of the Center. (FCC, 1999a)

TRAVEL TO CHINA AND COMPLETING THE ADOPTION

The acceptance of a referred child is formally acknowledged to the CCAA in writing, usually by the applicants' adoption agency. After indicating acceptance of a referred child, a formal notice of permission to travel, "Notice of Coming to China for Adoption," is issued to the prospective parents. At this point, "prospective parents may then proceed directly to the city in China where the Civil Affairs Bureau with jurisdiction over the appropriate Children's

Welfare Institute is located. Thereafter, a series of interviews of the prospective adoptive parent(s) will occur; a contract will be signed with the Children's Welfare Institute; the contract will be registered with the Civil Affairs Bureau; and a notarized adoption decree will be issued" (U.S. Department of State, 1999). The Chinese Civil Affairs Bureau also issues a notarized birth certificate and either death certificates for the child's parents or a certificate of abandonment from the Children's Welfare Institute. A Chinese passport and exit visa are also obtained at this time.

The last phase of the Chinese adoption process involves travel to Guangzhou to complete the INS visa process. First, a medical exam is completed. The exam is usually a simple procedure conducted by a U.S.–approved physician that lasts no more than fifteen minutes. Second, an interview at the consulate is required. Interviews are scheduled in advance by the agency responsible for overseeing the adoption process. During this meeting with U.S. consulate staff, parents are required to submit all necessary paperwork, including Forms I-600 and I-864, evidence of legal abandonment, and evidence that a Chinese court has finalized the adoption. In addition,

the Department of State Consular Officer who adjudicates the child's immigrant visa application is required to conduct an investigation, called the "I-604 Orphan Investigation," prior to issuing an immigrant visa for the child. The purpose of this investigation is two-fold: (1) to verify the orphan status of the child and (2) to ensure that the child does not suffer from a medical condition of which the adoptive parents are not already aware and willing to accept. (National Adoption Information Clearinghouse, 1998)

The final step involves returning to the U.S. consulate, usually the day following the interview, to receive the child's completed visa packet. The sealed visa packet must be handed unopened to appropriate INS officials at the port of entry upon arrival back in the United States.

POSTPLACEMENT REQUIREMENTS AND ISSUES

Once the adoptive family returns home and begins to settle into a new routine, a couple of final legal issues need to be resolved. In the past a permanent alien registration card, usually referred to as a "green card," was sent to the family six to eight weeks following the return home. Once the green card was received, parents could apply for a social security number for the child. The process, while relatively simple, required a number of documents, including the Chinese adoption certificate, the child's passport, the green card, a parent's driver's license, and the original Chinese birth certificate.

Many parents consider readopting the child in the United States. While the legality of adoptions completed in China are recognized by U.S. courts, readoption reestablishes legal ties between parents and their child, as well as allowing the state to register and issue a birth record for the child. The ability to simultaneously change the child's legal name is a secondary benefit. In some states, intercountry adoption from China is considered final and readoption is not possible.

Until recently, the final legal issue involved in intercountry adoption from China was applying for and securing U.S. citizenship for the adopted child. This process was initiated by submitting a completed Form N-643, "Application for Certificate of Citizenship in Behalf of an Adopted Child," and accompanying documents related to the adoption and immigration to the INS. This requirement changed on October 12, 2000, when the Child Citizenship Act of 2000—cosponsors of the bipartisan bill were Senators Don Nickels (R–OK) and Mary Landrieu (D–LA), and Representatives Lamar Smith (R–TX), Sam Gejenson (D–CT), and William Delahunt (D–MA)—passed the Senate, having earlier passed the House of Representatives. On October 30, 2000, President Bill Clinton signed the bill into law, which went into effect on February 27, 2001. The act grants automatic citizenship to all internationally adopted children under eighteen years of age who have been admitted to the United States as lawful permanent residents and are in the legal and physical custody of at least one parent who is a U.S. citizen. Parents will no longer be required to submit the Form N-643 application to have their child naturalized. Specific regulations pertaining to the bill were not available at the time of printing (Joint Council on International Children's Services, 1999, n.d.).

NOTES

1. The U.S. Department of State Bureau of Consular Affairs general flyer on international adoption is available via the Consular Affairs homepage at http://travel.state.gov/ or the main State Department home page at http://www.state.gov/ under the subheading "Travel." The flyer contains general guidance about selecting an adoption agency.

2. China's Adoption Law was originally established by the Seventh National People's Congress of the People's Republic of China on December 29, 1991, and went into effect on April 1, 1992. Amendments to the Adoption Law were approved by the Ninth National People's Congress on November 4, 1998, and went into effect April 1, 1999. Among other things, the Adoption Law provides specific definitions for categories of adoptable children. Children eligible for adoption in China usually fall into one of three categories: orphans, abandoned children, and children whose par-

ents are incapable of caring for them because of unusual hardship. A fourth category, special needs, is also used and refers to a child with a diagnosed medical condition, often considered minor (e.g., a prominent birthmark) or correctable (simple cleft lip).

3. The most recent statistics on waiting periods are available at http://homepages.wwc.edu/staff/stirra/waiting.htm.

Chapter 4

"And Baby Makes Three": Attachment and Adjustment Issues

> But for all the possible problems in getting used to their new adoptive home, we hasten to point out that children tend to be incredibly resilient. If they weren't, then virtually every child adopted from a foreign country, indeed every child adopted after any transitional foster care, would be a child at considerable risk. But in fact the evidence suggests that the great majority of these children adjust quite normally.
> Brodzinsky, Schechter, & Henig, 1992, p. 37

Jim and Nancy had waited a long time—over eighteen months in fact—for the day when they finally started on their trip to China to receive their daughter. They had decided to name her Sarah. Their anticipation had been building as they counted down the final few days. The car ride from home to the airport, the plane ride to Hong Kong, and the train ride to Guangzhou, China, were all a blur. There were periods on the trip when they felt as if they were dreaming; it seemed as if time stood still.

After thirty-six hours en route, they arrived at their destination, Nanchang in Jiangxi province. Still unpacking their clothes at the hotel, Jim and Nancy—along with the other couples in their travel group—were informed that the children had arrived from the orphanage. As each travel-weary couple huddled in front of their hotel room, orphanage workers appeared from around the corner and delivered the children. As they received their daughter, Jim and Nancy realized that they were finally parents.

The emotion was overwhelming. But rather than making the immediate bond they had imagined and hoped for, they struggled for the better part of the next two weeks to make a connection, to form an attachment, with Sarah. Jim and Nancy recalled the concern they felt over their daughter's inconsolable crying, sporadic hair pulling, and her generally stressed appearance and behavior. Over the next two weeks, Jim and Nancy saw slow but steady progress; at first a smile, then tentative attempts at play, and in just a few more days, full interaction with her parents. Although difficult, the foundation for developing a secure and loving attachment between parents and child was established by the time the family returned home.

While Jim and Nancy's experience is not necessarily representative of other adoptive parents, many parents experience some initial adjustment difficulties once they accept their adopted daughter or son. The literature is vague about common or abnormal attachment experiences with intercountry adoptees, although our own research suggests that a wide variety of normal experiences exist. Concerns about initial adjustment are also accompanied by questions about longer-term adjustment. Do children adopted from China develop positive self-concepts, address issues connected to their minority status, and emerge from adolescence in ways similar to their majority peers? This chapter addresses these types of questions by focusing on several issues of critical concern for parents who have adopted internationally: parent–child attachment, and the adjustment and development of intercountry adoptees in childhood.

ERIKSON'S PSYCHOSOCIAL STAGES OF DEVELOPMENT

There are many ways to conceptualize the initial and long-term adjustment made by intercountry adoptees. We follow the lead of past authors—in particular, Kirk (1988) and Brodzinsky (1987)—by applying Erikson's model of psychosocial development to understand the types of adjustment issues faced by Chinese adoptees. Erikson (1963) believed that individual development is shaped by a series of eight stages or phases that cover the entire lifespan, from infancy through adulthood, although we focus only on the first five stages, ranging from infancy through adolescence. Each life stage represents a conflict between two competing outcomes. One or the other of these outcomes is realized when attempts are made to resolve predetermined developmental tasks or challenges referred to as "dilemmas of identity." These universal and observable crises include trust versus mistrust, autonomy versus shame and doubt, initiative versus guilt, industry versus inferiority, ego identity versus identity confusion, intimacy versus isolation, generativity versus stagnation, and ego intensity versus despair. Progress through each stage is partly influenced by the degree of success experienced in previous stages and is iterative. Like clothes in a washing machine that periodically surface and submerge, "We are forever struggling with the issues we seem to have resolved at an earlier period of life" (Brodzinsky et al., 1992, p. 15).

Kirk (1988) and Brodzinsky (1987; Brodzinsky et al., 1992) used Erikson's life stages model to construct a framework for understanding adoption-related tasks faced by adoptive parents and children. Issues specific to intercountry adoption can also be acknowledged and understood within Erikson's enhanced framework. Thus, we identify tasks that may result from racial or ethnic differences and cultural heritage issues specific to children adopted from China (see Table 4.1). While speculative, we have drawn information from studies that examine the outcomes of Korean and other intercountry adoptees in order to shed light on the various life-stage challenges that might be experienced by Chinese adoptees now and in the future, and how they might be resolved.

In infancy, the main psychosocial crisis is the development of trust (trust versus mistrust). A basic sense of trust is gained when a child can predict and depend on her own behavior and the behavior of others. Typically, trust results from ongoing, positive, and consistent interactions between a child and her primary caretakers. A sense of trust is essential for developing attachments between children and caregivers. If a proper balance of trust and mistrust is achieved, hope—that is, the strong belief that things will work out—is nurtured (Boeree, n.d.).

Brodzinsky (1987) proposed a number of adoption-specific tasks that present themselves during infancy. Parents must resolve any conflicts that have developed between their expected and actual parental roles (e.g., infertility), as well as make adjustments to accommodate a new child in the family. Likewise, adopted children must adjust to the transition to a new home and family, and develop secure attachments with their adoptive parents and siblings.

Additional tasks arise for parents and children involved in intercountry adoption. Most parents are faced with decisions about how, or even if, to acknowledge their child's cultural heritage, as

Table 4.1

Psychosocial Tasks Associated with Parent–Child Adjustment in Intercountry Adoption

Erikson's psychosocial tasks	Adoption-related tasks (parents)	Adoption-related tasks (child)	Culturally influenced tasks for adoptive parent and/or child
Infancy *Trust vs. Mistrust*	• Resolve feelings regarding infertility • Cope with uncertainty of adoption • Adjust to transition of child in home • Find appropriate role models; develop realistic expectations of adoptive parenthood • Cope with social stigma on adoption • Develop secure attachment relationships	• Adjust to transition to adoptive home • Develop secure attachment relationships	• Depending on age, child may adjust to new culture; foods, language, schedules, expectations, etc. • Deal with loss of privacy for entire family (approach by strangers) • Cope with the social stigma regarding transracial or transcultural adoption • Determine how or if to acknowledge parent–child differences
Toddlerhood *Autonomy vs. Shame and Doubt* Preschool years *Initiative vs. Guilt*	• Cope with the anxiety and uncertainty of initial discussion about adoption • Create atmosphere in which questions about adoption and race can be freely explored	• Learn about birth and reproduction • Adjust to initial information about adoption	• Recognize differences in physical appearance • Adjust to knowledge about and expression of Chinese heritage

Erikson's psychosocial tasks	Adoption-related tasks (parents)	Adoption-related tasks (child)	Culturally influenced tasks for adoptive parent and/or child
Middle childhood *Industry vs. Inferiority*	• Help child master meanings of adoption • Help child in initial stages of adaptive grieving • Maintain atmosphere where questions about adoption can be freely explored in light of complications brought about by the grief process	• Understand meanings and implications of being adopted; sense of loss or grief • Search for answers regarding origin and reasons for relinquishment • Cope with stigma of adoption • Cope with peer reactions to adoption • Cope with adoption-related loss(es)	• Cope with physical differences from family members • Understand the meaning of being in a racial minority • Develop awareness of cultural heritage
Adolescence *Ego Identity vs. Identity Confusion*	• Help adolescent cope with genealogical bewilderment • Help adolescent grieve for the lost self (and loss of birth parents and origins) • Maintain atmosphere where questions about adoption can be freely explored in light of the complications associated with grief process	• Explore meanings and implications of being adopted • Connect adoption to sense of identity • Resolve family romance fantasy • Cope with adoption-related loss, especially related to the sense of self	• Realize search for biological parents is impossible • Connect race and cultural heritage to identity development • Cope with physical differences from family members and most of society • Develop racial identity

Note: Adapted from "Adjustment to Adoption: A Psychosocial Perspective," by D. M. Brodzinsky, 1987, *Clinical Psychology Review*, 7, 24–47; *Being Adopted: The Lifelong Search for Self*, by D. M. Brodzinsky, M. D. Schechter, and R. M. Henig, 1992, New York: Anchor Books; *Exploring Adoptive Family Life*, by H. D. Kirk, 1988, Port Angeles, WA: Ben-Simon.

well as the most appropriate ways to acknowledge and contend with racial or ethnic differences between themselves and their adopted child. Parents also need to address the negative social stigma often connected to transracial (transcultural) adoption, and the loss of privacy that occurs when strangers approach family members to inquire about their adopted child. Depending on the child's age at the time of adoption, her developing sense of trust—primarily with Chinese orphanage or foster caregivers—may be severed, causing potentially serious problems, including the need to reestablish the adopted child's sense of trust through building secure parent–child relationships (Brodzinsky, 1987).

The toddler (autonomy versus shame and doubt) and preschool years (initiative versus guilt) represent the age groups of Erikson's (1963) next two stages. These stages represent the initial attempts of children to establish their independence and begin physical and psychological separation from parents or caregivers. The phrase, "I can do it myself," typifies a toddler's initial steps toward autonomy. Toddlers' (one to two years of age) activities are primarily focused on developing control of physical skills such as language and manipulating things in the environment. If successful (i.e., a proper balance of autonomy and shame and doubt is achieved), the young child develops a sense of determination.

Preschoolers three to five years of age continue to expand their sense of autonomy by becoming more assertive and initiating, rather than merely imitating, actions needed to achieve self-developed goals. A gradual awareness of social institutions and role expectations help develop the child's sexual identity. A rudimentary conscience also begins to emerge. A positive balance of initiative and guilt and doubt results in a sense of purpose (Boeree, n.d.; Brodzinsky, 1987; Kirk, 1988; University of California, Irvine, n.d.).

At some point during the toddler and preschool years, parents usually begin to talk to their child about being adopted and, in the case of intercountry adoptees from China, their cultural heritage, although it is not always easy to do so. "In adoptive families, the child's strivings for autonomy and initiative are complicated by one of the most difficult tasks faced by adoptive parents—telling the child that he or she is adopted" (Brodzinsky, 1987, p. 33). Parents are often ambivalent about talking to their children about adoption because it acknowledges that a biological link is missing and tends to accentuate the gap between family and child. Even so, the reactions of adoptive children to knowledge of being adopted are usually quite positive during these early developmental stages. Positive feelings about adoption are further reinforced by parents' adoption stories that emphasize the happiness of parents and child.

According to Brodzinsky and colleagues (1992), Erikson's first three developmental stages provide the context for introducing the idea of adoption to a child even though he or she cannot fully understand it. The ways that parents introduce, discuss, and cope with adoption-related issues early in a child's life are important, because these interactions establish the patterns and support received when dealing with adoption issues later in life.

Primary tasks during middle childhood from six to twelve years of age expand the child's world to include school, friends, and society at large. The quality of results, including skill mastery and understanding, are increasingly important criteria for successful task completion. A strict adherence to rules and standards is usually observed. Children want to be recognized for the results of their work and seek the satisfaction of self and others (Boeree, n.d.; Brodzinsky, 1987; University of California, Irvine, n.d.).

In middle childhood, adopted children gradually acquire a fuller understanding of what it means to be adopted. They come to realize that their birth family lives in China and start to identify factors that resulted in being abandoned. A sense of loss is often felt for the first time during this period. "Now the child can infer the flip side of her beloved 'adoption story'—that for her to have been chosen, she first had to have been given away" (Brodzinsky et al., 1992, p. 18). Trolley (1995) has noted that while the major loss for any adopted child is loss of biological parents, intercountry adoptees encounter additional losses, including separation from preadoption caretakers and a severing of contact with the child's birth country and culture. The loss of one's roots and identity may cause the child difficulty in establishing a sense of self and birth heritage. The adopted child may also be exposed to negative social reactions "as the differences in ethnicity between the country of birth and country in which the child resides [become] apparent . . . prejudice, discrimination, and racism may further impede the child who is adopted internationally from a sense of belonging" (p. 259).

The most observable consequence of adoptees' sense of loss—including separation from caregivers when adopted as young children, and during middle childhood and adolescence when the full implications of being adopted are realized—is the act of grieving. It is sometimes difficult for new adoptive parents to detect and successfully respond to the grief initially experienced by young children, primarily because of the child's lack of expressive skills. In addition, a child's grief can be manifest in many ways:

[Children] in this age group may go through the stages of grief that older children and adults experience including denial, often expressed by the "searching" behavior that indicates that the child expects the previous caretaker to return; anger, expressed often by uncontrollable crying; depression, or withdrawl, and disinterest in food or play; and reorganization, or acceptance of the new situation. These stages may not be sequential and may repeat themselves. (Melina, 1998, p. 29)

Brodzinsky (1987) used the term "adaptive grieving" to describe the expression of grief (e.g., confusion, anger, uncertainty) that occurs as a normal reaction to the loss experienced by adoptees as they become aware of what it means to be adopted. "The behavioral and emotional patterns associated with this process are well known. Shock, denial, protest, despair, and eventual recovery or reintegration are commonly observed, although not necessarily in such a clear and orderly progression" (p. 36). While it is impossible to dismiss the sense of loss and grief adopted children experience, Trolley (1995) was optimistic by noting that out of the grief process older children may develop a more clearly defined self-identity that incorporates an increasingly mature perspective on the roles of biological and adoptive parents, birth heritage and adoptive culture, and the value of family and relationships.

Adolescence is a time when basic issues of self-identity, independence, and physical maturity are explored and resolved. Erikson (1963) coined the term "identity crisis" to describe the often turbulent process that adolescents experience when trying to determine who they are and how they fit into society. Successful resolution of the identity crisis occurs when adolescents determine how various aspects of their life fit together and contribute to their overall definition of self.

A primary goal of adolescence is separating from one's family and venturing into the adult world; to define oneself as a unique individual while still maintaining ties to family. This particular process is complicated for adoptees, who have both biological (genetic influences) and adoptive (environmental influences) families. Westhues and Cohen (1997) explained that "these young people have to contend with all of the usual challenges of adolescence plus being adopted, and most often being placed in a family that has a different ethnic and racial background than their own" (p. 48). The added challenges that adopted adolescents encounter can result in greater difficulty forming a complete and stable sense of self (Brodzinsky, 1987). "If the task of the preschooler is to understand *how* adoption happens and the task of the child in middle childhood is to explore *why* it happened and what it says about her that she was adopted, the task of the adolescent is to determine how adoption has shaped her in specific ways. What does it mean that she has had *these* adoptive parents? This upbringing? And, in particular, what does it mean that she had *these* birth parents?" (Melina, 1998, p. 111).

The process of identity development can also be complicated for children adopted from China by the child's racial minority status in the United States and her Chinese cultural heritage. Again, Melina (1998) notes the types of problems typically encountered:

For teenagers who were adopted transracially or internationally, the questions are the same but involve more layers. What does it mean to have been raised in this culture? What is their relationship to other people of the same racial or ethnic background? What beliefs, customs, or attitudes do they have that may be different from those of other people of their racial background? What experiences have they had that are influenced by their racial or ethnic heritage and not understood by their adoptive families? (pp. 111–112)

Other issues related to racial and ethnic difference include experiences of and ways to effectively cope with discrimination, prejudice, and racism.

ATTACHMENT

There are few topics in the adoption literature that generate as much interest and, at times, controversy as the issue of attachment. Even the definition of attachment—as well as a commonly although incorrectly substituted term, "bonding"—has generated considerable discussion. According to Watson (1997), a clear distinction should be made between bonding and attachment. Bonding refers to a significant relationship between people that happens without the knowledge, intent, or conscious effort of those involved.[1] Attachment, on the other hand, is a learned ability where psychological connections between people are (1) nurtured over an extended period of time, (2) developed through two-way (mutual) interaction, and (3) result in people having significant meaning to each other. Unlike bonding, which is essentially an unconscious act, attachment is an emotional relationship that requires reciprocal interaction, is based on learned trust, and requires time—weeks or even months—to develop (Brodzinsky et al., 1992). There are two essentially distinct theoretical approaches that exist to explain the notion of attachment (Richters & Waters, 1991): Freud's psychoanalytic theory, touted, most notably, by Bowlby (1969); and social learning (social control) theory. The next sections briefly describe these two theories and discuss their distinct implications for domestic and intercountry adoption.

Bowlby's Attachment Theory

The person most clearly identified with the subject of attachment is John Bowlby (1969) who used an ethological approach—the study of animal behavior to explain and understand human behavior— and a grounding in psychoanalytic thought to conclude that "attachment behavior evolved from an instinctual survival mechanism designed to keep caretakers close by. He proposed that humans were born with the instinctual drive for attachment" (Watson, 1997, p. 162). Thus, for Bowlby attachment is primarily a function of survival and protection. Through early interaction between infants and caregivers, children develop a cognitive model of themselves, their caregivers, and their world that acts as a filter for interpreting all subsequent experiences (Groze & Rosenthal, 1993).

A component of Bowlby's (1969) theory with direct implications for adoptive relationships is the belief that attachment is a developmental process that requires a critical period, usually the first six months of life, to become established (Johnson & Fein, 1991). If attachments do not occur during this critical period, the child is at a considerable disadvantage for developing attachments in the future. Proponents of Bowlby's attachment theory argue that adoption placements that occur after the critical six-month period are most at risk of attachment difficulties or disorders, such as children developing less-secure attachments to their adoptive parents (Portello, 1993). In a theme that we see consistently throughout adoption literature in both domestic and intercountry adoptees, the older the child at the time of placement the greater the likelihood of attachment difficulty (Fancott, n.d.).

Social Learning Theory or Social Control Perspective of Attachment

The psychoanalytic explanation of attachment, particularly the reliance on ethological studies and importance of bonding during a critical period, have been challenged by a number of scholars and practitioners. Herbert (1988) argued that if the bonding model were correct, attachments between adopted children and parents would not happen. Crnic, Reite, and Shucard (1982) reasoned that while ethological studies on imprinting and other types of "animal" bonding might appear to be similar to human phenomena, there is no evidence that results of ethological studies are applicable to human relationships. Similarly, Brodzinksy and colleagues (1992) argued against applying ethologically derived theories like Bowlby's (1969) to explain the process of attachment: "The fact that while many lower animals do indeed show a biologically-based bonding during critical periods soon after birth, the scientific evidence for such bonding in human infants is weak" (p. 32).

An alternate perspective, social learning theory, takes the position that attachment is a learned pattern of behavior, a social bond. Attachment behavior is believed to originate in the interaction between parent or, more generally, caregiver, and child. Interaction is especially important during the first three years of life, and acts as a catalyst in shaping the behavior and psychological and emotional connections between parent and child. Groze and Rosenthal (1993) explained, "The closer the parent–child relationship, the greater the attachment and identification the child feels with the parent. Higher levels of attachment result in behaviors that are congruent with the parental value system and that increase affection between parent and child" (p. 6).

Unlike the psychoanalytic perspective, social learning theory does not grant a unique status to mother–child attachments. Rather, a focus is placed on attachment to a limited number of caregivers that could include mother but also a host of others, such as father, foster parent, or institution worker. Another important aspect of social learning theory is the notion that adoptees, as well as others separated from birth parents or early caregivers, can develop new and equally strong attachments with other people in their lives. Melina (1998) explained, "The child who has been able to form attachments in the past will form new attachments more easily than the child who has never felt an attachment, because he has already learned to trust" (pp. 64–65). Finally, attachment is seen as an outcome of early childhood development rather than as a determinant (Richters & Waters, 1991).

Children must learn the skill of making attachments during the first years of their life and do so as a result of mutual interaction with a limited number of primary caretakers. Once learned, the skill of making attachments is transferable, but since an attachment is made by choice and conscious effort, it can be ended by choice or by atrophy. . . . Children must learn to disengage from attachments just as they had to learn to make them. Disengagement skills involve learning to cope with loss and are acquired once a child has established the capacity to make attachments—usually sometime during the third year of life. (Watson, 1997, p. 165)

It is interesting that despite the implications that attachment issues hold for the success of adoptive relationships, particularly in intercountry adoptions where children are usually older at the time of placement, relatively few empirical investigations have been conducted. The limited information that is available on attachment in adoptive families presents conflicting results about whether adoptive attachment is more or less secure than in nonadoptive situations. To further complicate matters, many studies have been criticized for methodological and conceptual flaws (Portello, 1993).

Do adoptive parents and children develop weaker and less-secure attachments than nonadoptive families? Two studies that have examined this issue and are free from fatal design flaws clearly indicate that adopted children are highly capable of developing attachments with adoptive parents and siblings that are as strong and secure as those found in nonadoptive families. The first investigation (Singer, Brodzinsky, Ramsey, Steir, & Waters, 1985) provides, perhaps, the best evidence that attachments between adopted infants (thirteen to eighteen-month-olds were studied) and mothers do not significantly differ from those of nonadopted families. The investigators did find a statistically significant difference between nonadoptive (biological mother and child) and adoptive families when mother and child were of different races. However, a more naturalistic follow-up investigation revealed no differences between the two groups, leading Singer and colleagues to conclude that their original results indicating a difference based on racial differences were probably the result of an experimental artifact in the study rather than a reflection of true differences between the groups.

Benson, Sharma, and Roehlkepartain (1995) conducted an investigation designed to ascertain the mental health and service needs of 881 adolescents who had been adopted as infants. The study is noteworthy because (1) the design relied on a representative sample, (2) adopted adolescents and their adoptive parents were directly surveyed, and (3) it spanned four states with forty-two public and private adoption agencies involved. Among other findings, the study revealed extremely high rates of strong attachment between adoptive adolescents and parents, demonstrating that "adopted adolescents are as deeply attached to parents as are their non-adopted siblings" (p. 2). In fact, over 80 percent of adolescents indicated being strongly attached to one or both of their adoptive parents. Benson and colleagues concluded that "attachment, which is strong among the vast majority of families in this study, is an important precursor to positive identity and psychological health, both of which are commonplace among the adolescents in this study" (p. 4).

In summary, then, from a social learning (social control) perspective—the position we take to understand attachment-related issues in adoption—adoptees are highly capable of forming strong, secure, and long-lasting attachments to adoptive parents. Watson (1997) contends,

If infants get consistently good care from a limited number of caretakers in the context of mutually interactive relationships, by the time they are three years old they have learned both how to become attached and how to manage separation from those whom they have become attached. The capacity to make attachments once learned is never lost. Children who have not had this kind of care during these three years, and that is true of most children who come from foster care or adoption beyond that age, usually have attachment disorders. (p. 169)

The move by Chinese orphanages over the past several years to place children in foster care rather than have them remain institutionalized prior to adoption is one of several likely reasons for relatively lower reported prevalence rates of attachment disorder for children adopted from China. In contrast, high prevalence rates of attachment disorders have been noted for intercountry adoptees from Eastern European countries such as Romania and Russia. In these cases, children have often received poor or no prenatal care, usually remain institutionalized until adopted, have multiple caretakers, receive limited interaction with others, and are provided inconsistent care (Mainemer, Gilman, & Ames, 1998). Although proportionally few attachment-related problems have been identified in Chinese adoptees, some problems do exist. The next section provides the perceptions of several adoptive parents at their first meetings with their children, and briefly discusses the types of attachment problems exhibited by intercountry adoptees.

Secure versus Insecure Attachment

The vast majority of Chinese adoptees are capable of developing strong and secure attachments with their adoptive parents; however, some experience difficulty. Attachment problems are usually thought of as representing a continuum or as having multiple levels, with securely attached children on one end and completely insecure (unattached) children on the other (Groze & Rosenthal, 1993). Secure attachments are important in helping children cope with stressful situations and in developing expectations about others that form the basis for subsequent social relationships and concepts of self (Johnson & Fein, 1991). Common problems that result from difficulty in forming attachments include retarded social–behavioral, cognitive, emotional, and conscience development; difficulty making and maintaining friendships; and difficulty accepting responsibility (Keck & Kupecky, n.d.).

As a result of her innovative and seminal work, Mary Ainsworth (1973, 1979) and her colleagues identified three distinct types or patterns of attachment: secure, anxious–avoidant, and anxious–ambivalent (resistant). Children who are securely attached express affection, cry or show distress when separated from their mothers, seek their mothers when distressed, and are easily comforted by their mother when reunited. Ainsworth reported that about three-fourths of all children in her studies exhibited secure attachment. Children with insecure attachment are characterized by a lack of distress during parental separation. They are at times demanding and clingy, but just as likely to ignore or avoid their caregiver (parent). Children with insecure attachments are just as easily comforted by strangers as by their own parent. A third group, labeled with anxious–ambivalent (resistant) attachment disorder, display distress even when their mother is in close proximity. These children often exhibit conflicting behaviors when reunited with caregivers. Children often seek contact and comfort from their caregivers (are clingy and demanding), but receive little if any comfort. Instead, they often display passive or aggressive hostility (Brodzinsky et al., 1992; Groze & Rosenthal, 1993; Parent Network for the Post-Institutionalized Child, 1995; Pendry, n.d.).

Attachment of Parents and Their Children Adopted from China

The topic of attachment was not a focus of our investigation when we initiated data collection. However, we received a considerable number of comments and general queries on this topic from survey respondents. As a result, we included several questions about attachment in follow-up contacts made to select adoptive parents. The experience of one adoptive couple, Ken and Sheila Mayes, was particularly poignant, and illustrates (1) how attachments often develop between Chinese adoptees and their early (preadoption) caregivers, and (2) the potential confusion and misunderstanding these early interactions can cause for adoptive parents.

The Mayes, a professional couple in their early forties, remembered the first several days after receiving their daughter, Katie, from orphanage workers in China as being very difficult. It was apparent that Katie missed her foster mother terribly. She would continually search for the foster mother, cried often, and initially rejected most of Ken and Sheila's attempts to comfort her. During the most difficult times both Ken and Sheila remember expressing their anger at the foster mother's care for their daughter and for "allowing" Katie to become attached to her. "Why would she allow such a strong attachment to occur knowing that her care was only temporary?" The situation was so emotional that Sheila remembers crying, "What has that woman [the foster mother] done to our child?"

Now, almost two years after the completion of the adoption process, the Mayes have a strong and secure attachment to their daughter, and vice versa. Ken and Sheila now smile about their misplaced anger and undue concern about attachment. They are now able to see the attachment between Katie and her Chinese foster mother as an extremely positive indicator of Katie's ability to develop deep and secure attachments. According to Sheila, they had expected an immediate bond with Katie and when that didn't occur they became concerned, perhaps panicked. While it has been gradual—and will be an ongoing process—a strong attachment has developed between adoptive parents and child that has been built on learned trust and mutual interaction. This is thanks in no small part to a woman and her family in China who also loved and cared for Katie and taught her how to develop attachments to others.

For parents, developing an attachment to their adopted child might actually begin years before the actual adoption. Dreams of a family, making the decision to adopt from China, receiving a referral picture of "their" child, and thoughts about what the future has in store for their child place firm connections between parent and adoptive child. However, actually meeting their child face to face brings thoughts and dreams back to reality. Those first meetings seemed to hold particular importance to the parents in our study and practically all respondents described their thoughts and actions during this time. Clearly, first meetings are as varied as the children and parents involved. However, they are almost always intense emotional experiences. Lucy B.'s first meeting with her daughter at an orphanage in Guangdong province was once such meeting:

I was soooo in love with her referral picture. . . . But, when we actually saw her, it was a little hard for me. The weather was hot and humid, we were still tired from the long flight over, and the emotions of the daughters was overpowering. Whereas I knew I loved her instantly as she was my daughter, I did not feel that I was in love with her. She looked different than her referral picture and the pressure of everything got to me. The next day things were much better for me and I could see things more clearly. I look back on my reaction 9 months later and I have to say that the whole thing surprises me.

Kristina M. and her husband recalled a stressful first couple of days with their daughter Kathryn. She described their experiences once they arrived in Changsha, Hunan province:

We were told that our guide and our baby were waiting for us at the hotel. We were thrilled. She, however, was not. She had been in foster care for six months (she was 8 months old at the time of the adoption), then taken by two strangers for a long trip, then handed off to two even stranger people—us. She was dressed in the usual seven layers of sweaters and we chose not to undress her too quickly. We tried to feed her but she wasn't interested. We walked a lot that night. My husband spoke in a soothing tone to her. I sang to her, the same song over and over again. She finally cried herself to sleep in my husband's arms.

In contrast, some parents reported very smooth first meetings. Janet F. attributed the easy transition with their daughter, Jessica, to the fact that she had spent her first nine months in an orphanage and hadn't become attached to any particular caregiver during that time. Debbie T., on the other hand, believes it was her daughter's attachment to a foster mother who cared for her deeply that helped with the transition and with her daughter's happy and curious nature.

Karen R. and her husband, who have adopted two daughters from China, described for us the very different types of experiences they had when meeting their adopted children for the first time. Their first daughter was six months old when they met and was happy, alert, and attentive. "When handed to me she looked straight into my eyes and blew bubbles." In contrast, their second daughter was sixteen months of age when adopted. When handed to Karen, the child "screamed and kicked! I was not prepared for her to be like this the entire time in China—luckily this did not happen." Speaking from her experience with two adoptions, Karen shared her thoughts on attachment with us: "We knew to take the bonding [issue] one step at a time. I have seen other families so wanting their child to attach to them right away that the child becomes overwhelmed—which she is anyway—and the bonding becomes slower."

ADJUSTMENT IN CHILDHOOD AND PREADOLESCENCE

The initial and long-term adjustment of domestically adopted children has long been a topic of interest and concern for researchers, but what about children adopted from abroad? How do intercountry adoptees fare? For example, do intercountry adoptees have a more difficult time negotiating developmental tasks than individuals adopted domestically or nonadoptees? To be more specific, are children adopted from China at greater risk for problems with psychological adjustment or behavioral difficulties?

Research on international adoption by U.S. families remains limited, although "a fair number of studies have been carried out in Europe. [Unfortunately] most are not available in English and many are not published" (Tizard, 1991, p. 747). This trend is changing, albeit slowly, since first proclaimed by Tizard a decade ago. The available research on intercountry adoption has primarily focused on the initial and long-term adjustment of adopted children from Korea in the 1970s and a more diverse population including adoptees from Vietnam and Cambodia in the 1980s. And while most of the early research indicates generally positive outcomes, empirical findings on the adjustment of international adoptees is still considered inconclusive by some (Wilkinson, 1995).

The need for data about initial and long-term development of children adopted from China was brought home to us in these frank comments of one concerned adoptive mother:

As a parent of two Chinese children I'm much more concerned about the many developmental issues our children face because of institutionalization and its effects including the after-effects of trauma, as well as sensory integration dysfunction and attachment problems/attachment disorders. These are the issues which frequently leave parents feeling isolated and as if there must be something wrong with their parenting and are issues which are too seldom acknowledged by the adoption community, particularly the Chinese adoption community.

Despite claims to the contrary, recent empirical investigations appear overwhelmingly supportive of the benefits of intercountry adoption to both family and child (Bagley, 1992; Bartholet, 1993a; Brodzinsky, 1993; Brodzinsky et al., 1992; Melina, 1998; Simon & Altstein, 2000; Westhues & Cohen, 1997). Most domestically adopted children lead happy, normal lives, have friends, grow up, attain meaningful careers, and have families of their own. Similarly, the vast majority of intercountry adoptees adjust quickly and function well in their adoptive homes. They, too, live full and complete lives (Altstein & Simon, 1991; Tizard, 1991).

Yet there are also predictable conflicts that adoptees may face, such as genealogical bewilderment, problems with identity formation, and difficult parent–child relationships (Kim, 1995). The existence of transcultural and, in most cases, transracial adoption raises concerns that are unique to intercountry adoptees. Brodzinsky (1987) believed that the ways adoptive parents acknowledged and tried to cope with these concerns largely determined an adopted child's overall pattern of adjustment.

A look at past investigations can help to shed some light on developmental and adjustment-related concerns of children adopted from China. We rely, to a certain degree, on general (domestic) adoption issues, intercountry adoption issues that are conceptualized as representative of a homogeneous population despite including adoptees from a variety of birth countries, and intercountry adoption of Asian children, primarily Korean, many of whom were adopted in the 1960s and 1970s.[2] Many of these investigations have drawn criticism for being fragmented, processing narrow and short-term research foci, or containing research design and method flaws (Brodzinsky, 1987; Dodds, 1999; Gorman, 1999). A lack of longitudinal data on intercountry adoption from China is also problematic. Yet even with these concerns, the data consistently shows positive outcomes for intercountry adoptees. In the following section we focus on several concerns, including (1) the medical condition of adoptees upon their arrival in the United States and (2) the behavioral and psychological adjustment of adoptees in childhood and preadolescence. Adjustment issues specific to adolescence (e.g., identity formation) are discussed extensively in Chapter 8.

Medical Condition of Chinese Adoptees

Concerns about the initial and long-term physical and mental health of intercountry adoptees occupy a prominent place in the minds of many pre- and postadoptive parents. Reports of abandoned or orphaned children facing adverse social circumstances, inadequate nutrition, poor pre- and postnatal care, and long-term institutionalization—particularly children from Romania and other Eastern European countries—highlight the need for obtaining reliable information. Unfortunately, no large-scale or longitudinal studies of the medical conditions of Chinese adoptees have been reported to date. Smaller-scale investigations that focus on the health issues of Chinese adoptees are becoming more common. However, much of what we currently know about the health of intercountry adoptees from China is preliminary, fragmented, obtained from studies relying on narrow time frames, and based on a belief that all intercountry adoptees belong to a single, homogeneous group (Johnson, n.d.).[3]

The risk for disease can be fairly high in institutionalized settings as a result of crowded living conditions that cause infections to spread quickly. The situation is often aggravated by limited access to professional medical care. Miller (1999) noted that the incidence of medical problems among all intercountry adoptees, but particularly children from Eastern Europe, is substantial. The situation is further complicated by a high number of intercountry adoptees who do not receive proper medical evaluations. Miller noted the high probability that many medical or behavior problems go undetected. Despite the potential for serious health problems, anecdotal evidence (e.g., descriptions of personal experience like those found in Liedtke and Brasseur, 1997) and the few published reports indicate that, as a whole, most Chinese adoptees are extremely healthy. While relatively minor medical problems and developmental delays are common, few children exhibit serious physical, psychological, or behavioral disorders upon their arrival in the United States.

Several clinical reports covering the medical condition of Chinese adoptees are available on the World Wide Web. By far, the most complete treatment of the topic we found was in a review conducted by Aronson (1999). Aronson relied on her research and clinical practice when summarizing much of our current knowledge about the health of Chinese adoptees. She concluded that the general good health and limited incidence of long-term medical problems reflect the excellent physical health of most Chinese adoptees. Triseliotis and colleagues (1997), among others, confirmed Aronson's claim that most of the identified medical problems of Chinese adoptees were easily resolved with proper diagnosis and treatment.

Not surprising, a list of the medical problems commonly diagnosed in adoptees from China reflects the common health issues faced by all Chinese children regardless of their institutionalization status. This fact led Aronson (1999, n.d.) to urge that adoptive parents become aware of and understand the specific health issues commonly found in their child's birth country, as well as the unique medical problems that can result from being institutionalized. She identified the top five medical problems found in children living in China, and hence Chinese adoptees, as malnutrition, rickets, anemia, lead poisoning, and asthma. Other health concerns frequently mentioned include tuberculosis, hepatitis B, and bacterial or parasitic intestinal infections.[4] Aronson also reported on the prevalence rates for several serious health problems found in some Chinese adoptees: lead poisoning (13% had elevated levels of lead in their bloodstream), tuberculosis (8% of adoptees tested positive), and hepatitis B (these prevalence rates are similar to those reported by Johnson and Traister, n.d., who found that 3.5% of the Chinese adoptees they studied responded positive to a heptaitis B surface antigen test).

In a separate study, Dr. Nancy Hendrie (n.d.) examined the overall health and behavioral adjustment of 263 children adopted from China. Her study spanned a six-year period in the early to mid-

1990s and included children from twenty-eight different Chinese orphanages located in a total of eight different provinces. Excluding children previously identified as having special medical needs, few adoptees were diagnosed with serious diseases such as hepatitis B (prevalence rate between 5 and 10%) or tuberculosis, and no cases of AIDS were diagnosed. Hendrie concluded that developmental lags were almost inevitable with intercountry adoptees. Even so, relatively few children she evaluated had experienced severe delay. Most diagnosed problems were quickly reversed after adoption. In her sample, only a small handful of families ($n = 8$) indicated moderate to severe behavior problems with their child. Only one child was diagnosed with severe attachment disorder upon arrival. Subsequent reports about this child indicated that the problem had been successfully resolved. Hendrie asserted that Chinese adoptees were "for the most part extraordinarily healthy, and have done incredibly well adjusting to their new families" (p. 4).

Johnson and Traister (n.d.) conducted a three-year investigation in which they studied the medical conditions of 154 newly adopted children from China. Ninety percent of the adoptees were female and had arrived in the United States at ten months of age, on average. The incidence of infectious diseases like hepatitis B, AIDS, and syphilis was fairly rare (less than 5% of all adoptees). Blood levels for lead were normal in over 90 percent of those tested ($n = 31$), and only slightly elevated for the remainder. Nineteen children in six areas of development were assessed, with abnormalities found in one or more of the areas for two-thirds of this group. Strength and gross motor skills were most often affected. Most developmental delays were quickly reversed, however, after the child's arrival in the United States.

The positive findings for Chinese adoptees stand in stark contrast to the serious health and behavioral problems identified in many children adopted from Romania and other Eastern European countries. For example, Harnott and Robertson (1999) report that of thirty-five children adopted from Eastern Europe by parents in the United Kingdom, twenty-nine children experienced mild to significant problems with attachment that required frequent and sustained stimulation. A similar percentage also displayed some degree of behavior problems. A number of reasons have been posed to explain the positive outcomes for Chinese children, although the most plausible ones seem to be the young age when most Chinese children are adopted and the limited exposure to orphanage life resulting from increased use of home foster care in the months preceding adoption.

Developmental Delay, Psychosocial and Behavioral Conditions, and Adjustment

Incidence of Developmental Delay in Chinese Adoptees

Reports of growth and developmental delays are common in studies of intercountry adoptees (Serbin, 1997). The recent medical reports about children adopted from China (Aronson, 1999; Johnson & Traister, n.d.; Miller, 1999) indicate that as many as three-fourths of all Chinese adoptees experience some type of developmental delay for a period of time after adoption. Miller and Hendrie (2000) assessed the health and development status of 452 Chinese adoptees after their arrival in the United States and found frequent developmental delays, including height (39% of adoptees had delays of two or more standard deviations) and weight (18% of adoptees were two or more standard deviations below average). Medically, children from China were diagnosed with the following types of conditions: anemia (35%), hepatitis B surface antibody (22%), elevated lead levels (14%), and intestinal parasites (9%). Three-quarters of adoptees were found to experience significant developmental delay in at least one domain: social–emotional (28%), gross (55%) or fine motor skills (49%), cognitive (32%), language (43%), and global delay (44%). Miller and Hendrie concluded that "Chinese adoptees display a similar pattern of growth and developmental delays and medical problems as seen in other groups of internationally adopted children [but were] better than expected."

We were interested in determining if the adoptees in our survey followed this general pattern of initial delay, so we asked parents to estimate the developmental level of their adopted child immediately after adoption (initial) and at the time of completing the survey (current) in five areas: social–emotional, physical, eye–hand coordination, language, and learning. Initially, almost two-thirds of the adoptees in our sample experienced delay in one or more developmental areas, although very few exhibited current problems. As a whole, these results are encouraging and compare favorably with past findings reported by Miller and Hendrie (2000). While positive, the interpretation must be tempered by knowledge that we asked parents to estimate (1) whether a delay existed, and (2) the degree or severity of that delay. Obviously, the data are only as good as the estimates (and estimators), and we did not determine whether parents had the ability to make accurate judgments in each of the five developmental areas. However, other studies have used similar approaches to data collection (e.g., Saetersdal & Dalen,

1991; Verhulst & Versuluis-den Bieman, 1995), and we reasoned that estimates of development were likely to be informed ones given the demographic profile of most parents who pursue intercountry adoption (e.g., older, college education, higher socioeconomic status, etc.). Despite this limitation, our results do support previous investigations that have examined psychosocial and behavioral delays in intercountry adoptees.

A total of 133 parents (41.7% of those with valid responses on all development-related items) reported no developmental delays of any kind with their adopted children, either when first received or at any time following placement. The age of these children at the time of adoption ranged from three to fifty-two months, with the average age of placement just under one year (M = 11.8 months, sd = 7.3 months). Over three-fourths of children in this group (n = 105) were fourteen months of age or younger at the time of initial placement.

Remaining adoptees (n = 186; 58.3% of those with valid responses on all development-related items) experienced a delay in one or more developmental areas. These delays were categorized into two groups, those of a short-term nature (the delay was eliminated after a period of time in the adoptive home) or those experienced on an emerging or long-term basis. A composite summary of findings for adoptees' initial and current developmental delay is presented in Table 4.2. While over one-half of the adoptees experienced initial delays in one or more developmental areas, for the most part the severity of delay was not considered extreme. The majority of parents estimated their child's delay at or less than twelve months behind developmental norms.

A majority of adoptees who were developmentally delayed when first placed with their adoptive family (n = 128, 68.8%) had "caught up" by the time parents completed our survey and were now at or above expected attainment levels. Approximately one-third (n = 43) of children in this group experienced delay in only one or two areas, but over half (n = 68) experienced delay in four or all five areas. The overall magnitude of delay for these adoptees was fairly consistent across the five developmental areas we examined, ranging from an average of 4.1 months (sd = 3.5) for eye–hand coordination (fine motor skills) to 5.1 months (sd = 6.4) on physical development (gross motor skills). Children had spent, on average, around two years in their adoptive home at the time of the survey (M = 26.6 months, sd = 24.4).

The experience of Robyn T., a single mother of two Chinese daughters, presents a good illustration of adoptees who evidenced initial

Table 4.2
Parents' Indications of Initial and Current Developmental Delay in Children Adopted from China (in months)

| | Presence of delay | | | | Extent of development delay (in months) | | | |
| | No delay | | Delay | | | | | |
	n	%	n	%	M	sd	Range	Comments
Initial development								
Social-emotional	166	48.9	173	51.1	9.63	7.4	1–48	43.9% ≤ 6 mos., 81.5% ≤ 12 mos.
Physical	143	42.1	196	57.9	8.34	6.5	1–36	34.7% ≤ 4 mos., 68.4% ≤ 9 mos.
Eye-hand coordination	167	49.2	172	50.8	10.04	8.4	1–39	25.0% ≤ 4 mos., 66.3 % ≤ 10 mos.
Language	181	53.4	158	46.6	9.96	7.3	1–42	41.8% ≤ 6 mos., 77.8% ≤ 12 mos.
Learning	179	52.8	160	47.2	10.34	7.2	1–42	37.5% ≤ 6 mos., 76.9% ≤ 12 mos.
Current development								
Social-emotional	289	85.3	50	14.7	26.90	20.4	1–62	36.0% ≤ 12 mos., 74.0% ≤ 36 mos.
Physical	285	84.1	54	15.9	28.60	20.0	1–66	29.6% ≤ 12 mos., 68.5% ≤ 36 mos.
Eye-hand coordination	286	84.4	53	15.6	29.75	21.8	1–66	30.2% ≤ 12 mos., 69.8% ≤ 36 mos.
Language	178	82.0	61	18.0	25.01	20.1	1–66	32.8% ≤ 12 mos., 77.0% ≤ 36 mos.
Learning	290	85.5	49	14.5	31.08	21.7	1–72	30.6% ≤ 12 mos., 67.3% ≤ 36 mos.

delay at the time of adoption but soon erased their developmental problems. Robyn adopted her older daughter, Elizabeth, at fourteen months of age. Elizabeth was a bright and curious child who had an easy way of engaging others. However, she also exhibited trouble with grasping objects and balancing herself as she attempted to take her first steps. The results of several medical tests confirmed Robyn's initial hunch: Elizabeth's fine and gross motor development was about six months delayed. Although Robyn was concerned, she noted that her daughter's recovery was remarkably quick. Within a few months following their return from China, Elizabeth had caught up with her same-age peers. Robyn attributed her daughter's delay to the effects of institutionalization.

Other parents reported similar experiences with rapid development in delayed areas after returning home from China. For example, one mother explained, "Our baby has raced ahead developmentally in some areas, starting to read at 15 months, counts objects to 15, and knows shapes just to name a few." In another case, Jennifer K. reported, "We had Grace assessed by a pediatric physical therapist who said she was normal, but delayed. Her development was at about 9–10 months. She could not walk, sit up, crawl, roll over but she had great dexterity with her hands and could sit in a chair very well. She walked within 5 weeks of coming home. . . . She is very healthy now, and very bright and full of energy."

In a few cases, children were actually ahead of the developmental expectations for their age level at the time of adoption:

I had researched China since early 1996, had met many families from China, and traveled to China with a friend who adopted in 1998. I was prepared for a child who was small for age and developmentally delayed. With years of experience as a nurse in neonatal intensive care, I felt prepared to handle the situation. At adoption, our daughter was at the 50th percentile for weight and 75th percentile for height on the AMERICAN charts. She was on target developmentally. I've been running ever since.

Twelve children were not initially identified with developmental delays but were identified as being delayed later on, after varying periods of adjustment in their new home. Children in this group were younger than other adoptees ($M = 12.8$, $sd = 15.5$) at the time of adoption. Time elapsed since placement varied from three months to just under seven years ($M = 30.5$ months, $sd = 18.1$). Nine children in this group experienced difficulty with language, ranging from a delay of three months to over four years.

A group of forty-six children were initially identified as being developmentally delayed and continued to experience delay in one or more areas at the time of our survey. The age of this group at adoption was considerably higher than the remainder of our sample, ranging from five months to nine years ($M = 18.9$ months, $sd = 17.3$). These children had lived in their adoptive homes an average of just over two years ($M = 27.0$ months, $sd = 23.2$). Based on parents' estimates, at least two-thirds of adoptees' current developmental delays were less than twelve months behind same-age peers.

The extent of delay was considerable for half of the adoptees in the group experiencing delay in four or five areas. Twenty children experienced delay in all five areas. One mother in our sample attempted to explain her daughter's problems: "My daughter's delays have been very specific—not able to sit up by herself at 10 months but very strong in muscle tone and good fine motor skills at the same age. Her more recent delays are equally specific, i.e., high tested IQ but some specific frustrations in learning areas and emotional neediness." It is possible that some of these children were identified with special needs prior to their adoption. However, we did not ascertain whether or not this was the case.

The older age of these children and their higher degree of delay is consistent with reports that have documented similar situations.

Children who are adopted when older often face adjustment-related issues characterized by a more prolonged process of accommodation and assimilation into their new homes, communities, and cultures. It seems that language problems, in particular, are especially problematic for older adoptees (Wilkinson, 1995). "The sudden interruption of developing native linguistic competence in order to learn a strikingly different semantic and phonetic system is likely to reduce, at least initially, communication skills and tax overall learning capacity" (Kim, 1978, p. 480).

Adjustment of Intercountry Adoptees

What does the future hold for intercountry adoptees in terms of their adjustment; for example, emotional and behavioral development, psychological status, school achievement, integration, and so on? Does a general prognosis apply to all children, including those adopted from China? These types of questions frame our focus in this section. However, because intercountry adoption from the People's Republic of China is fairly new, the psychosocial adjustment and long-term outcome of this group of children is largely unknown. Therefore, we also examine a broader range of investigations that have examined these issues for children of domestic and international adoption (see Appendix A for a partial listing of relevant empirical studies). The results from comparative studies are applicable to Chinese adoptees to the extent that intercountry adoptees share similar experiences and developmental challenges. However, additional research focusing on unique aspects of Chinese adoption is required before definitive claims can be made about long-term adjustment.

Given these caveats, a picture is emerging from the body of literature on domestic and intercountry adoption about the initial and long-term adjustment of intercountry adoptees. However, the continued existence of inconsistent and contradictory results can challenge our ability to establish general conclusions (Benson et al., 1995; Brodzinsky, 1993; Tizard, 1991; Wilkinson, 1995).[5] Westhues and Cohen (1997) summarized their extensive review of the intercountry adoption literature, noting,

Although there now is a reasonable body of work addressing the question of how intercountry adopted children have adapted to their new countries, the results are as inconclusive as for domestically adopted children. . . . Some report that children who have been adopted internationally are likely to demonstrate adjustment problems. . . . Others suggest that difficulties are likely to be encountered only in the initial adjustment period. . . . Still others conclude that problems of adjustment are associated with placement at an older age . . . although some researchers find no such association. (p. 49)

Despite some findings to the contrary, most adoptees function well within the normal ranges of behavioral and psychological development. Intercountry adoptees develop a sense of belonging in their adoptive family, attain levels of self-esteem that are comparable to the general population, usually exhibit average or above-average academic achievement, and relate well to their peers (Altstein & Simon, 1991; Bagley, 1992; Westhues & Cohen, 1998a, 1998b). At the same time, however, intercountry adoptees may also be at increased risk for experiencing problems, particularly in later childhood when a fuller understanding of adoption forms, and during adolescence when identity formation is of primary importance (Brodzinsky et al., 1992). "Discontinuous mothering, unresolved grief at the loss of birth parents, failure to make an attachment to the adoptive parents, confusion about the meaning of adoption, and feelings of rejection and abandonment may place an adoptee at risk of emotional problems" (Melina, 1998, pp. 157–158).

Several studies have focused on the adjustment of adoptees during childhood, particularly during the preschool years. Rojewski, Shapiro, and Shapiro (2000) examined the behavior of forty-four children adopted from China (current age $M = 46.9$ months) and found no significant differences between adoptees and a normed U.S. sample on nine separate scales: aggression, anxiety, attention problems, atypicality, conduct problems, depression, hyperactivity, somatization, and withdrawl. Although adoptees' behavior was within normal ranges of functioning, adoptees older than three years of age were at increased risk of hyperactivity, aggression, conduct problems, and attention problems. The age of children at the time of adoption placement was not a significant determinant of behavior.

In a nationwide study conducted by D. S. Kim (1978), the long-term adjustment of 406 Korean adoptees in the United States was conducted, with particular focus on identity and socialization patterns. Results showed that Korean adoptees progressed well in all areas of life, reported a positive self-concept, and did not experience serious mental health problems.

Kim, Shin, and Carey (1999) compared the psychological adjustment of a small group of Korean adoptees ($n = 18$) with their adoptive siblings ($n = 9$) who were biological children of the adoptive parents. No significant differences were found for social or emotional–behavioral adjustments between biological and adoptive children. Kim and colleagues concluded that despite minor differences—slightly lower social competence scores for adoptees and higher internalization scores for biological children—these Korean adoptees adjusted quite well to their adoptive homes.

Saetersdal and Dalen (1991) studied the adjustment of 182 Vietnamese children who had been adopted by Norwegian parents and found that over half of the children experienced initial adjustment problems, including difficulties with eating and sleeping. As many as one-third of these children experienced problems considered serious. The high rate of initial developmental problems was attributed to, among other things, preadoption trauma caused by exposure to the Vietnam War. Despite the high prevalence of difficulty, a relatively high percentage of the adoptees did not experience any type of initial adjustment problems that the investigators found "remarkable." Equally important, a majority of delayed adoptees recovered from their initial problems, although recovery was more difficult for children adopted between one and three years of age.

Feigelman and Silverman (1983) investigated 298 adolescents adopted from Korea—a subgroup of a larger investigation—and concluded they "were especially well adjusted in their adoptive homes" (p. 237). Not only did 74 percent of the Korean adoptees feel well adjusted, only 9 percent required professional help with psychological adjustment problems. Approximately one-half of the children were above average in academic achievement (55%) and expressed above-average interest in their school activities (45%).

In 1979, S. P. Kim and colleagues studied the adjustment patterns and behavioral development of twenty-one Korean adoptees. Sixteen of these children exhibited behavioral symptoms severe enough to have their parents seek or think about seeking professional help, although only one child actually required psychiatric intervention. Temper tantrums, shyness and withdrawing behavior, excessive or frequent crying, and learning difficulties were the most commonly identified problems. Differences were also noted between children who were adopted either before or after the age of three years. Kim and his colleagues concluded that "the behavioral symptoms in the majority of children were considered only intensified, transient features of adjustment" (p. 424).[6]

While the initial adjustment and psychological development of intercountry adoptees appears to be generally positive, adoptees face an increasing likelihood of experiencing problems as they enter adolescence (Brodzinsky, 1993; Kim, 1978; Saetersdal & Dalen, 1991; Simon & Altstein, 1991; Wilkinson, 1995). In a series of studies on intercountry adoptees living in The Netherlands (Verhulst & Versuluis-den Bieman, 1995; Verhulst, Althaus, & Versluis-den Bieman, 1990; Versuluis-den Bieman & Verhulst, 1995), a significant increase in maladaptive behaviors—particularly delinquency and withdrawal—and a decrease in competencies were found for intercountry adoptees as they entered adolescence. Almost one-quarter of adolescent boys and one-tenth of adolescent girls exhibited deviant behavior. The authors were not able to attribute these problem behaviors to the age or medical condition of the child at placement, early abuse or neglect, or racial antagonism. Versuluis-den Bieman and Verhulst concluded that "it is possible that adolescence, characterized by its developmental increase of cognitive abilities, by its striving toward greater independence, its sexual maturation, and by its concerns over identity, may constitute a period of increased vulnerability for adopted children" (p. 1413).

Hoksbergen (1997) also found a significant increase in behavioral or emotional difficulties experienced by adoptees at the onset of adolescence: higher rates of internalized behavior problems for girls and externalized behavior problems for boys. However, unlike Verhulst and Versuluis-den Bieman (1995), Hoksbergen found age of placement to be a significant factor in determining the prevalence of such problems.

Other studies have also identified the importance of early versus late age placement on the long-term adjustment of intercountry adoptees. In their study of 174 Korean adoptees, Wickes and Slate (1997) found that children placed at an older age recorded higher math and honesty self-concepts than adoptees placed earlier in life. Verbal self-concept was negatively related to placement age. Bagley (1992) reported that Korean adoptees exhibited very good patterns of adjustment and high academic achievement. Levy-Shiff, Zoran, and Shulman (1997) did not detect any significant difference in the school adjustment, psychological adjustment at home (e.g., anxiety, depression, hyperactivity, and self-concept), or ability to cope with adoption issues between international and domestic adoptees in a sample of 100 Israeli families.

The overall news about development and adjustment issues for intercountry adoptees is positive. This is reflected in Tizard's (1991) comments that intercountry adoptees fare quite well physically, psychologically, and behaviorally in the initial years following adoption: "While the evidence is patchy and incomplete, it does suggest that in 75–80% of intercountry adoptions the children and adolescents function well, with no more behavioral and educational problems at home and at school than other children, and that they have close and mutually satisfying relationships with their parents" (pp. 754–755). Melina (1998) suggested that "when adoptees do have problems, it may be because they are struggling to make sense of the issues raised by their adoption, rather than because adoption itself is psychologically damaging" (p. 163).

Why do Chinese adoptees fare so well? To date, no one has attempted to systematically address this question. However, W. J. Kim (1995) considered a number of reasons why Korean adoptions have been considered successful over the years. These reasons may apply to children adopted from China, and provide us a starting point for understanding and future inquiry:

- Children may have been less traumatized prior to adoption than children from other countries. Early trauma can place a child at risk of later difficulties (Hoksbergen, 1997). One factor lowering the possibilities of severe trauma in Chinese adoptees is that children are not products or casualties of war, in contrast to many other groups of intercountry adoptees in the past. Several other factors may also reduce the incidence of trauma, including a greatly improved government structure in China to process intercountry adoptions, adoptions that occur at relatively young ages (often before the adoptee's first birthday), better institutionalized care, and an increased use of foster care prior to adoption.

- Confucian ethics value children a great deal, reducing possibilities of abuse or neglect.

- The strong notion that the earlier the adoption, the better the result. A number of investigations have examined the role of age on adjustment. Many, although not all, studies found age at adoption a significant factor in successful adoptee adjustment (e.g., Brodzinsky, 1987; Hoksbergen, 1997; Kim, 1995; Kim et al., 1979; Kim et al., 1999; Simon & Altstein, 1991; Tizard, 1991; Wickes & Slate, 1997; Wilkinson, 1995).

- The preponderance of adopted Chinese girls. "Boys, adopted or nonadopted, tend to be more vulnerable than girls to a number of psychological problems, especially disruptive disorders and academic problems" (Brodzinsky, 1987, p. 157).

- The characteristics of parents adopting children from China may have a positive influence. Most U.S. parents adopting children from China are older and presumably more mature, reflect higher socioeconomic status, experience stable marriages, are college educated, and are more adept at coping with stress (Brodzinsky et al., 1992; Register, 1991; Serbin, 1997).

SUMMARY

The good news about initial adjustment and early development suggests that the prognosis for the long-term adjustment of Chinese adoptees during adolescence and into adulthood is bright, although at least one author, D. S. Kim (1978), is skeptical of reports that document the successful adjustment of intercountry adoptees, in particular Korean adoptees, and is apprehensive about the prospects of this group for achieving positive long-term outcomes. Kim argued that the pervasive influence of racial and cultural differences often present in intercountry adoption place the long-term adjustment of adoptees in jeopardy:

Although making a good initial adjustment, these adopted foreign children, during the long-term socialization process, are forced to face an inferior status consistently ascribed to ethnic minority group members. Empirical data seem to confirm the impression that the so-called good adjustment of these children is being accomplished at the cost of their unique ethnic cultural heritage and identity, partially reinforced by parents' innocent, yet inapt, expectations. (p. 485)

Given the relatively young age of most Chinese adoptees, only time will tell whether or not these children will be significantly influenced by the negative experiences of discrimination and bias they are likely to encounter in adolescence and adulthood. However, many scholars have suggested that difficult issues faced by intercountry adoptees, such as identity formation and dealing with racism, can be made easier if parents acknowledge their adopted child's birth culture and heritage. Chapter 5 examines several topics that are relevant to forming perceptions about the value adoptive parents place on acknowledging cultural heritage and the various methods they rely on to help them in this effort.

NOTES

1. Four types of bonding have been identified. Genetic bonds reflect the built-in sense of connection that people share through a common ancestry and certain inherited common characteristics. Birth bonding involves the shared experience of pregnancy and birth between a mother and child. Traumatic bonding occurs when strangers unexpectedly experience a common traumatic event that connects them to each other. Transference bonding refers to an immediate, unconscious connection two people feel for one another, drawing two strangers together for reasons that neither can explain (Watson, 1997).

2. Findings from Korean adoption studies of both children and adults spanning more than forty years may provide initial, albeit general, expectations for the initial and long-term adjustment of Chinese adoptees. Wickes and Slate (1997) posited that findings from studies of Korean adoptees may be generalizable to other Asian groups because of the common issues they share in being labeled an ethnic minority. While there are similarities between Korean and Chinese adoptees, important differences exist as well. From the 1950s through the 1970s, a vast majority of Korean chil-

dren were adopted, primarily for humanitarian reasons by parents with biological children, while parents of Chinese adoptees are often childless due to infertility and cite the desire for a child as a motivating factor in adopting. Korean children were originally available for intercountry adoption as a result of military conflict. In China, complex political, social, and familial forces interact with burgeoning population growth to motivate some parents to abandon their children in the face of government birth-restriction policies. Korean adoptees were escorted to the United States by caregivers, minimizing parents' contact with the child's birth country or culture. In contrast, Chinese adoptions are carried out in China, requiring parents to travel and experience their child's birth country and culture. Finally, Korean children were often adopted at older ages than are Chinese children (Gorman, 1999; Tessler et al., 1999). The degree to which these differences influence data interpretation or application of past findings from one group of adoptees to another is unclear.

3. While intercountry adoptees do share certain characteristics, "the very attempt to present them as one group is a risky assumption due to significant ethnic/social/cultural differences among their native countries" (Gindis, n.d., p. 1).

4. In her pediatrics practice, Deborah Borchers (1999), an adoptive mother of two daughters from China, reports observing a number of Chinese children with treatable infections and conditions at the time of their adoption, such as rashes, lice, scabies, ear infections, impetigo, and skin infections. Yet despite these minor medical problems and negative media reports concerning the deplorable conditions in Chinese orphanages, Borchers emphasizes that "it was obvious the caretakers cared for the children in very loving ways, meeting the childrens' basic needs of warmth, food, and changing diapers" (p. 1).

5. Inconsistent and contradictory results found in the adoption literature are generally explained by methodological problems identified with the research, including (1) the use of clinical samples that severely limit the generalizability of results, (2) an overreliance on small sample sizes, (3) frequent failure to use control or contrast groups, (4) no distinction between early- and late-placed adoptees, and (5) failure to use valid and reliable instruments (Brodzinsky, 1993; Kim, 1995). In addition, "children in the studies have also been of different ages at placement, different ages at the time the data were collected, and have come from different countries of origin" (Westhues & Cohen, 1998b, p. 49).

6. A number of clinically based adoption studies have reported that a higher proportion of adoptees receive professional mental health or psychiatric counseling than found in the general population. Grotevant and McRoy (1990) observed that "adopted children are referred for psychological treatment two to five times as frequently as their nonadopted peers. . . . This finding has been replicated in countries as widely dispersed as Great Britain, Israel, Poland, Sweden, and the United States" (p. 167). Brodzinsky and colleagues (1992) explained that while adoptees under the age of eighteen account for less than 2 percent of the general population, they comprise unexpectedly high percentages of children who receive mental health

counseling (5%), require psychiatric hospitalization (10 to 15%), or are identified in school systems as perceptually, neurologically, or emotionally impaired (6 to 9%). Jenista and Chapman (1987) compared adopted and nonadopted children referred for mental health counseling and found that behavioral and emotional problems increased for adoptees as the child's age of placement increased. Even then, however, reported problems usually fell within the normal ranges of all children clinically referred. A common explanation for this phenomenon is that adoptive parents may be more aware, willing, and financially able to access these types of services. Melina (1998) suggested that as a result of their intensity and concern, adoptive parents may intervene (i.e., seek professional help) at the first sign of trouble. Conversely, there may be "a clear tendency among adoptees not only to seek professional help but also to need it. And we believe the increased vulnerability of adoptees to psychological problems can be explained largely by their experience of loss" (Brodzinsky et al., 1992, p. 10).

Chapter 5

Addressing Chinese Culture and Heritage

It's not just your child who will make the transition to a new culture, but you, too. . . . My daughter was born in China and is an American. I was born in America and I am an adopted Chinese.

Alperson, 1997, pp. 101, 106

When a child is adopted from another country, the adoptive family becomes multicultural in every sense of the word, not for just a short while but for generations to come. But what does it mean to be a multicultural family? And what's the big deal about culture anyway? Once children are adopted from China, or anywhere else for that matter, their home is in the United States. Shouldn't they be taught (socialized) to fit into American society? Besides, most adoptees were too young to remember much of their Chinese origins and heritage anyway, right?

Questions about if, when, how, and how much to acknowledge the birth cultural heritage of intercountry adoptees are difficult but extremely important to answer. The task of finding answers is compounded by a lack of consensus on the best or most appropriate ways to acknowledge adoptees' cultural heritage or differences that exist between family and child. So what options are available to parents? Some adoptive parents are anxious to assimilate their child into the dominant culture, to minimize any differences, and have the child "fit in." Other parents, however, have enthusiastically conveyed aspects of their child's birth heritage to them, such as food, music, and stories (Tizard, 1991). Some disagreement exists among adoptive parents about whether acknowledging Chinese culture and heritage to adopted children is necessary for them to grow up with a positive self-identity (Tessler, Gamache, & Liu, 1999). However, literature reviews (e.g., Grotevant, 1997b; Hollingsworth, 1998) suggest that the ways parents cope with physical and cultural heritage differences between themselves and their adopted child (e.g., connecting upbringing, physical appearance, and Chinese heritage) can have considerable influence on adoptees' personal and ethnic identity during adolescence.

The bulk of this chapter is devoted to examining the views and practices of adoptive parents toward acknowledging (or rejecting) Chinese cultural heritage in their families. We present findings from our Web survey that describe how parents (1) view the role of Chinese culture in the life of their families, (2) recognize special events related to the adoption, and (3) introduce Chinese cultural heritage to their adopted children.

DISTINCTIONS BETWEEN CULTURE AND HERITAGE

Our investigation focused on how parents acknowledge and socialize their adopted children to their Chinese birth culture and heritage. This particular issue is significant and may influence children's long-term psychological adjustment and self-identity development. But what do the terms "culture" and "heritage" actually mean? A clear distinction can and should be made between the two concepts because of the implications each hold for parents (and families) of children adopted from China.

Culture is a difficult term to clearly define. In fact, there is no single definition that is universally agreed to by scholars (Segall, 1986). With that said, however, most definitions describe culture as a comprehensive approach, a sum total of living, used by a group of people to help them interpret and negotiate the world. Culture includes a shared system of ideas and meanings that are both explicit and implicit. Halsall (1995) notes that the concept of culture includes an understanding of works of art, literature, and history of a society, "but also less tangible aspects such as attitudes, prejudices, folklore. . . . Culture is almost as much what is NOT talked about as what IS talked about" (pp. 1–2). A number of cultural components have been identified. In addition to the basic facts, assumptions, and mental habits of a society, other cultural elements include collective values, laws, rules, social categories, tacit models of interaction and behavior, rituals and ceremonies, fundamental ways of thinking about societal and personal roles, government, economic life, religion, and social structures (Ebrey, 1981).

LaFromboise, Coleman, and Gerton (1993) provide a behavioral definition of culture that suggests must do the following in order to be culturally competent individuals: "(a) possess a strong personal identity, (b) have knowledge of and facility with the beliefs and values of the culture, (c) display sensitivity to the affective processes of the culture, (d) communicate clearly in the language of the given cultural group, (e) perform socially sanctioned behavior, (f) maintain active social relations within the cultural group, and (g) negotiate the institutional structures of the culture" (p. 396). This definition reflects the difficulty (and complexity) that exists in developing cultural competence, especially if an individual is not raised in a particular culture.

What is Chinese culture? While a complete description of Chinese culture and all that it entails is beyond the scope of this text, a brief summary may help place the dilemma identified by one of our survey participants in perspective (viz., the apparent inability of American parents to socialize their adopted children in Chinese culture). She noted, "We teach a 'heritage' or teach *about* Chinese culture (history, art, values, etc.). But 'culture' as I understand it, is learned through the daily living of values and attitudes."

Chinese culture represents a culmination of over 5,000 years of writing, urbanization, artistic achievements, and politics, and is influenced by numerous issues, such as the size of the population and the government's efforts to control future growth, communism, increased capitalism and trade with the rest of the world, and so on. A prevalent attribute of Chinese culture is the focus on hierarchical interpersonal relationships with strong respect and loyalty to family and authority. The needs of the family and family honor are placed ahead of personal interests and concerns. Humility and modesty in social interactions are also highly valued. Most Chinese value a collective rather than individual orientation, reflected in a reliance on family members for support and comfort when important decisions are made. Issues of honor and avoiding a "loss of face" also are very important. In many cases, elaborate, subtle, and complex forms of interpersonal communication, including nonverbal cues, have been developed to uphold these cultural values (Leung, 1987).

Chinese culture, or any culture for that matter, can be acquired only by living in and belonging to the culture; that is, by awareness of and participation in history, institutions, rituals, and everyday practices (LaFromboise et al., 1993). In fact, more deeply ingrained aspects of a culture—the way people view the world, the way they interact with one another (including gender roles) the way they interpret their life experiences and their roles in the world—can be difficult, perhaps impossible, to acquire from an outside perspective. Given this understanding, children adopted from China cannot actually be socialized to their birth culture per se without actually living and sharing Chinese perspectives, values, and beliefs.

Many of the participants in our study understood and discussed the distinctions between Chinese culture and heritage. For example, one adoptive father gave us a particularly clear, albeit direct, description of how culture and heritage differ and their application to American families with children from China:

[Culture and heritage] aren't the same thing. As Westerners, it is IMPOS-SIBLE for most of us to expose our children to ANY Chinese culture, although we can help them understand their Chinese heritage. We simply weren't raised in China and thus don't have the qualifications to impart Chinese culture. We can, however, teach about her Chinese heritage, since we are literate and can read books about China right along with most literate people and can convey what we read to our daughter [but] she'll NEVER understand the culture.

One adoptive mother shared similar beliefs about parents' inability to socialize their children in Chinese culture. She notes that a key element of socialization, a society that reinforces and supports Chinese culture, is absent in the United States: "Still, I do not believe that we really 'teach our kids to be Chinese' only to know about, [and] be proud of their 'Chinese heritage' as Chinese-born children raised in the US. . . . In fact, our kids cannot be 'socialized' to have Chinese values, habits, etc. unless we as parents begin acting like parents in China act, [and] our families develop the structures and behaviors of families in China."

Even if cultural socialization of adopted children from China was possible, a Chinese American mother who recently adopted a daughter from China raised several concerns about the apparent incompatibility of certain Chinese-held values and beliefs with her American-held ones:

"Culture" does not just mean art, food, history, music, etc. Culture also means values, perspectives, attitudes, religion, etc. Unfortunately, this kind of culture is very difficult to transmit, and I believe that many parents might be unwilling to transmit this type of culture. . . . Should an adopting American parent transmit the Chinese cultural religion (Buddhism or some other) to their child or an American cultural religion? Chinese culture often suggests that a child should be relatively silent, not speaking unless spoken to, subjugating her own desires and impulses to a greater societal good. Should American parents transmit this to their adopted child or should they encourage the American values of independence, relative outspokenness, and individuality? These are parts of Chinese culture that are difficult for an American parent to transmit, [and] maybe they shouldn't transmit it.

Despite the limitations on socializing children in Chinese culture, a sense of Chinese heritage—legacy, inheritance, or tradition—can be attained if parents provide opportunities for their children to observe and understand Chinese artifacts, stories, festivals, spoken and written language, traditions, beliefs, and so forth. Tessler and colleagues (1999) used the term "bicultural socialization" to indicate a goal more limited than learning a different culture. They proposed that the real goal of families with children from China should be to provide their children with positive experiences and opportunities that are associated with China, allowing them to develop a sense of belonging and identity.

This perspective seems appropriate and reasonable for parents who have adopted children from China. Register (1991) offered some examples of heritage that parents could pass on to children adopted from other countries:

The features most evident are distinctive foods, holiday rituals, music, and dance, and assorted artifacts, especially folk arts and costumes. . . . These more obvious elements of cultural heritage are, indeed, the ones most accessible to adoptive families. . . . These features which Roy Brower calls "the trappings of a culture" make for great fun, and they give the children something concrete to identify as their own and to display to their classmates at school. . . . I find it ironic that this is probably teaching them less about [Korean] culture than about American consumerism and the importance it places on owning material things. (pp. 165–166)

COPING WITH FAMILY–CHILD DIFFERENCES AND PATTERNS OF ACKNOWLEDGING BIRTH CULTURE AND HERITAGE

The unique nature of adoption often presents families with an awareness that differences exist in the roles of biological and adoptive parenthood. Bartholet (1996) observed that "we place an extremely high value on the right to procreate and the related right to hold onto our birth children. We place relatively little value on the right to develop and maintain parenting relationships that are not based on blood. There is an essentially absolute right to produce a child, but no right to adopt" (p. 264).

Noted Canadian sociologist H. David Kirk (1964, 1984, 1985) introduced the concept of "role handicap" to describe the differences between biological and adoptive parenthood. He maintained that for biological parents, society maintains a number of role-related rules and expectations: for example, parents gradually prepare for the arrival of a baby, the decision to conceive and give birth to a child is an independent one that does not require agency or government permission, the baby is automatically considered a member of the family even before birth, and there is engagement in a variety of activities, rituals, and interactions designed to integrate the baby into the family. In contrast, few clearly defined, adequate social role expectations exist for adoptive parents. However, a number of "gray areas" exist, such as the conflict between a couple's infertility and a generally assumed ability to conceive, the uncertainty of the adoption process (adopters must prove to governmental agencies they have the ability to be parents), and conflicting role obligations related to disclosure of adoptive status to the child.

Melina (1998) pointed out that while role expectations for adoptive parents and families are "different from the majority of families in society, they are common among adoptive families and therefore normal" (p. 155). She identified a number of areas that are "normal" for adoptive families:

It is normal for adoptive families to have experienced losses for which they must grieve. It is normal for us to have children who are physically dissimilar from us. . . . It is normal for us to be anxious or overprotective because of our experience with loss and the unpredictability of adoption. It is normal for other people to scrutinize us because our model of forming a family is different from the cultural model. It is normal for us to respond to that scrutiny by feeling defensive, by withdrawing, or by projecting an overly positive image. . . . For those who were adopted [internationally], it is normal to have a sense of racial identity that is different from the majority of people of the same racial group. (p. 155)[1]

The way that adoptive parents choose to handle role dilemmas can have considerable influence on an adoptive child's long-term adjustment. Clarification of adoptive-parent roles may be even more strongly affected by international adoption, where children look different physically and represent cultural histories distinct from their parents (Kirk, 1984; Trolley, Wallin, & Hansen, 1995). Grotevant (1997b) observed that differences in physical appearance and cultural–ethnic heritage between adoptive parents and children cannot simply be ignored, because they are constantly being raised through social interactions with others.

How do parents address the issues of adoption and birth culture that are presented through intercountry adoption? Are there strategies or approaches that parents, family members, and adoptees use to successfully acknowledge and adjust to differences? The next several sections will address these and related questions using the work of Kirk (1964, 1984, 1985) as the basis for understanding how parents cope with the unique tasks, challenges, and conflicts that distinguish adoptive families from nonadoptive ones. Changes made to Kirk's model by subsequent scholars, Dalen and Saetersdal (1987) and Brodzinsky (1987), are also considered. Finally, we expand the notion of coping strategies to include the decisions that parents make about whether to maintain cultural connections with their adopted child's birth heritage, and if so, how.

Kirk's Model of Coping Strategies

Kirk's seminal book on adoption, *Shared Fate* (1964), advanced the idea that parents choose one of two opposing strategies to help them resolve the inherent differences between themselves and their adopted child. He called these complementary coping patterns "rejection of differences" and "acknowledgment of differences" (see Figure 5.1). Parents who reject adoption-related differences are likely to encourage their adopted child, and others as well, to forget the fact that they are adopted. Any physical, cultural, or racial–ethnic differences between child and parent are either denied, ignored, or flat-out rejected. Often, parents deny differences as a way to take the sting out of an unpleasant situation (i.e., adoption) by simulating nonadoptive family life as much as possible (Kirk, 1984). While parents may be trying to help, a rejection of differences often inhibits open communication among family members and intensifies a belief in the adopted child that "different is deviant." As a result, a child's adjustment may be more difficult, complicated even more by an unspoken message that adoption is something to be ashamed of and kept hidden.

Other adoptive parents openly acknowledge differences that exist in their family. In some cases, parents may feel as if they don't have much choice but to address the adoptive nature of their family and their child's origins, given the obvious physical differences between parent and child (Trolley, 1995). When differences are acknowledged, opportunities for family members to openly explore their feelings about adoption are created, open lines of communication are developed and maintained, and, as a result, trust and posi-

Figure 5.1
Three Separate Models of Parental and Adoptee Patterns of Coping with Difference

A. Linear model depicting parental patterns of coping with difference in adoptive homes: *Acknowledgment of Difference — Rejection of Difference* continuum

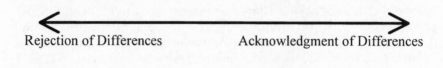

B. Three-dimensional model for understanding the dilemma faced by intercountry adoptees and parents

C. Model explaining parents' reactions to culture and racial-ethnic differences of intercountry adoptees

Acknowledging the differences

Stressing the differences   Rejecting the differences

Note: From (A) *Shared Fate*, by H. D. Kirk, 1984, New York: Free Press; (B) "Transracial Adoption in Norway," by M. Dalen and B. Saetersdal, 1987, *Adoption & Fostering, 11* (4), 41–46; (C) "Adjustment to Adoption: A Psychosocial Perspective," by D. M. Brodzinsky, 1987, *Clinical Psychology Review, 7*, 24–47.

tive attitudes toward the unique characteristics of each family member are nurtured and valued. Empathy with the circumstances of a child's abandonment can also be established, creating a family environment that encourages children to inquire about the circumstances surrounding their adoption. Open communication creates an environment that can lessen adoptees' sense of fear and guilt over their origins, abandonment, and adoption (Brodzinsky, 1987).

Kirk (1984) believed that acknowledgement of differences was critical for the positive psychological development and long-term adjustment of adoptees. Conversely, parents' decisions to reject differences are more likely to result in problems with adoptee self-identity and psychological adjustment. While this relationship is linear in nature (Kirk, 1985, termed it a "a bipolar pattern"), the two coping styles are not mutually exclusive. Because parents' coping patterns are to some degree reactions to societal or cultural pressures, families can vary in how they cope, acknowledging some differences but rejecting others.[2]

Dalen and Saetersdal's Dimensional Model of Coping Strategies

Although Kirk (1964) originally proposed his idea of coping patterns to explain how adoptive parents dealt with differences in role expectations, parallels have been drawn to explain ways that parents and children cope with cultural and racial–ethnic differences in transracial and intercountry adoption. Dalen and Saetersdal (1987) felt that many intercountry adoptees experienced a double bind—a paradox—living in a "psychological no-man's land because they at the same time both belong and do not belong [to either birth or adopted cultures]. Their position is marginal" (pp. 43–44). As a result of the physical characteristics of children adopted from China, society will often identify and treat them, at least initially, as Asian rather than American. A distinctly different physical appearance will probably result in Chinese adoptees needing to explain their "Chinese-ness" to many Americans and their "American-ness" to many Chinese (Tessler et al., 1999). This reality places additional importance on the strategies that parents use to cope with differences in the family and how they prepare their children to cope with and successfully resolve encounters with discrimination and racism.

Deciding how to treat differences between parents and children adopted from other countries is not unique to the United States. Similar to the United States, parents in Canada and many Western European countries have chosen intercountry adoption as a means to build families. For example, during the period from 1968 to 1975 a number of children from Vietnam, either abandoned or orphaned in the Vietnam War, were adopted by Norwegian families. A study by Dalen and Saetersdal (1987) applied Kirk's (1964) coping-strategies model in an effort to explain how these Vietnamese adoptees handled the racial–ethnic and cultural differences between themselves, their adopted families, and Norwegian society. In the course of their investigation, Dalen and Saetersdal concluded that Kirk's original model was incomplete and did not adequately explain adoptees' situation. They increased the complexity of the original theory by adding a third dimension they termed "stressing the differences" (see Figure 5.1), referring to "those psychological mechanisms that enhance, underline, and stress the ethical and psychological differences in such a way that they overshadow other, perhaps equally strong, traits in the adoptees' psychological make-up" (p. 45). In a sense, stressing the differences can be viewed as an extreme form of acknowledging differences between adoptive parents and child.

Dalen and Saetersdal (1987) also believed that coping patterns were not static but fluid and dynamic, influenced by a wide range of social (e.g., environment) and personal factors (e.g., personality and existing relationships). The combination of (1) the influence of context and personal factors, and (2) the three-dimensional model better illustrates the complexity involved in coping with cultural and racial–ethnic differences: "An individual might easily be put into a situation where A (acknowledgement of difference) will be the dominating factor within the family, B (rejection of difference) in the school, and C (stressing the difference) in the social situation outside the family and school arenas" (p. 46). The competing pressures caused by three separate value systems and the subsequent need to successfully cope with all three dimensions can often create ambiguous and controversial situations for parents and intercountry adoptees, resulting in greater difficulty establishing a clear self-identity.

Brodzinsky's Curvilinear Model of Coping Strategies

Brodzinsky (1987) also applied Kirk's (1964) description of parent coping patterns to explain how adoptees deal with differences that result from adoption. Independently, Brodzinsky came to the same conclusions as Dalen and Saetersdal (1987); that is, development and use of coping patterns is actually more complex than originally hypothesized by Kirk. Based on his clinical impressions, Brodzinsky described a third pattern in which some parents took the acknowledgment of differences to an extreme, an insistence of differences. Rather than reflecting a linear relationship among the three dimensions—acknowledgment, rejection, and insistence of differences—he proposed a curvilinear relationship (see Figure 5.1). On one end of the continuum an insistence on differences describes parents who stress the differences between themselves and their adopted child to the point that they become a major focus of the family; this is taking an acknowledgment of differences to the extreme. Stressing differences can result in feelings of disconnectedness or disengagement among family members. On the opposite end of the continuum are adoptive parents who reject any differences and find it difficult to allow individuation among family members. "In between these two extremes are the majority of adoptive families—families that take a moderate position on the rejection—acknowledgment continuum" (Brodzinsky, 1987, p. 43).

Brodzinsky (1987) also believed that coping patterns are dynamic, not only in response to different contexts, but also as family members grow and mature intellectually, emotionally, and physically. For example, adoptive parents' coping patterns often change as their children progress from infancy through childhood and adolescence. During infancy differences may be downplayed in order to build family relationships. In childhood, coping patterns may gradually change to acknowledge differences and recognize the child's adoptive status and, during adolescence, the child's racial–ethnic identity: "It is assumed that the rejection-of-difference pattern is more likely to be manifested during early periods of the family life-cycle and that with development there occurs a shift in parental coping toward greater acceptance of the differences inherent in adoptive family life" (p. 42).

Tessler and Colleagues' Approaches to Bicultural Socialization

So far we have examined three increasingly complex explanations of the strategies that families use to cope with differences inherent in adoptive situations. Another perspective that is relevant when considering how parents cope with differences in children adopted from China is the approach used to introduce and nurture a sense of cultural and ethnic heritage in adopted children. We believe the explanations of (1) coping with differences and (2) acknowledging heritage are quite similar and briefly turn our attention to this issue.

Tessler and colleagues (1999) outlined four approaches commonly used to introduce and nurture a sense of culture and heritage in children adopted from China: acculturation, alternation, assimilation, and child's choice. These models of cultural adaptation "roughly correspond to major categories that have been used to model patterns of immigrant adaptation in the United States to a second culture" (p. 106), and when viewed broadly reflect the major explanations of cultural composition in the United States: melting pot, separatism, or cultural pluralism. These approaches also conform, to some degree, with the three main coping styles identified in Brodzinsky's (1987) revised model of familial coping strategies. The approaches to acknowledging cultural heritage presume the availability of two distinct sets of ethnic characteristics from which to choose. "The construction of confident and effective social identities will depend on how conflicts between competing standards are resolved" (Tessler et al., 1999, p. 106). Tessler and colleagues referred to this process as "bicultural socialization."

One socialization strategy that some parents employ is "assimilation," the idea "that the standards of American culture are 'privileged' and that a positive self-identity can best be achieved by fully accepting the perspectives of the dominant majority in the United States" (Tessler et al., 1999, p. 106). Assimilation reflects a belief that the United States is a great melting pot where immigrants from around the world come to start new lives. However, in exchange for the opportunities that the United States offers, immigrants are expected to "fit in," to let go of old cultural ways and beliefs and accept "American" cultural values and practices.

An obvious advantage to assimilation is that people with quite diverse backgrounds can be molded into a single society, all sharing common ideas and beliefs, all working toward common goals. But critics of the melting pot idea argue that individual cultural identities, beliefs, and practices are devalued and must be discarded in order to be a part of the new culture; people give up everything, including the definition of who they are and where they came from individually and collectively.

A second socialization approach, "acculturation," describes an individual who finds "it necessary to learn the new ways of the United States, [although] he or she also will retain some elements of his or her own culture" (Tessler et al., 1999, p. 107). Acculturated individuals are competent in the dominant culture, but because of their physical differences are assigned minority status by the larger society.

The concept of "alternation," a third approach, describes people who are competent in two different cultures and can operate competently in both, depending on the context (Tessler et al., 1999). The ability to interact competently in two cultures is also a major component of cultural pluralism, the idea that people of all different cultures should be able to participate in and enjoy the benefits of mainstream U.S. culture while simultaneously maintaining their birth cultures and heritages.

A fourth approach identified by Tessler and colleagues (1999) was called "child choice." Parents choosing this approach emphasized "the importance of the child's choice with respect to nurturing Chinese identity" (p. 113). The types and degrees of activities reflecting Chinese heritage made available to adopted children are monitored and adjusted by parents to reflect their children's levels of interest and expressed wishes.

CONSOLIDATED CONCEPTUAL FRAMEWORK DEPICTING EMPHASIS ON CHINESE HERITAGE

As we developed the conceptual and theoretical framework for our investigation, we first relied on the work of Kirk (1964, 1984, 1985) and his successors. While not designed specifically for understanding intercountry adoption, the focus on differences applies to most families with children adopted from China in several ways: for example, in dealing with parental roles before and after adoption, physical differences between family and adoptee, children raised as American but treated as Chinese by society, and the inability of parents to help children cope with potential discrimination.

The work of Tessler and colleagues (1999) was also important for several reasons. First, they applied concepts traditionally used in studies on immigrant adaptation to a different culture to the socialization efforts of parents with children adopted from China. This particular application of cultural theory expanded our own understanding of how parents cope with adoption-related difference and acknowledge their children's cultural heritage. We also considered Tessler and colleagues' approach because the focus of their investigation was quite similar to ours, and we wanted to expand on the results obtained in their investigation.

Our combined model describing the presence and emphasis of Chinese heritage in families with children from China (see Figure 5.2) is based on Brodzinsky's (1987) notion of a curvilinear relationship between the insistence–acknowledgment–rejection of adoptive family–child physical and heritage-related differences. We try to avoid the term culture (or bicultural) and the possible confusion its use can bring, instead preferring the term cultural heritage or, simply, heritage. The three dimensions of Brodzinsky's coping-strategies model are viewed in a more general fashion—not focusing strictly on parents' coping patterns or approaches to bicultural socialization—by stressing the amount of emphasis families place on cul-

Figure 5.2
Combined Model of Socialization (Coping) Strategies for Families with Children from China

Balance Chinese heritage with U.S. culture

⊙ Recognition of Chinese culture and heritage is dynamic
and changes over time as adoptee's interest changes

⊙ Family-child differences are acknowledged but not
over-emphasized

⊙ Alternation model

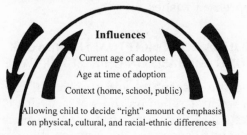

Influences

Current age of adoptee

Age at time of adoption

Context (home, school, public)

Allowing child to decide "right" amount of emphasis
on physical, cultural, and racial-ethnic differences

Maximize presence of heritage

⊙ Extreme emphasis on Chinese heritage

⊙ Child is competent in American culture but
is always identified initially as being Chinese

⊙ Family-child differences are emphasized

⊙ Desire for child to be competent in American
and Chinese cultures (equal status to both)

⊙ Acculturation model

Minimize presence of heritage

⊙ Reject or ignore child's Chinese heritage

⊙ Family-child differences are minimized

⊙ Focus almost exclusively on American culture;
awareness and ties to birth culture are discouraged

⊙ Assimilation model

tural heritage, and the degree to which artifacts and activities indicative of one's heritage are present in the home and everyday family life.

We have attempted to reflect the dynamic nature of parent–child interactions by highlighting personal and contextual factors such as the age of the child when adopted, current age, and the setting. Tessler and colleagues' (1999) fourth approach to Chinese socialization, child choice, is included in our model. However, we view it as an influence on parents' decisions to acknowledge or reject Chinese heritage rather than a bona fide socialization strategy. Most parents in our survey who wanted to gauge their actions on their child's interest reported providing some emphasis on Chinese culture until the child could decided for herself.

The strategies parents use to cope with family–child differences, represented by the insistence–acknowledgment–rejection-of-differences continuum, are positively related to the degree of emphasis placed on Chinese culture and heritage in the home, and vice versa. Parents who reject differences in their adopted child are likely to minimize the emphasis on their child's birth culture. Conversely, parents who maximize the presence of Chinese heritage in their home, whether intended or not, are likely to stress the differences between themselves and their child. A similar relationship can also be drawn with the socialization approaches described by Tessler and colleagues (1999). For example, in households where Chinese heritage is stressed the characteristics of an acculturation model are likely to be observed; that is, there are attempts to learn and be competent in two distinct cultures, although physical differences serve as a consistent reminder of minority (Chinese) status. While these relationships were speculative, we found them plausible and supported through our analysis.

PARENTS' THOUGHTS ABOUT EMPHASIZING CHINESE CULTURAL HERITAGE

Several questions in our investigation were directed at ascertaining parents' thoughts about the benefits and importance of exposing adopted children to their Chinese heritage. First, the frequency that parents engage in discussions about adoption and Chinese heritage with their children is discussed. Second, we examine parents' beliefs about the benefits and importance of acknowledging Chinese heritage to their adopted child.

Adoption and Cultural Heritage

Kirk (1964, 1984) claimed that the most constructive strategy for dealing with adoption is to acknowledge the differences that exist in parental roles and between family members and adopted child. In most intercountry adoptions, ongoing parental acknowledgment of the adoption is likely to occur, simply because of physical differences. It is difficult to deny a child's intercountry adopted status or suppress the issue of adoption when the child is physically different from her parents (Trolley et al., 1995). Thus, understanding how adoptive families with children from China deal with the issue of difference is an important one to consider.

Generally, most parents in our study felt they acknowledged adoption and the Chinese cultural heritage of their child on an occasional or more-frequent basis (see Table 5.1). We felt, however, that parents would probably adjust their patterns of acknowledging adoption and cultural heritage based on their children's ability to comprehend the complexity of these two topics. To examine this possibility, we divided parent responses into three comparable groups based on the distri-

Table 5.1
Frequency of Acknowledging Adoption and Cultural Heritage

Items	Never		Seldom		Occasionally		Frequently		Quite often		M	sd
	n	%	n	%	n	%	n	%	n	%		
Ages 2-26 months												
Discusses adoption with child	28	27.2	10	9.7	25	24.3	21	20.4	19	18.4	2.93	1.5
Discusses birth cultural heritage with child	12	13.3	15	16.7	37	41.1	14	15.6	12	13.3	2.99	1.2
Frequency of exposure to birth cultural -heritage	3	2.9	8	7.8	40	38.8	33	32.0	18	17.5	3.83	3.1
Ages 27-46 months												
Discusses adoption with child	10	9.3	12	11.1	27	25.0	41	38.0	18	16.7	3.42	1.2
Discusses birth cultural heritage with child	9	8.5	28	26.4	34	32.1	22	20.8	13	12.3	3.02	1.2
Frequency of exposure to birth cultural heritage	0	0.0	16	14.5	29	26.4	35	31.8	30	27.3	3.72	1.0
Ages 47 months and older												
Discusses adoption with child	1	0.9	0	0.0	15	13.4	62	55.4	34	30.4	4.14	0.7
Discusses birth cultural heritage with child	3	2.7	15	13.6	40	36.4	34	30.9	18	16.4	3.45	1.0
Frequency of exposure to birth cultural heritage	0	0.0	8	7.1	23	20.5	37	33.0	43	38.4	4.21	2.0

Note: Totals may not equal 100 percent due to missing data and rounding error.

bution of adoptee ages at the time of survey completion: two to twenty-six months of age ($n = 109$), twenty-seven to forty-six months ($n = 110$), and forty-seven months and older ($n = 112$).

Distinct acknowledgment patterns were identified for adoptees in different age groups. Parents with infants and toddlers (two to twenty-six months old) were less likely to acknowledge adoption than parents with older children. Slightly less than two-thirds of parents with young children (twenty-seven to forty-six months old) acknowledged issues related to adoption on an occasional or frequent basis (i.e., frequency ranged from once every other month to once or twice monthly). Parents with older children (forty-seven months old or older) were likley to address general adoption-related issues on a frequent (once or twice monthly) to quite-often basis (one or more times weekly).

As expected, parents also increased the frequency of their family discussions about Chinese cultural heritage as their adopted children grew older. The least frequent discussions occurred with the youngest adoptees (younger than twenty-six months of age) where 41.1 percent of parents reported having only occasional discussions. Almost one-third of parents in this group ($n = 27$) reported having only one or two family discussions per year about cultural heritage. The frequency of discussion was higher for families with older children. Two-thirds of the parents ($n = 69$) with children twenty-seven to forty-six months of age and over three-fourths of parents with older children ($n = 74$) reported having occasional or more-frequent discussions about Chinese cultural heritage.

Most adoptees, regardless of age, received some degree of exposure to Chinese cultural heritage. For example, 49.5 percent of the youngest children were exposed to cultural artifacts and events on a weekly or daily basis, while 59.1 percent of children between twenty-seven and forty-six months of age and 71.4 percent of the oldest age group experienced similar levels of exposure to their Chinese cultural heritage. While we expected this type of acknowledgment pattern, no prior information was available to show how parents react to the dual concerns of acknowledging adoption and cultural heritage to their children adopted from China.

Perceived Benefits and Importance of Chinese Heritage

The next series of questions we posed were designed to determine the views of adoptive parents toward the benefits and importance of maintaining some emphasis on Chinese heritage for their adopted children. As with our previous analysis of parental acknowledgment, we anticipated that parents' responses might vary based on the age of their adopted children, which would serve as a general indicator of ability to comprehend the complexities inherent in intercountry adoption and understanding Chinese cultural heritage. As before, adoptees were divided into three age groups: two to twenty-six months of age ($n = 109$), twenty-seven to forty-six months ($n = 110$), and forty-seven months and older ($n = 112$). We expected to see fairly strong and consistent beliefs about the positive aspects of providing children with exposure to their birth culture and heritage. Our results support this expectation (see Table 5.2). Regardless of their adopted children's ages, almost all parents agreed or strongly agreed with statements asserting the positive benefits and importance of exposing their children to their birth heritage. Most parents also felt that recognition of Chinese heritage would be relevant in the development of their children's personal identity. We noted a tendency for parents with children in the two older age groups (twenty-seven months or older) to respond with "strongly agree" more than parents with the youngest children. In general, however, most parents agreed that acknowledging their children's Chinese cultural heritage was both important and beneficial.

Table 5.2
Importance and Benefits of Acknowledging Cultural Heritage

Items	Strongly disagree		Disagree		Agree		Strongly agree		M	sd
	n	%	n	%	n	%	n	%		
Ages 2–26 months										
It is *beneficial* to expose adoptee to Chinese culture.	2	1.9	0	0.0	47	44.3	57	53.8	3.50	0.61
It is *important* to expose adoptee to Chinese culture.	2	1.9	0	0.0	49	46.7	54	51.4	3.48	0.61
It is *important* for adopted child to identify with both American and Chinese cultures.	3	2.8	7	6.6	42	39.6	54	50.9	3.39	0.74
Recognition of Chinese culture is/will be *relevant* to our adopted child's personal adjustment.	0	0.0	10	9.6	64	61.5	30	28.8	3.19	0.59
Recognition of Chinese culture is/will be *relevant* to our adopted child's development of personal identity.	2	1.9	4	3.8	60	57.1	39	37.1	3.30	0.63
Ages 27–46 months										
It is *beneficial* to expose adoptee to Chinese culture.	0	0.0	1	0.9	36	33.3	71	65.7	3.65	0.50
It is *important* to expose adoptee to Chinese culture.	0	0.0	2	1.9	32	29.6	74	68.5	3.67	0.51
It is *important* for adopted child to identify with both American and Chinese cultures.	2	1.9	6	5.7	35	33.0	63	59.4	3.50	0.69
Recognition of Chinese culture is/will be *relevant* to our adopted child's personal adjustment	0	0.0	9	8.6	47	44.8	49	46.7	3.38	0.64
Recognition of Chinese culture is/will be *relevant* to our adopted child's development of personal identity.	1	0.9	8	7.5	42	39.6	55	51.9	3.42	0.68
Ages 47 months and older										
It is *beneficial* to expose adoptee to Chinese culture.	2	1.9	1	1.0	34	33.0	66	64.1	3.59	0.62
It is *important* to expose adoptee to Chinese culture.	2	1.9	1	1.0	35	34.0	65	63.1	3.58	0.62
It is *important* for adopted child to identify with both American and Chinese cultures.	2	2.0	5	4.9	39	38.2	56	54.9	3.46	0.69
Recognition of Chinese culture is/will be *relevant* to our adopted child's personal adjustment.	1	1.0	8	7.7	49	47.1	46	44.2	3.35	0.66
Recognition of Chinese culture is/will be *relevant* to our adopted child's development of personal identity.	3	2.9	2	1.9	49	47.6	49	47.6	3.40	0.68

Note: Totals may not equal 100 percent due to missing data and rounding error.

Awareness and Knowledge of Chinese Cultural Heritage

Adoptive parents, for the most part, recognized the important and beneficial role that acknowledging Chinese cultural heritage plays in adoptees' lives. Parents were also sensitive to their child's ability to understand issues related to both adoption and birth heritage, as reflected in an increased frequency of acknowledging these issues as adoptees grew older. Another facet of these concerns is families' knowledge and awareness of Chinese cultural heritage (see Table 5.3). Parents perceived that their adopted children's

Table 5.3
Adoptees' Awareness and Family Knowledge of Chinese Cultural Heritage

	None		Slight		Adequate		A great deal			
	n	%	n	%	n	%	n	%	M	sd
Ages 2–26 months										
How aware is your adopted child of her Chinese cultural heritage?	57	58.8	19	19.6	11	11.3	10	10.3	1.73	1.03
How knowledgeable are you and your family about Chinese cultural heritage?	1	1.0	43	41.7	47	45.6	12	11.7	2.68	0.69
Ages 27–46 months										
How aware is your adopted child of her Chinese cultural heritage?	14	13.1	44	41.1	28	26.2	21	19.6	2.52	0.96
How knowledgeable are you and your family about Chinese cultural heritage?	1	0.9	50	45.5	46	41.8	13	11.8	2.65	0.70
Ages 47 months and older										
How aware is your adopted child of her Chinese cultural heritage?	1	0.9	12	10.7	36	32.1	63	56.3	3.44	0.72
How knowledgeable are you and your family about Chinese cultural heritage?	0	0.0	28	25.0	66	58.9	18	16.1	2.91	0.64

Column group header: Level of awareness and knowledge

Note: Totals may not equal 100 percent due to missing data and rounding error.

awareness of their birth heritage was directly related to their age. Over one-half of responding parents with the youngest children (*n* = 57) felt their children were relatively unaware of their Chinese background. Conversely, over half of parents with the oldest children (*n* = 63) felt their children were very aware of their cultural heritage.

When asked about their level of knowledge concerning Chinese culture and heritage, a majority of parents reported having slight to adequate knowledge. Parents of children in the two younger age groups were equally divided between these two knowledge levels. Parents of the oldest adoptees, however, were twice as likely to indicate having an adequate knowledge of Chinese cultural heritage.

Acknowledging Chinese Heritage

Like Tessler and colleagues (1999) before us, we found that practically all parents had assigned some degree of importance to maintaining the presence of Chinese cultural heritage in the lives of their adopted children. Preadoption counseling and research, questions from Chinese adoption officials about adoptive couples' intentions to maintain a connection between the child and Chinese culture, and personal characteristics like higher socioeconomic status, advanced education, and emotional and intellectual maturity are likely contributors to this finding. However, stated degree of importance does not necessarily translate into behavior. Ultimately, parents must initiate discussions about adoption and Chinese heritage and provide culturally relevant events and activities for their children. Some of the written and oral feedback we received clarified the issues that surrounded parents' decisions to minimize, maximize, or balance the importance placed on American culture and Chinese heritage.

Minimizing the Presence of Chinese Heritage

While few in number, some adoptive parents did choose to minimize or totally eliminate the presence of Chinese culture and heritage: language, festivals, names, art, and so on. The focus of these parents was almost exclusively on socializing their child in American culture. Little if any relevance between the child's birth and adopted cultures was recognized. If maintained, the child will eventually lose any meaningful connection she may have had to her birth country and culture. This adaptive approach incorporates ideas described by Kirk (1984, 1985) and others about the rejection of differences, and Tessler and colleagues' (1999) use of assimilation to describe parents' predominant focus on American cultural values and practices.

Trolley and colleagues (1995) hypothesized that rejection of Chinese culture "may stem from adults' lack of understanding of the culture of origin, or their own bias towards American superiority as unconsciously perpetuated in the common euphemism 'the adoption of foreign children'" (p. 468). Another possibility is a belief that emphasizing Chinese culture may result in their child's isolation or increase the possibilities of facing discrimination from the majority culture.

Participants in our study expressed a variety of opinions about the role that Chinese culture plays in their families. One participant felt strongly that while exposure and knowledge of Chinese heritage would be available, she would not make her daughter "live as a 'Chinese' person now that she is American." Mary Petertyl (1996) reacted in a similar manner to a question posted on an e-mail listserv that asked, "How much culture is enough for children adopted from China?"[3]

I think we are setting ourselves up for failure if we think force-feeding Chinese culture and language will somehow make them feel more whole or connected. They will be American Chinese (accent on the American). They will not be like older immigrant Chinese who have one foot in China and one in American. Nor will they be like American-born Chinese, who often live a "double-life," if you will, blending into the American culture with ease, but still immersed in authentic Chinese culture from their China-born parents. Our daughters will be more like the children of American-born Chinese; Chinese face, American heart. While I do think a sense of heritage is important, our daughters' sense of identity won't come from constantly looking back to China, it will come from making them feel at home in our homes, like they belong there because they are our daughters.

Religious belief was another factor cited as an influence on the amount of emphasis placed on Chinese cultural heritage in adoptive families' homes. One parent stated, "We will not introduce Chinese culture because she will only know being Jewish since she was a young baby when we got her and knew nothing of Chinese culture. She is a very special child and we are honored to be her parents. We would not do anything to make her feel different or separate from us (such as Chinese cultural things that are unfamiliar to us)."

Another Jewish mother also points to the potential problems that religious beliefs can pose when deciding if and how to acknowledge a child's birth culture. However, unlike the previous mother, this woman describes how to best recognize and accommodate the various cultural perspectives represented in her family: "Our family is Jewish, so we are actually incorporating THREE cultures into our family: Chinese, Jewish, and standard American culture. It is sometimes a delicate balancing. And one that I haven't seen addressed much in the literature."

Family residence was cited by a couple of parents as critical to the amount of emphasis placed on Chinese heritage. Geographically isolated areas provide few opportunities for exposure to Chinese people and activities and tend to diminish the emphasis placed on Chinese heritage. One respondent who had hoped to expose her daughter to Chinese heritage summed up the difficulty that a rural location can pose: "We live in a small town where there are very few Chinese families and no adopted Chinese girls. We have almost no activities etc. that are Chinese-related. . . . It is difficult."

Maximizing the Presence of Chinese Heritage

Parents who place a heavy emphasis on Chinese heritage purposively construct a Chinese cultural identity for their child, similar to the stress or insistence on differences coping strategy described by Brodzinksy (1987). A prominent factor of this approach is a belief that a strong grounding in the child's birth culture is essential for establishing a strong, positive self-identity. Based on LaFromboise and colleagues' (1993) definition and Tessler and colleagues' (1999) work the acculturation model best describes this approach to acquiring knowledge of Chinese heritage. Parents who stress Chinese heritage assume that it is possible and desirable to have their child be knowledgeable and competent in two different cultures. In most cases, a hierarchical relationship between U.S. and Chinese cultures is not assumed—equal status is assigned to both cultures.

One issue we raised while examining written survey responses was the motivation of parents to choose one particular approach over another. Why do parents choose to emphasize Chinese culture? One adoptive mother explained it to us this way: "I hope we are doing our best to expose our daughter to Chinese culture. I feel it is in her best interest to do so. I know several Korean-born adoptees and this is one area they wish their parents had stressed more. I want my daughter to be fluent in Mandarin. I feel it will be essential for her growth into adulthood both for her personal [and professional] identities."

At least one parent placed a heavy emphasis on Chinese heritage to counteract the limited knowledge and exposure to Chinese cultural heritage: "I could not accurately answer your question on the importance of American AND Chinese culture as being American and growing up American, 99.9% of my child's exposure is American culture. I have to work exceptionally hard to try to move that percentage just a few points, so we do EVERYTHING we can for Chinese exposure."

The following list of Chinese-related experiences described by an adoptive mother in our study illustrates the types of activities that parents seek and the amount of effort that can be expended when Chinese heritage is stressed:

We celebrate Chinese New Year at home and at school. My daughter takes Chinese language lessons at a local Chinese cultural center, has a Chinese language tutor once a week, and attends Chinese acrobatics class at a local Chinese arts center. She plays frequently with other children adopted from China. However, despite all of the above, she feels uncomfortable in her school environment which is primarily Caucasian and resents being "different."

For some parents the heavy emphasis they place on Chinese heritage can be a pivotal consideration in many family decisions, including where the family lives, who they are friends with, or where they go to school:

[We] are planning on starting a Chinese preschool in the area with the help of Chinese families living close by. We are also members of the local FCC group and will be more active in that organization as our daughter gets a little older. We live in a part of the city that has several Asian children in the school system and will continue to live in this area for that reason. We have appreciation for the Chinese culture and plan to vacation in China with our daughter several times as she grows up. Our hope is that she'll have exposure to real life in China.

Parents who maximize the emphasis placed on Chinese heritage discuss similar types of opportunities that are available for exposing and teaching their adopted child about her birth culture and heritage. Socialization to Chinese heritage can be supported in numerous ways, such as attending playgroups comprised of other children adopted from China, celebrating Chinese festivals like Chinese New Year, and interacting with Chinese children and adults living close in neighborhoods or the community.

One activity that was discussed in fairly emphatic terms by some respondents and also tends to polarize people's responses is Chinese language classes. One mother flatly declared that "we want to bring more Chinese culture into [Emma's] life, [and] we will when she starts walking. Our next step is to enroll in Chinese language classes, we would hate for her to not be able to speak Chinese." Not all parents believe that enrolling their child in Chinese language classes is a necessary or important activity, but regardless of one's personal position, the topic is likely to ignite sparks of contention. One parent wrote, "A flashpoint for many people who have adopted Chinese children seems to be Mandarin acquisition for the child, not just cultural exposure. Not sure why this is so frightening for some unless it is the level of commitment required."

Not all parents eagerly embrace the challenges and opportunities associated with acknowledging Chinese culture to their adopted child. Some respondents, like Bob W., expressed negative feelings about adoptive parents who stress Chinese heritage in their home. Bob's thoughts articulate the difficulty with non-Chinese parents establishing a Chinese identity for their adopted child:

We have friends with adopted children who try to socialize them as Chinese. I think it is the height of stupidity when this happens. Here you have people who have taken a 10–14 day trip to China and think they are the *end all and be all* as it relates to understanding Chinese culture and their ability to transmit this knowledge to their child and others. They say they are going to celebrate the Red Lantern Festival or Chinese New Year. . . . It seems rather ridiculous when they really have no idea about this celebration other than on the surface. . . . They try to make their children Chinese, when in fact, they are living in a much different culture.

Balancing the Presence of Chinese Heritage and American Culture

Most parents we have talked with try to find a balance in the emphasis placed on their child's birth heritage and adopted culture; they take the middle road (Benson, Sharma, & Roehlkepartain, 1995). Tizard (1991) explained that "parents must find a difficult balance that neither sets their child apart as being different, nor denies the child's origins" (p. 502). In an article from *China Connection*, a national newsletter for China-adoptive families, Bob Crawford (1998) elaborated on the difficulty many experience when trying to determine what constitutes balance: "Too much emphasis on things Chinese and being Chinese is likely to create, in the child, feelings of exclusion or being different; too little attention to things/ being Chinese is likely to create the impression that this aspect of the child's identity is not valued nor an appropriate subject for discussion" (p. 1). Alienation and identity confusion are risks that parents commonly associated with placing too little emphasis on adoptee birth culture. Positive aspects of emphasizing Chinese culture included adoptees who develop strong self-identities and are comfortable and competent in both American and Chinese contexts.

Of course, the nature of balance is a somewhat relative decision that can vary considerably from one household to another. However, common themes in balancing cultural emphasis included (1) the acknowledgment of adoption and Chinese heritage and (2) a realization that the child will be competent in only one culture, American. An additional consideration for many parents is an awareness that while their child will for all intent and purposes be American, they will always be identified as being Chinese because of their physical differences. These themes parallel the primary elements of the alternation model (LaFromboise et al., 1993; Tessler et al., 1999).

The following comments by an adoptive mother reveal the delicate balance that sometimes exists between birth and adopted cultures. Her thoughts also reveal how emphasis may change in response to the child's age:

My attitude is that my daughter is American now and will grow up with essentially the same culture as the Caucasian kids around her. But other people will see her as Chinese, so it would be good for her if she's familiar with Chinese language and culture. We're doing a lot of it now while I call the shots, to give her a solid background that she can build on when/if she ever wants to. As she grows up, she will have more say in what her activities are, and I expect the Chinese-focused activities to get proportionally less time.

Finally, there are those parents who would like to acknowledge their child's birth culture but are uncertain about the best ways to do so. We found Terri Culp's (1996) candid remarks on the World Wide Web and include them to illustrate that feeling of uncertainty. Terri declared that she was

still sitting on the fence with regards to the cultural issue. I agree with wanting my child to be proud of her Chinese heritage but I question the value of expending a lot of effort to maintain her heritage. If I get her a Chinese caretaker and make a special effort to keep her in touch with her Chinese roots, won't this make her feel different from her playmates who probably won't all be Chinese? . . . When she is older if she wants to learn about China I will readily encourage her but I don't plan to spend a lot of effort learning Chinese. . . . I don't know where the line is drawn between keeping her in touch with her native heritage and overemphasizing it to the point of making her feel "different." . . . We seem to be placing too much emphasis on people's differences and not the similarities.

ACKNOWLEDGING ADOPTION AND
CHINESE CULTURAL HERITAGE

Celebrations of Adoption-Related Events

The use of rituals and traditions are common ways that most of us recognize important events in our lives and reestablish our connections to one another and to a common history or heritage. Rituals, like celebrating adoption-day anniversaries, are equally important in adoptive families, where they provide family members a means of acknowledging the adoption. They can also be helpful to parents by promoting a sense of entitlement (Rosenberg & Groze, 1997). We asked parents the types of events they celebrated to commemorate their child's adoption. The events we initially identified represent important milestones in the intercountry adoption process. Celebration of the day in China when parents first saw and held their child, referred to by many as "Gotcha Day," was the most frequently celebrated of all adoption-related events (see Table 5.4). The other five adoption-related events were recognized in some formal way by only a small number of parents. Readoption in the United States was the least likely event to be singled out and celebrated.

Almost half of the respondents celebrated only one of the six adoption-related events ($n = 163$, 48.1%), most likely the day they

Table 5.4
Frequency of Family Celebrations Recognizing Special Adoption-Related Events

	Responses			
	Yes		No	
Special adoption-related events	n	%	n	%
Do you and your family celebrate the anniversary of				
receiving referral packet from China?	52	15.3	261	77.0
Gotcha day?	254	74.9	56	16.5
Chinese adoption?	73	21.5	231	68.1
arrival home from China?	53	15.6	256	75.5
readoption in the United States?	21	6.2	268	79.1
U.S. citizenship?	35	10.3	244	72.0

Note: Totals may not equal 100 percent due to missing data and rounding error.

received their child in China. The next largest group of parents (n = 74, 21.8%) reported celebrating two separate adoption events. Again, while Gotcha Day was likely to be identified, there was no discernible patterns on the next most recognized anniversary. Interestingly, 16.2 percent (n = 55) of those responding did not recognize or celebrate any of the adoption events we had listed. We had expected this number to be much lower. Replication of this particular aspect of our investigation would be quite useful, not only to clarify our quantitative results, but to determine the specific ways that celebrations are observed and reasons that some parents have for not recognizing specific anniversaries.

The anniversary of Gotcha Day was clearly viewed as a very special time to reflect quietly on past experiences and celebrate the joy of being a family. Parents talked of "spending special time" together or of taking "the day off from work and spending it together as a family." The entire day is often set aside for remembering and celebrating the adoption. The ways that parents recognize and celebrate the day are amazingly similar. Typically, the day is family centered, spent just with the immediate family, close friends, or, perhaps, with other families included in the same China travel group. Some families mark the day with a special meal at a favorite restaurant, almost always Chinese. Families watch videos and look at pictures of their trip to China. They also retell stories, told hundreds of times before, about the first meeting between parents and child or other aspects of the first few weeks spent together as a new family. Some children receive special gifts, usually small but with special meaning, to symbolize the child's Chinese heritage. A low-key "party" with ice cream and cake is sometimes held to celebrate and distinguish the day from other important days. Many families celebrate the day they received their child and the finalization of the Chinese adoption at the same time, since they almost always occur on the same day or within a few days of each other.

Parents tend to recognize the other important events in their child's adoption from China with intimate, simple, and family-centered celebrations. The same elements and activities described for Gotcha Day celebrations—eating at a special restaurant or reminiscing about the adoption—are also used to recognize these other special days.

Acknowledging Chinese Culture

Much of the research we reviewed for this book indicates, to one degree or another, that acknowledging a child's birth cultural heritage is important for the development of positive self-esteem and personal identity. We posed several questions to adoptive parents about recognizing Chinese heritage in their homes. Responses were arranged on a five-point Likert-type scale with a low score of 1 indicating "Never" and a high score of 5 assigned to "Quite often."

We first asked parents about the frequency with which they recognized and celebrated Chinese holidays and cultural heritage. Tessler and colleagues (1999) explained that many U.S. adoptive parents emphasize Chinese cultural celebrations rather than traditional Chinese values and practices of Confucian ethics such as modesty and deferring to parental authority. They also tend to pick and choose those holidays or festivals that suit them, usually ignoring political holidays. Approximately half of our respondents indicated occasionally (i.e., approximately once every two months) celebrating Chinese holidays or festivals like Chinese New Year and Lantern Festival or the Autumn Moon Festival. Another quarter of the sample said they recognized Chinese holidays once or twice yearly (see Table 5.5). These results are not too dissimilar from those reported by Simon and Altstein (1991), who found that about 75 percent of the parents in their sample engaged in some culturally related activities.

One way that parents transmit aspects of cultural heritage is through use of cultural artifacts, such as books, music, art, food, language, cultural ceremony, and clothes that reflect the child's country of origin. We asked parents about how often they used these types of cultural artifacts to teach their adopted children about Chinese cultural heritage (see Table 5.5), and noted several interesting patterns of response. Books were the most used means of learning about Chinese heritage. Over half of the adoptive parents

Table 5.5
Recognition and Celebration of Chinese Heritage

Items												
	Never		Seldom		Occasionally		Frequent		Quite often			
	n	%	n	%	n	%	n	%	n	%	M	sd
Celebration of Chinese holidays?	11	3.2	94	27.7	155	45.7	50	14.7	14	4.1	2.88	0.86
Methods (medium) for teaching about Chinese heritage												
Reading materials and stories	6	1.8	31	9.1	100	29.5	110	32.4	74	21.8	3.67	1.00
Videos and movies	28	8.3	59	17.4	147	43.4	61	18.0	21	6.2	2.96	1.00
Art	37	10.9	85	25.1	95	28.0	48	14.2	52	15.3	2.98	1.24
Music	47	13.9	67	19.8	92	27.1	54	15.9	59	17.4	3.03	1.31
Toys	42	12.4	61	18.0	111	32.7	50	14.7	53	15.6	3.04	1.25

Note: Totals may not equal 100 percent due to missing data and rounding error.

(54.2%) reported using books or stories at least two or more times monthly. Parent's responses on the frequency of using music and toys to teach Chinese heritage were very similar, each reflecting a fairly normal distribution pattern. Slightly less than one-third of parents reported using either music (28.3%) or toys (30.3%) frequently or quite often. Videos and movies were only used occasionally by 43.5 percent of adoptive parents. Similarly, half of the parents (53.1%) only seldom or occasionally used art as a way to teach their adopted child about Chinese heritage.

Contact with Chinese Children and Adults

Parents and professionals involved in transracial and intercountry adoption have often assumed that the degree and quality of adoptees' social integration with people from their own cultural (ethnic) group is critical for positive ethnic identity development. This belief is based on positive relationships that exist between ethnic identity and (1) the ethnic composition of one's neighborhood and (2) family involvement in the social life and cultural practices of a particular ethnic group (Phinney, 1990). Carstens and Julia (2000) identified seven social systems where integration with a minority reference group can occur: neighborhood, school, friendships, religious affiliation, recreational activities, communities, and with cultural artifacts. Ideally, daily exposure and interaction with people of the child's ethnic group would occur in integrated neighborhoods (playmates and peers), and schools (students and teachers; Melina, 1998). In practice, transracially or intercountry adopted children tend to live in predominantly white neighborhoods and attend predominately white schools with little or no opportunity for encounters with people of the same race–ethnicity (Feigelman & Silverman, 1983; Freidlander, 1999; Zuniga, 1991).

Unfortunately, few studies are available to inform practice relating to social integration and involvement. The few available studies suggest that about half of the families of intercountry adoptees place a premium on living and socializing in integrated social environments (Trolley et al., 1995; Westhues & Cohen, 1998a, 1998b). Carstens and Julia (2000) categorized adoptive families according to high, medium, and low degrees of ethnoracial integration. Families with a high level of integration stressed the importance of socialization and developed strategic plans for broadening their existing sociocultural environments. Neighborhoods, schools, and other community structures were significant systems of support for these families. Families that maintained moderate levels of integration frequently cited an ethnic restaurant or recreational events (e.g., cultural fair) as a focal point for social connections. Low levels of integration reflected families who emphasized cultural artifacts—books, art, music and dance, clothing, or toys—but downplayed the importance of social interaction.

How does a greater or lesser involvement with Chinese individuals and communities influence adoptees? Again, we have precious little information from which to draw conclusions. The several studies we were able to locate on this topic presented mostly positive outcomes when adoptive families lived in diverse, integrated communities. McRoy and Zurcher (1983), for example, posited that active involvement in a culturally diverse community was a critical issue in developing a positive racial identity. Feigelman and Silverman (1983) reported that African American adoptees who lived in wholly integrated environments and had frequent interaction with the members and institutions of the African American community were more likely to espouse a positive racial identity. However, they were no better adjusted than African American adoptees living in segregated (white) settings. In a recent investigation, Feigelman (2000) compared the adjustment of inracially adopted white young adults with transracially adopted Asian, Latino, and African American young adults. He found that adoptive-family decisions about where to live had a substantial impact on adoptees' adjustment and identity development. In addition, "Transracial adoptive parents residing in predominantly White communities tended to have adoptees who experienced more discomfort about their appearance than those who lived in integrated settings" (p. 180).

Not many of our respondents directly addressed the benefit of maintaining close interpersonal and community connections to Chinese people and neighborhoods. However, one adoptive mother voiced her experiences: "We noticed a big shift in our daughter's self-esteem and interest in discussing Chinese heritage when we began to expose her to Chinese adults. She had rejected advances of Chinese adults when first adopted, but it awakened her when we took the initiative to invite a Chinese friend to go on a picnic with us."

In contrast to studies revealing positive effects, Westhues and Cohen (1998a, 1998b) found that having family friends or living next to neighbors of the same ethnicity as their adopted child did not result in any significant differences in adoptees' level of comfort with their ethnicity when compared to adoptees who did not experience this type of integration.

While the long-term consequences of living and interacting with people from diverse cultural backgrounds is not presently known, we felt the issue was an important one to consider. Family contact with Chinese American children (peers) and adults (possible role models or mentors) was examined in each of three areas: social events, school, and neighborhoods. Parents reported similar patterns of contact for Chinese children and adults (see Table 5.6). In term of social events, just over one-quarter of parents indicated their children had monthly or weekly contact with Chinese American children (29.5%) and adults (27.7%). A majority of the sample indicated only seldom or occasional social contact with Chinese children (58.4%) and adults (64.0%).

Contact with Chinese children and adults in day-care or school settings was most likely to be an all-or-nothing proposition. Approximately one-fourth of the adoptees reportedly had no contact or weekly interaction with Chinese children or adults. In contrast, the same general proportion of adoptees had weekly or perhaps even daily interaction with Chinese American peers and adults.

Responses about the degree of contact with Chinese Americans in neighborhoods revealed an interesting pattern. First, about one-third of adoptive families lived in integrated neighborhoods and had monthly or weekly interactions with their Chinese American neighbors. As one parent explained, "We are very blessed to live in a city where there are over 22 nationalities represented. We live, work, attend church with, and are friends with many people who are Chinese. . . . Our adopted daughter has as many Chinese friends as American. We also have several friends who have blended fami-

Table 5.6
Contact with Chinese and Chinese American Children and Adults

Items	Never		Seldom		Occasionally		Frequent		Quite often		M	sd
	n	%	n	%	n	%	n	%	n	%		
How often adopted child comes in contact with Chinese *children* at												
culturally related social events?	21	6.2	76	22.4	122	36.0	60	17.7	40	11.8	3.07	1.09
day care, preschool, school?	93	27.4	53	15.6	42	12.4	24	7.1	91	26.8	2.89	1.64
home or in the neighborhood?	57	16.8	55	16.2	76	22.4	61	18.0	63	18.6	3.06	1.38
How often adopted child comes in contact with Chinese *adults* at												
culturally related social events?	13	3.8	71	20.9	146	43.1	53	15.6	41	12.1	3.12	1.02
day care, preschool, school?	80	23.6	57	16.8	46	13.6	23	6.8	98	28.9	3.01	1.62
home or in the neighborhood?	53	15.6	55	16.2	74	21.8	55	16.2	69	20.4	3.11	1.40

Response options (spanning header above Never/Seldom/Occasionally/Frequent/Quite often)

Note: Totals may not equal 100 percent due to missing data and rounding error.

lies (i.e., American and Chinese)." It appears from our responses, however, that the remaining two-thirds of families lived in less-diverse areas and had little to no contact with Chinese children and adults. Several parents explained their limited interaction with Chinese communities as a result of geographic location rather than lack of interest or desire: "We live in a small, rural farming community. . . . The population here is mostly Caucasian and our daughter is the only Chinese person in her school. While we do make an effort to learn about and expose our family to things Chinese, the opportunities here are very sparse, and must be sought out." Other parents with limited interaction or contact with Chinese people made special efforts to connect with them: "I have been very active in starting an Asian Cultural Group, primarily for adoptive families in our own area. We have frequent activities and have attracted Asian inter-married families and some Asian families. This has been very important, since we live in a very nondiverse community with few Asian residents."

SUMMARY

The literature is fairly clear about the importance of acknowledging and celebrating the cultural heritage of intercountry adoptees. In fact, all family members can reap the benefits gained when differences are recognized. Not only is communication enhanced; a sense of trust is likely to emerge, and positive attitudes and values among family members can be nurtured. Acknowledging cultural heritage also provides the basis for strong positive self-esteem, which is essential in identity development. A sense of cultural heritage may also play a critical role in being able to react to racism and discrimination.

While there is wide support for acknowledging Chinese cultural heritage, considerably less agreement is found when considering the right amount of attention or best ways to acknowledge cultural heritage. We adapted the work of several scholars—Kirk (1984), Dalen and Saetersdal (1987), Brodzinsky (1987), and Tessler and colleagues (1999)—to explain the range and implications of alternatives parenting approaches. This perspective places parents' decisions about recognizing cultural heritage differences on a curvilinear continuum, with rejection of differences on one extreme and stressing differences on the other.

Most parents in this study attempted to provide a balanced approach toward acknowledging their child's Chinese heritage. Their decisions were often based, in part, on the child's age and ability to comprehend. Parents with children around two years of age (actually, twenty-six months) or younger were least likely to acknowledge cultural heritage issues, while parents with children four years of age (forty-seven months) or older were most likely. The most variability in perspective and approach seemed to be shown by parents with children in the middle, those between the ages of two and four years.

One aspect of our findings that may become more of a prominent issue in years to come, particularly during adolescence, is the interaction with Chinese children and adults. Approximately two-thirds of families did not live in an integrated, diverse neighborhood or community. While many argue that interaction with same-race peers and adults is critical to experiencing positive role models and acquiring a sense of pride in one's race, it remains to be seen if the limited contact reported here will have a negative influence on self-identity development.

In the final analysis, is it necessary that all children adopted from China learn to speak Mandarin or know how to celebrate tradition Chinese festivals? Probably not. What is important is recognizing the contribution that cultural heritage plays in the lives of children from China, and achieving some sort of balance that supports a child's uniqueness but does not stress differences to the point of isolating the child from other family members or segments of the community. A number of parents clearly stated that their efforts were not intended to replace or diminish the importance of the dominant culture of the home or community, but to extend it.

NOTES

1. Sharma, McGue, and Benson (1996) also claimed that the "role handicap" experienced by adoptive (infertile) parents was normal (they actually used the term "normative") for this group. Kirk (1997) strongly objected, asserting that the use of the concept of role handicap to explain common experiences of adoptive parents "is utterly alien to me, and I have not seen that use of 'normative' in any sociological work" (p. 230). Kirk claimed that confusing the psychological and sociological meanings of terms like role handicap and normative presented problems when trying to understand this particular aspect of his theory.

2. In presenting his ideas on acknowledging and rejecting differences in adoptive families, Kirk (1984, 1985) found that some adoptive parents expressed certain beliefs that were not clearly aligned with either end of the coping-strategies continuum. He referred to a certain type of these views, those that constructed or sustained fictional explanations of the adoptive relationship, as myth. Parents construct myths as a way to cope with the uncertainties and discomfort presented by adoptive situations, to define the origin of the adopted child's status and legitimacy in the family, as well as to establish the parents' role in the adoptive relationship. In any culture, societal myths help people understand, justify, and legitimize their life experiences. Myths serve as a way to cover certain inconsistencies created by historical events. They also help to establish and extend people's sense of meaning and destiny. The ultimate questions addressed by myth are those that ask "Who am I?" "Who are we?" and "Where did I (we) come from?" Likewise, adoption-based family myths shape parents' expectations. They are constructed as ways to introduce a sense of stability during unsettling circumstances and lessen painful situations. "The myth sustains at the beginning and supports through certain crises" (Kirk, 1984, p. 63). While Kirk (1985) initially believed that the introduction of myth into the adoptive family was comparable in form and outcome to other attempts at rejecting the differences between adopted child and parents, he later modified his perspective to suggest that myth might serve a useful function early in the establishment of the adoptive relationship:

There might be exceptions to an all-or-nothing mode of coping. I came to think about people who took a very young infant and who could, for a while at least, indulge in all the long-desired experiences of being parents pure and simple. . . . Until the toddler's concepts with language use, the adopters can indulge in the immediate gratification of rejection-of-difference. They can do so with impunity as long as they are aware of the necessity to shift their behaviors to A/D [acknowledging differences] patterns when the time comes. (p. 53)

Kirk (1984, 1985) identified several prominent myths of origin, including the notion that fate or the direct intervention of God was instrumental in bringing the adopted child and family together. In stating the belief that "our child was meant for us," focus is placed on the adoptive parents. Their role is defined as legitimate. The statement also provides a sense of entitlement to the newly formed relationship that resembles the entitlement automatically present with birth children. Myths can also be principally focused on defining the adopted child's status within the family. The notion of the "chosen child"—the parents looked throughout the world for just the right child and found or chose the adopted child—is a commonly expressed myth. Here, the general theme reflects the notion that of all the children in the world the adopted child was specially selected for a particular family (Hartman & Laird, 1990). The perfect child was found. A variation of the chosen-child theme portrays international adoption as a rescue mission and the adopted child as a lucky survivor (Register, 1991). The National Adoption Information Clearinghouse (1999d) warns that telling an adopted child she is special or chosen can be problematic. Such communication can be burdensome for the child, who may worry about living up to such an ideal. Several societal myths about adoption also influence the short- and long-term adjustment of adoptive families. Power and Eheart (1995) believe the most potent myth about American families is that they consist of concerned, loving people who can overcome any adversity with love and who live happily ever after. When examined closer, Power and Eheart suggest that the connection of two factors, love and need, are at the heart of the adoption myth in contemporary society: "Parents unconditionally love their children (biological and adopted); children without parents need families in which they are loved; therefore, if parents can be found to adopt these children, the children will receive love, and they will ultimately have a happy family life—a 'forever family'" (p. 106). For families involved in intercountry adoption, the introduction of complex societal concepts like race and cultural heritage add additional demands to those already placed on parents as they attempt to establish both nuclear and extended family connections. As the demands on family expand, so too does the need to find coping strategies that facilitate the process. Typically, adoptive parents know very little about the circumstances surrounding their Chinese child's abandonment. For example, the insight of parents in our study was limited primarily to the information contained in official documents received in China. While specifics differ (e.g., location where abandoned or the person who found the infant), a general pattern is discernible. An infant, almost always a female, is found on the doorstep of a government building, in a train station, near a food market, on the side of a road, or in another publicly accessible location. In rare instances a note is attached to the child's clothes indicating a birth date or, even more infrequent, a message from a birth parent. The limited information available between the time of a child's birth and abandonment to the time of adoption represents a significant void in understanding answers to questions of self-identity and shared history. Sometimes adoption professionals construct myths to ease the anxieties created by this lack of information about the circumstances surrounding the child's birth and abandonment. Karen, the mother of a fourteen-month-old daughter from China revealed that "[Our daughter] was probably left early in the morning just before workers came in. The [birth] mother was probably somewhere close by to make sure she was alright our adoption representative told us." This observation may or may not be correct. We simply don't know. While the statement was intended to alleviate undue concerns, some experts argue that presenting this type of scenario to an adopted child—for example, "Your birthmother loved you but . . ."—establishes a dilemma where love becomes equated with abandonment, thus creating the potential for problems with attachment. Register (1991) urged a balanced approach to the discussion of a child's origin: "While it is important to guard against ethnocentrism, we must not be so leery of making judgments that we end up romanticizing their heritage" (p. 173). Mary G., an adoptive mother, took a different approach when discussing the issue of abandonment with her Chinese daughter, Jennifer. Rather than rely on some mixture of reality and myth, Mary stressed the reality and avoided reliance on the abandonment myth: "I am leery of the psychobabble that says create a happy scenario and say that your birth parents had an adoption plan for you. I don't know the truth. . . . I just don't know and I don't want to create a rosy picture where there may be none. My approach now is to explain it honestly but minimally. Not dwell on it or fabricate happiness. . . . It [is] a fact of life." Another myth advanced by adoptive parents reflects their child's birth culture. Many parents of children adopted from China are, no doubt, familiar with the ancient Chinese belief of the "red thread." According to the belief, "An invisible red thread connects those who are destined to meet, regardless of time, place, or circumstance. The thread may stretch or tangle, but will never break."

3. We did not collect data from any active listserv (e.g., post-adopt-china), but adhered to the position that individuals using an e-mail list "own" the content of messages they post (Michalak & Szabo, 1998). Thus, any unauthorized use of information from a listserv would constitute a violation of copyright law. In the specific case of Mary Petertyl (1996), the quote we cite was posted on an accessible (open) Web site with a variety of other information about children adopted from China, and not on a listserv. Thus, we treated this particular quote, both in narrative citation and reference listing, as we have all other information available on the World Wide Web.

Chapter 6

Race, Discrimination, and the Reactions of Strangers

We do look different and we have become a minority family, potentially subject to criticism, odd remarks and prejudice from people of all races.

Adomavicius, n.d.

Intercountry adoption in North America is largely a transracial and transcultural phenomenon (Carstens & Julia, 2000). Reitz (1999) estimates that approximately 65 percent of all intercountry adoptions in North America involve children and parents of different racial backgrounds. This figure probably underestimates racial differences in families who adopt children from China, since practically all parents are white, middle- or upper-class individuals in their late thirties or forties. Over 90 percent of the parents in our sample fit this general description. Racial differences between parents and Chinese adoptees give rise to a number of questions. Is the existence of racial differences between parents and adoptees an issue? How do racial and cultural heritage differences affect adoptive families? Should parents attempt to minimize racial differences in their families and in essence become color-blind to race and culture? Do adoptees face predictable problems as a result of being a minority child in a majority household? Does the intercountry adoption of children from China in the United States and Canada raise issues or concerns from Chinese or Chinese American constituencies?

This chapter examines the issue of race and how racial differences affect those involved in intercountry adoption from China. In our race-conscious society, the rhetoric on this issue can be contentious and highly charged. Perry (1996) observed, "There is no question that the subject of transracial adoption is complex and potentially volatile. However, successful discussions can provide opportunity to increase understanding of different doctrines and policy issues, as well as understanding of complex cultural and political issues that inevitably rise in a diverse society."

This chapter, then, outlines the positions of supporters and opponents, and examines the empirical evidence on transracial adoption. Where possible, we draw parallels to Chinese adoptees. Since we found only a small handful of empirical studies and scholarly articles that spoke directly to the issue of race in intercountry adoptions of children from Asia (mostly Korean)—experiences with discrimination, racism, stereotypes, and prejudice—we have relied on empirical findings from past studies conducted with adoptees of various minority groups as a way to establish a context for discussing our findings and a reference point for future studies.

ARGUMENTS FOR AND AGAINST TRANSRACIAL ADOPTION

When transracial placements first began to occur in large numbers at the end of World War II, they provoked little debate.[1] At that time, the focus of transracial adoption was both international and humanitarian in nature and widely viewed as an appropriate response to countries ravaged by war. Later, in the 1950s, adoption of children who had been abandoned or orphaned by the Korean War was generally applauded or simply ignored. In fact, throughout the early to mid-1960s most professional advocacy groups and adoption professionals supported the notion of transracial adoption. However, in the early 1970s negative sentiment about domestic transracial adoption, specifically the increasing number of African American children placed in white households, began to surface.

In an effort to eliminate increasing numbers of black child–white family adoptions, the National Association of Black Social Workers (NABSW)—a professional organization founded in 1968 to ensure the welfare, survival, and liberation of people of African ancestry through black community control and accountability of self to the black community (http://www.nabsw.org/)—issued a historic position statement in 1972 declaring their "vehement opposition" to the practice. Neal (1996) explained that the resolution did not reflect racial hatred, bigotry, or a belief that white families could not love African American children. Rather, the position was based on experiences of unfair treatment and discrimination, and "directed at the child welfare system that has systematically separated Black children from their birth families." Largely as a result of the NABSW's political agenda, transracial adoption (specifically black children in white adoptive homes) became an extremely sensitive issue and was severely curtailed; it remains so to the present despite federal legislation prohibiting adoption placement based on race.[2]

The notion of psychological harm to adoptees, fueled by an inability of white parents to provide necessary racial socialization, forms the basis of most opposition to transracial adoption (Alexander & Curtis, 1996; Feigelman & Silverman, 1983; Hollingsworth, 1997; Simon & Altstein, 1995). Zuniga (1991) claimed that white parents of transracial adoptees usually live and interact in predominantly white "systems" (e.g., neighborhood, groups of friends, schools, communities). Thus, adoptees are cut off from minority systems where they could develop cultural and racial–ethnic identity and learn the emotional and sensitive subtleties of perceptions and reactions essential for minority children's survival in a racist society. Critics charge that in such cases a minority child "will adapt and develop as a White child, feeling and identifying as a White" (p. 20). It is argued that a child's lack of identification with her race (ethnicity and culture) is likely to lead to identity problems and an inability to deal with individual and institutional racism when it occurs.

Despite the persistence of rhetoric against transracial adoption, empirical evidence amassed over several decades has consistently found no basis for the ideological claims of opponents (e.g., Altstein & Simon, 1991; Bagley, 1993a, 1993b; Bartholet, 1998; Feigelman & Silverman, 1983; Grow & Shapiro, 1974; McRoy & Zurcher, 1983; Simon & Altstein, 1972, 1987, 2000). In fact, over twenty years ago, Feigelman and Silverman (1983) concluded,

The consistent findings of all these studies is that approximately three-fourths of transracially adopted children adapt well in their new homes, and less than a quarter have moderate-to-serious maladjustment problems. The studies of racial awareness, identification, and self-esteem of transracially adopted children have not indicated any evidence of problems among these children. . . . The social and psychological adjustments of Black transracial adoptees were comparable with those of in-racially adopted White adoptees. (pp. 236–237)

Recently, based on the results of their nearly thirty-year investigation of transracial adoption, Simon and Altstein (1995) concluded that transracial adoptees show no special problems. "We have observed Black children adopted and reared in White families and have seen them grow up with a positive sense of their Black identity and a knowledge of their history and culture" (p. 21). The case supporting transracial adoption can also be made from a legal perspective. Bartholet (1993a), a noted legal scholar on adoption practice, has indicated that "there is no compelling necessity for racial matching. . . . Placing more of these children with white families poses no threat to the existence of that [black] community or to the preservation of its culture" (p. 108).

While the focus of this book is not on a narrowly defined view of transracial adoption (i.e., black child placed in a white home), it is instructive to briefly examine the criticisms that have been used in response to an impressive body of empirical and clinical data showing the benefits of transracial adoption. Some of the more prominent criticisms levied against transracial adoption studies have included (1) a reliance on the responses of adoptive parents, (2) limited availability of appropriate comparison groups (sample bias), (3) concern with researchers who overstate or blatantly misinterpret their findings, (4) the position that a lack of negative empirical evidence does not necessarily indicate a lack of harm to adoptees, and (5) a biased cultural perspective in which research has represented the dominant white culture and a preeminent European worldview to frame the problem, identify relevant variables for measurement, and decide how to interpret results for an historically oppressed minority (Alexander & Curtis, 1996; Courtney, 1997; Goddard, 1996; Harrison, 1996; Hollingsworth, 1997; Rushton & Minnis, 1997, 2000).

It is likely that a number of the studies conducted on transracial adoption have suffered from one or more of the criticisms that have been identified. Yet despite the probable flaws in some studies, the body of adoption literature, conducted by a diverse group of researchers over a considerable time frame, overwhelmingly endorses transracial adoption (Simon & Altstein, 2000): "The studies provide no basis for concluding that placing black children with white rather than black families has any negative impact on the children's welfare" (p. 102). We examine specific studies that support this conclusion later in this chapter.

The arguments for and against transracial adoption are similar to those that frame the issues concerning intercountry adoption (see Chapter 2). Critics of intercountry adoption raise national and international concerns about removing children from one country and placing them in a very different country and culture. Predominant arguments against intercountry adoption include (1) loss of heritage, connection to birth country, and ethnic–racial identity experienced by adoptees (i.e., cultural genocide), (2) the exploitation of people living in weak, poor countries by citizens of wealthy and powerful nations, and (3) the inability or unwillingness of adoptive parents to nurture an appreciation of their children's birth culture and heritage in their adopted children. However, as is true with findings on transracial adoption, charges of harm to adoptees who are placed with mixed-race families is without merit.

Views of Transracial and Intercountry Adoption Involving Children from China

Societal and Scholarly Perspectives

The literature is relatively silent on the issue of transracial and intercountry adoption (Carstens & Julia, 2000; Kim, 1995).[3] When compared to the attention received by African American adoptees, intercountry adoptees in transracial situations, Chinese adoptees in particular, have received minimal attention. Why? Several possibilities exist. The heightened controversy and subsequent attention that surrounds the transracial adoption of African American children tends to generate interest and a certain sense of drama that promotes greater research efforts in that particular direction (Courtney, 1997; Silverman & Feigelman, 1990). Some investigators (e.g., Bartholet, 1998; Courtney, 1997; Tizard, 1991) have suggested that parents' decisions to pursue, as well as investigators' decisions to not study, intercountry adoption reflects the pervasive racism in the United States. The logic goes something like this: Adoptive parents prefer to adopt Eastern European or Latin American children because they are most likely to pass as white, while African children are least preferred (Feigelman & Silverman, 1983). Asian-born adoptees benefit from this societal view toward race and adoption. "Public and private opinion does not seem to discriminate [against] Asian-born children, who somehow are seen to assimilate despite obviously different appearance from their White parents" (Reitz, 1999, p. 343). Researchers, too, appear to favor the study of African American adoptees, possibly because they represent the most marginalized of adoptee groups.

An underlying, although incorrect assumption reflected in much of the scholarly and clinical literature is that intercountry adoption poses problems that are identical to those encountered in the domestic adoption of African American, Hispanic, and Native American children by white families. This assumption is another possible explanation for the limited degree of inquiry into intercountry adoption (Ryan, 1983; Tizard, 1991). Intercountry and transracial adoptions are viewed as similar, if not identical, resulting in diminished inquiry on intercountry adoptees.

D. S. Kim (1977) is one of the few investigators we found that challenged the fundamental practice of intercountry adoption with Asian children. In a study of 406 U.S. families who had adopted one or more children from Korea (most were adolescents at the time of the study), he found the majority of adoptees identified very little with Korean culture and heritage but held positive self-concepts when compared to other adolescents. In his remarks, Kim was particularly critical of parents' motives in pursuing intercountry adoption. He wrote, "The noble cause of raising other people's children seems to embrace a new element of self-righteousness, if not outright selfishness" (p. 479). His concern was tempered somewhat by the knowledge that Korean adoptees showed positive initial adjustment, although even here he seriously questioned the long-term outcome for these individuals: "[Adoptees] are forced to face an inferior status consistently ascribed to ethnic minority group members. Empirical data seem to confirm the impression that the so-called good adjustment of these children is being accomplished at the cost of their unique ethnic cultural heritage and identity, partially reinforced by parents' innocent, yet inapt, expectations" (p. 485). Almost two decades later, W. J. Kim (1995) echoed these concerns about the intercountry adoption of Korean children.

Views of Parents, Chinese Citizens, and Chinese Americans

Our understanding of how adoptive parents, Chinese citizens, and Chinese Americans view intercountry adoption from the People's Republic of China is minimal and difficult to determine. Are adoptive parents aware of controversies that surround transracial and intercountry adoption in general and from China in particular? How do parents and others cope with race-related problems? How do members of Chinese and Chinese American communities view intercountry adoption from China?

In one of the few investigations that has examined the perspectives of individuals involved in adoption from China, Tessler, Gamache, and Liu (1999) provide some preliminary answers to these types of questions. They describe the North American media as taking a generally positive, prointernational stance toward Chinese adoption. Although parents' motives for adoption are sometimes questioned by reporters and others representing the media, the most common themes voiced by media outlets revolve around (1) parents rescuing abandoned babies from deplorable conditions in Chinese orphanages, and (2) efforts of American parents to teach their adopted children about their Chinese cultural heritage.

Positive reactions are also typically expressed by Chinese scholars and government officials, who position intercountry adoption as a humanistic effort that has resulted in a greater understanding between Western countries and China. In a speech at the Seminar of the Adoption Organizations of the Four Scandinavian Countries, Guo Sijin (1999), director general of the China Center of Adoption Affairs, expressed his views about intercountry adoption:

We have not only helped those children who lost their parents find happy homes, but also helped those families which needed children realize their cherished dreams. At the same time, the intercountry adoption has enabled us to promote understanding and friendship between us and the adoptive countries and thus further enhancing the friendly relations between us. It is our firm conviction that through intercountry adoption, those children will become friendly ties and bridges of the people-to-people envoys of friendship between China and foreign countries in the twenty-first century. (p. 3)

In perhaps the only published report by Chinese scholars, Huang (2000) indicated that while not opposed to foreign adoption of abandoned or orphaned Chinese children, many Chinese citizens find it hard to understand the motives of foreign adoptive parents. Huang suggests that the difficulty results from many cultural differences between people living in the United States and the PRC:

People in China often ask me why those *Lao Wai* (meaning foreigners) come here to adopt their children. Why don't they give birth themelves? Why don't they adopt in America? Is it possible that they will raise these girls in America to be guinea pigs in experimental tests of drugs? Is it possible that they will raise these girls for servants or arranged marriages or even prostitutes? Do these foreigners without children know how to care for the babies? These suspicions showed that many Chinese people just don't understand why Americans adopt children from China. (p. 2)

After interviewing fifty adoptive families in New England and New York, Huang concluded that all of the Chinese adoptees were healthy, happy, and an integral part of their families.

Most Chinese citizens appear to be genuinely supportive of intercountry adoption (Chinese President Jiang Zemin is, himself, adopted). "Adoptive parents themselves report no suspicions concerning their motives from the Chinese people they meet on the street and in hotels [in China]. . . . The response is uniformly positive" (Tessler et al., 1999, p. 144). We can attest to this through our own experience while traveling in China. Seldom did we leave our hotel in Nanchang or Guangzhou without people approaching us, smiling at our daughter, and giving the "thumbs-up" sign indicating their approval. Several times Chinese citizens who spoke English stopped us and talked about the warm regard held by most Chinese people toward foreign adoptive parents. The general comments of parents who responded to our survey indicate very similar experiences and impressions.

We probably know the least about the views of Chinese Americans toward intercountry (and transracial) adoption of children from China. This situation is, by itself, interesting when you consider the impassioned arguments made by members of the African American community in opposition to the transracial adoption of black children into white families. There is some evidence that the positive or neutral perceptions of Chinese Americans are confounded by social class (i.e., views become more positive as social class and community standing increases).

Tessler and colleagues (1999) speculated that the "segment of the Chinese American community that appears to be most receptive to and interested in the adopted children and their families are second- and third-generation Chinese American professionals and scholars who are themselves rediscovering pride in their Chinese roots" (p. 146). Given our current lack of understanding about how Chinese Americans view the transracial and intercountry nature of children adopted from China, investigation of this topic appears warranted. A focus of this line of inquiry could be determining how people's perceptions toward intercountry adoption influence their actual or perceived roles in providing support to adoptees seeking connections to their Chinese cultural heritage.

What, then, about adoptive parents? How do they view the issues that surround intercountry and transracial adoption? Supporters of transracial and intercountry adoption tend to downplay political concerns and emphasize the right of each child to feel safe and loved in a caring family environment. Not unexpectedly, practically all of the adoptive parents who responded to our study voiced their support for transracial adoption. The arguments they used to support their position were ones repeated numerous times in the professional literature (i.e., every child has a right to a loving and caring home). Several parent comments reflect this point of view:

- "I believe that a child brought up with love and understanding in a loving home is the most important factor. Ideally having contact with others of the same racial heritage is important and opportunities should be provided and encouraged. But I don't feel it is crucial to be in a same race family."
- "All kids deserve parents no matter what."
- "Children need homes. Some families are not properly prepared or concerned with interracial issues as much as they should be, but a home is always better than an orphanage."
- "The most important thing for any child to have is a safe and loving environment to be raised. They need to know what unconditional love is and race certainly should not matter."

A few parents chose to simply ignore or deny the potential problems that racial differences pose, as expressed by one mother who flatly responded, "I do not believe that race is an issue." An adoptive father expressed this view: "I do not understand what all of the race-based problems are about anyway. Most of the people who are greatly concerned by this apparently care way too much about what other people think. I intend to raise my daughter as mine, of course she will know she is a little different from me on the outside, but that is all."

Some respondents were cognizant of the underlying issues inherent in transracial adoption, as evidenced by these representative comments:

- "Given how race-sensitive our society is, it probably makes sense to give preference to same-race adopters. But different-race adopters are a heck of a lot better than an orphanage."
- "It's not for everybody. As a parent you have to be comfortable that there is a part of your child that belongs to something you'll never belong to. You also have to be willing to do the work it takes to make those connections for your child; it just doesn't happen automatically and its hard work."
- "You have to be comfortable with difference and to value difference and find it interesting. And, be willing to experience yourself as a minority, so that your kid can be in the majority sometimes. All these things require time and energy beyond the 'ordinary' hard work of parenting [and] addressing adoption issues with a child."
- "I think there are cases and occasions where it [transracial adoption] can cause problems for the child (teasing, identity problems, etc.), but overall I think the benefits outweigh the negative side. Also, I think there are fewer problems for Chinese adoptees than for Black adoptees."

RACE AND RACISM

Does race (viz., racial differences) really matter in the adoption of children from China? The literature indicates that racial differences inherent in transracial adoption and, more important, the way that adoptive parents deal with these differences can be critical factors in determining a child's long-term adjustment and sense of identity. Bartholet (1998) claimed that "to say that 'race is not the most important factor in defining who they [adoptees] are or who their friends will be' seems to ignore the realities that in certain circumstances race is the defining factor for people of color." However, it is also true that race usually does not matter to people whom race favors, including parents—white and either middle or upper-middle class—who adopt children from China. This general phenomenon may partially explain why over half (n = 198) of the adoptive parents in our survey indicated that racial differences between themselves and their adopted children were not important. The response of parents can be interpreted several ways.

Parents may not see their child as Chinese, but simply as their daughter (or son). In fact, a number of comments we received attested to this fact. One mother admitted, "I sometimes forget she doesn't look like me and then I'm startled to have it brought to my attention." Another parent confessed, "It might sound crazy but we often forget that our daughter is Chinese. . . . [We] just see our daughter." Some parents simply choose to ignore racial differences entirely: "To us, it is a non-issue, because it is obvious." "This is *not* an important issue."

Others appeared frustrated over the question. One respondent declared, "Frankly, this angers me! Who gives a damn if your kid has blonde hair or blue eyes? It's what a person carries inside of them that counts." One mother even used humor as an expression of her feelings about racial differences between herself and her child: "I am happy to say that my daughter will not have to contend with the family thighs!"

By far the most common response to racial differences between parent and child was mention of how children were actually like their parents, both physically and in other ways, such as personality, mannerisms, and so forth. "Our kids look and act just like us, or so we think so." "Our daughter looks so much like me it is uncanny!" "People tell me how much my daughter and I look alike—which we do in a very general way." "Ironically, my daughter looks very much like me." Whether these comments reflect (1) parents' rejection of differences between themselves and their adopted children (Kirk, 1984, 1985), (2) an attempt on the part of parents to not appear bigoted or otherwise race conscious toward their children, or (3) a belief by parents that their children will be evaluated on their own merits rather than by their skin color (Melina, 1998) is not known.

A large number of parents who adopt transracially often start out color-blind, minimizing the emphasis on race and racial differences in the family. While at first thought this effort may seem positive, avoiding racial issues in the home can actually perpetuate racism (Register, 1991). Instead, adoptive parents are encouraged to identify racial issues in order to help their adopted children understand and cope with the racism they will inevitably encounter in their lives.[4]

Racism can be encountered in a number of different ways, from relatively minor experiences such as teasing and insulting comments to more serious forms of prejudice, discrimination, and even physical attack. When asked if they or anyone in their family had experienced discrimination, bias, or prejudice as a result of adopting a child from China, over three-fourths of our respondents ($n = 260$) indicated they had no prior experience with racism. It was common for those who had one or more encounters to mention dirty looks and stares, derogatory racial slurs, and ignorant and invasive comments. Several respondents were questioned about their motives and abilities as parents: "Why didn't you adopt a child from the U.S.?" "[I was told that] I am not a *real* parent so [I] do not have an opinion that matters on [the issue of] parenting." Still others report more disturbing experiences. One mother reported, "[We] had a person call us up telling us to take the child back to China where it belonged." Another mother noted that her "5 year-old was called *fried rice* on the bus and came home very upset." In perhaps the most extreme case, another parent explained she was "terminated by her employer who does not believe in transracial adoption."

Racism is not always overt and confrontational. It can take seemingly benign forms as well (Register, 1991). For instance, stereotypes about the superior intelligence or mathematical skill of Asians serve to predefine individuals and establish narrowly defined expectations of acceptable behavior based on race. Lavish praise and comment on the "exotic" beauty of Chinese children (e.g., the "China Doll" syndrome), can be viewed as a form of stereotyped thinking. Many parents have heard these types of comments in reference to their adopted children. Other types of positive expectations are reflected in these two comments we received from adoptive parents: "People assume she will be smart or a good gymnast or a computer wizard when she grows up." "Day care thought she should be potty-trained earlier because 'They are so much smarter than our White children.'"

Although racism in any form is unacceptable, it is encouraging to note that less than 20 percent of parents reported having such experiences and most of the racism reported was mild in form. Whether these promising findings will continue to reflect the experiences of children adopted from China and their families in the future is largely unknown. However, based on past studies (e.g., Dalen & Saetersdal, 1987), the incidence of racism and bigotry is likely to increase as children grow older and parents are less able to shelter and protect them from discrimination. One aim of a longitudinal investigation on children adopted from China might be the examination of experiences with racism and bigotry at different ages and their influence on development and identity.

With the near certainty that intercountry adoptees will encounter some form of racism in their lifetime, all members of the adoptive family "may find themselves for the first time at the receiving end of racism or bigotry vis-à-vis their children" (Vonk, Simms, & Nackerud, 1999, p. 504). How do parents who represent the mainstream react to this situation? How can parents—who reflect values, practices, and beliefs of the majority culture—adequately prepare intercountry adoptees to cope with racism and discrimination? Answers to these questions assume an even greater importance when we acknowledge that a majority of parents who pursue intercountry adoption "have little personal insight into what it is like not to be White and of European Christian heritage in a society dominated by people of that type" (Register, 1991, p. 156).

Helping children adopted from China or elsewhere to successfully cope with racism and bigotry is a critical, albeit complicated, proposition. While different ideas exist about how best to address the issue, almost everyone agrees that children must be adequately prepared to deal with negative experiences that result from racial difference. Melina (1998) summarized a commonly held belief: "It is important for us to prepare our minority children when they are young to deal with prejudice. That means helping them develop a healthy ethnic identity and survival skills for a racist world" (p. 225). The problem of preparing Chinese adoptees may go unrecognized by parents who often do not witness let alone personally experience racist actions because of their status as members of the majority culture. Register (1991) notes that it is important to remember that "separate from our children, we pass as ordinary Americans. Separate from us, they are still visibly out of the mainstream" (p. 156).

Opponents of transracial adoptions have long argued that white parents cannot possibly prepare a child to cope with negative societal reactions. Ryan (1983) noted that some white parents are likely to reject the idea that Asian Americans and other children with lighter skin color are subject to the same types and intensity of racism as African American youth. They will, in effect, simply ignore the potential for or actuality of racism. Simon and Altstein (1991) showed that ignoring actual or potential racism is not a wise decision, since only 39 percent of the adolescent adoptees they studied had never experienced a situation where "people were nasty or unpleasant about your racial differences." Negative race-related experiences commonly identified by the remaining participants in Simon and Altstein's longitudinal investigation included name calling at school (46%), insulting remarks made by people in public (26%), and racial jokes or insulting remarks made by friends or teacher (28%).

Parents without direct experience with racism often react inappropriately when their child reports its occurrence. Simon and Altstein (1991) reported that 63 percent of adoptees had told their parents about a racially related incident. Adolescents reported that most parents downplayed the incident. "We feel angry, frightened, eager to soothe. A common response is to tell the child that everybody gets picked on for something or other" (Register, 1991, p. 160). This type of approach, while appropriate for members of the majority culture, does not help adoptees understand that racism is not an individual experience directed at them personally, but rather is a reaction to a group (Winston, 1995). (A more complete look at the influence of race on self-identity can be found in Chapter 8.)

LIFE IN A FISHBOWL: THE REACTION OF STRANGERS

In their book *Being Adopted: The Lifelong Search for Self*, Brodzinsky, Schechter, and Henig (1992) relate the story of an adolescent Korean adoptee who complained that when he and his family went out in public together they were instantly recognized as an adoptive family because of racial differences. The young man exclaimed, "It's like living in a fishbowl!" The loss of privacy and feelings of being on display that result from the physical differences between adoptees and family members are common experiences for practically all intercountry adoptees and their families.

In our study, 90 percent (*n* = 306) of parents said that they had been approached by strangers, most on numerous occasions. Encounters with strangers seemed to occur anywhere and any time adoptive families were in public with their adopted children. One mother admitted that she understood how pregnant women must feel when people rub their tummy. "It's as if an open invitation exists that says, 'Ask me.'"

Whether encounters occurred at the grocery store, a shopping mall, a restaurant, in church, on the street, in an airplane, or at a carnival, they were for the most part positive. While encouraging, it is important to consider that even positive exchanges can take their toll on adoptive families. "Questions arising out of benevolence, curiosity, ignorance, or intolerance can leave the family, often the child, feeling vulnerable or different" (Trolley, 1995, p. 263).

Parents often encountered people who expressed their curiosity about their child's origin, her relationship to the family, age at the time of adoption, and other questions related to the parent's experiences of adopting from China. Even though most public encounters were positive experiences for adoptive parents, the exchanges they had with strangers could be characterized, at times, as interesting: "Is your daughter Chinese?" "People sometimes ask if my husband is Chinese? When I say no, you can really see the wheels spinning." "How much did you pay for her?" "When I tell them she is from China, they often comment about China not liking girls and what a 'saint' I am from 'saving her.' I make an effort to correct them on both of those points." "[I'm] usually asked where she is from. After I say Kennesaw, I might add that she was born in China." "A common one I hate is when asked where she is from. I respond 'Philadelphia' (where we are living). Response: 'No, where is she *really* from?'"

Sometimes strangers are interested in the process or related personal experiences with adoption from China: "I find it happens most with someone who longs to adopt, or someone who has a connection with someone who has adopted internationally." "A gentleman stopped me in a store to ask where my daughter was from. It turned out that he and his wife had just completed their adoption dossier to send to China." "Many people comment about someone they know with an adopted daughter from China and [we] immediately feel a bond because of this similarity."

Most recently we were in the bookstore and my daughter and I had gone by this particular gentleman a couple of times and he was grinning at us. We later sat next to him for coffee and while our daughter was helping Dad bring coffee to our table, the gentleman asked if she was our daughter. I said "Yes," and then he told me that he and his wife had arrived from China with twins two weeks ago. I should have recognized that goofy grin!

The frequency of encounters was an issue for only a relatively small number of parents. This was a typical comment: "Numerous times I have been approached by people of all ages, races, and genders wanting to know if my daughter was adopted." Other adoptive parents noticed the relative frequency of strangers' comments about their child's appearance (viz., beauty): "A lady came up to us at a fast food restaurant and said 'Your daughter is beautiful. Is she adopted? (Yes) Where is she from?'" "Our child is very beautiful and appealing. People are very taken with her and occasionally ask questions." "In almost every public setting we go with her, people tell us how beautiful she is and some ask questions about her adoption." "Almost daily someone approaches her and tells us/her how pretty she is."

Unfortunately, not all encounters with strangers are positive. We received a small number of descriptions about the negative encounters a few adoptive parents had experienced. Sometimes strangers questioned the motives of adoptive parents: "I have even had people ask me why I ever would want to do such a thing." "Why did you decide to adopt from China when there are plenty of kids in the USA that need good homes?" One mother related a story about the reaction of a fellow shopper: "One woman came up to me in the grocery store from the back . . . her face looked shocked as she noticed [my daughter] was Chinese. She stated, 'Oh my, she's Chinese!'" "Walking down the street . . . a lady looked at us and [our daughter] and said 'Bastards!'"

Parents have had other race-related encounters with both strangers and family, although they are often referred to as minor. Dirty looks and stares seemed to be taken in stride. However, more negative and invasive actions and comments were also reported. One parent was disturbed by the racist reaction of a stranger who asked if her daughter was Chinese. When told that she was, the stranger proceeded to denounce China and indicated he had no respect for the Chinese people. In fact, he made it quite clear to the adoptive mother he hated the Chinese immensely. Fortunately, most of the other racial incidents reported to us were not as negative or confrontational, although their effects on parents were equally upsetting. "People ask if she speaks Chinese and pretend to talk Chinese to her." Derogatory names, kids pulling the sides of their eyes, and taunting by peers were other examples of negative race-based actions experience by some of the adoptees.

One's immediate family is not always above making racial comments about the adoptive parents and child. One Asian American adoptive mother relayed this experience. "My family which is Japanese feels embarrassed that I had to go to China to adopt a child. They would have preferred that I go to Japan. My mother apologizes." Another mother described the reaction of her family to the announcement of her and her husband's decision to adopt a child from China. They asked, "What will you do if she grows up and wants to marry a White man? Does she eat a lot of rice?"

The willingness of strangers to approach adoptive parents and children appears to lessen as children get older. One parent noted, "When my daughter was much younger people at the mall or in the grocery store would ask where she was from and, less often, if she was adopted. It rarely happens anymore." "For whatever reason, it seems that this [being approached by strangers] has not happened as often as she [adopted daughter] has gotten older."

SUMMARY

There is little doubt that intercountry and transracial adoptions affect members of adoptive families as much as, perhaps more than, the children who are placed there. Some have noted that the status of adoptive families changes from being members of the dominant culture (and enjoying the perks associated with membership in the dominant culture) to one distinguished by its multiculturalism and its minority status. People who rarely if ever have experienced discrimination or racism can suddenly find themselves under closer scrutiny. Living life in a fishbowl can have negative effects if families are not prepared for the attention, both positive and negative, they are likely to receive as a result of adopting a child from China.

Parents with children from China need to be aware of how racial discrimination and prejudice can affect members of their family, particularly their adopted child. It is encouraging that, to date, almost all reported interactions with others have been positive and supportive. However, not all are. Are adoptive parents prepared, or even able, to help their Chinese children understand racism and ways to deal with it? Bartholet (1998) reminds us all that children who are assigned minority status must understand how they are viewed by others in order to protect themselves physically and emotionally from racism. Work remains to be done.

What about the future? What will happen to Chinese adoptees as they grow up and are no longer perceived as cute and innocent by our society? What can Chinese adoptees expect when, as adolescents, they begin to become more independent and lose the protective umbrella they enjoyed as members of mainstream families? Will uneasy relations and periodic tensions with the People's Republic of China affect the way adoptees are treated? Answers to complicated questions like these are unknown. A lack of response from the Chinese American community, a generally held societal view that people of Asian descent are a "model minority," limited empirical investigation in this area, and the sensitivity of racial issues in the United States make finding answers difficult, but important nonetheless.

NOTES

1. Although the term "transracial adoption" refers to the practice of placing any minority child in the home of an adoptive family of the majority culture, the bulk of the professional literature and ensuing debate on this topic has reserved the term and focus for the placement of African American children, and to a lesser degree Native American children, in white adoptive homes (Bausch & Serpe, 1997; Hollingsworth, 1997, 1998; Reitz, 1999). We use the term in its broader sense.

2. Federal legislation—the Howard M. Metzenbaum Multiethnic Placement Act of 1994 (MEPA; Public Law 103–382) and the Interethnic Adoption Provisions of 1996 (Public Law 104–188)—was enacted in the mid-1990s prohibiting any agency or service involved in adoption from delaying or denying the placement of a child based on the race, color, or national origin of either the child or the adoptive parents (Brooks, Barth, Bussiere, & Patterson, 1999; National Adoption Information Clearinghouse, 1999e). Unfortunately, passage of federal legislation has done little to moderate the positions staked out by those who oppose transracial adoption. In her book *Family Bonds: Adoption and the Politics of Parenting,* Bartholet (1993a) notes that the position of the NABSW is an isolated one and not indicative of the entire African American community:

There is no particular reason to believe that blacks as a whole would support these policies. The policies have been developed and are promoted by the leaders of one black social workers' organization in the absence of any evidence of general support in the black community and with little vocal support from any other organization. Reported surveys of black people's attitudes indicate substantial support for transracial adoption and very limited support for the NABSW's position or for the kinds of powerful matching principles embodied in today's adoption policies. (p. 109)

3. Here we are referring specifically to empirical investigations that primarily examine race and its impact on intercountry adoptees (e.g., discrimination, prejudice), to the exclusion of other relevant issues.

4. Undoubtedly, Chinese adoptees will experience some level of racial–ethnic hostility in their lives, although the effects of racism on intercountry adoptees is largely unexplored (Vonk et al., 1999). Information is available that suggests racism is a rather minor element in the lives of most Asian (specifically Korean) intercountry adoptees when compared with experiences of African American adoptees (Feigelman & Sliverman, 1983; Kim, 1978; Silverman, 1993). Even so, the potentially negative effects that racist attitudes can have on Chinese adoptees and their families cannot be ignored.

Chapter 7

Preferential Adoptions:
Family Size and Single Parenting

On the whole, Chinese adoptees are growing up in diverse familial arrangements and environments: with single- and dual-parent families; in urbanized, suburban, and rural settings; in multicultural community settings as well as homogeneous and isolated locales; and with childless families and families with biological and/or adopted children. We had not originally focused on adoption in families with other children present or with single parents, or expected them to emerge during our investigation, but they did. Their importance to a sizable portion of the community of families with children from China compelled us to consider them in greater detail. So, while our results are limited by the general nature of the data we collected, even these preliminary data extend our current understanding and establish a tentative direction for future inquiry on these topics.

Both of the adoptive-parenting choices mentioned here—single parenting and adopting a child from China into a home with other children—reflect a situation that Feigelman and Silverman (1983) referred to as "preferential adoption" (i.e., the choice to adopt a child that is motivated by reasons other than infertility). Preferential adoption represents a different pattern of adoptive relationship, one where the possible stresses and crises that typically accompany infertility are minimized or totally absent. "Such stresses seem to have a specially adverse impact on the well-being of children adopted by infertile parents" (p. 8). Preferential adoption, at least hypothetically, decreases the impact of potential crises: for example, uncertainty whether the parenting role is the same as "ordinary" biological parents, and decisions about acknowledging or ignoring physical (and perhaps also cultural, ethnic, etc.) differences between the adopted child and biological family members. As a result, a greater likelihood exists that preferential adoptive parents can focus the bulk of their attention and efforts on meeting the needs of the adopted child rather on attempting to meet their own needs.

In this chapter we examine the characteristics of parents involved in preferential adoption (from China) based on three distinct criteria. First, we take a look at parents that adhere to Feigleman and Silverman's (1983) original description of preferential adoption (i.e., reasons other than infertility). Two other parent or family circumstances are also likely to reflect preferential adoption: families with multiple children and single parenting. In both cases, purposeful choices are made to expand family size.

DECISIONS TO ADOPT BASED ON INFERTILITY

Many couples arrive at a decision to adopt a child because of infertility. Often this decision is a painful one, coming only after many months or, more likely, years of expensive, emotional, and, ultimately, failed efforts to conceive a child. The eventual realization of a couple's infertility conflicts with a societal assumption that married couples can and will conceive. Failure to do so often results in grief and a sense of inadequacy and loss. The imposition of different role expectations for parents with adopted children compound the difficulties in adjustment that parents experience (see Chapter 5 for a detailed explanation).

In their investigation, *Chosen Children: New Patterns of Adoptive Relationships*, Feigelman and Silverman (1983) argued that the unique experiences of infertile adoptive couples give rise to different motivations and interests in adoption than for couples with biological children who decide to adopt a child. To determine whether differences existed between infertile (also called traditional) and preferential adopters, Feigelman and Silverman studied a sample of 712 adoptive families; 60.5 percent were infertile, while the other 39.5 percent had one or more biological children. They compared traditional (infertile) and preferential adoptive families on several factors, reporting both similarities and differences between the two groups. Preferential adoptive fathers tended to be somewhat older, as a group, than traditional fathers. The age of mothers in the two groups, on the other hand, were not significantly different. Educational and occupational attainment was comparable for both groups. However, preferential adopters were three times more likely than traditional adoptive parents to have multiple children in the family: Of preferential families, 79 percent had three or more children living at home, compared to only 26 percent of traditional adoptive families.

In our study, infertility was cited as the primary reason for adopting a child from China by slightly less than half of the sample ($n = 156$). The remaining participants ($n = 161$) gave reasons other than infertility for deciding to adopt. Whether the difference in our sample composition is an indication of actual differences in the perspectives and motivation for pursuing intercountry adoption or simply an artifact resulting from our sampling method is unknown. However, it does seem worth further inquiry given the potential implications for both pre- and postadoption service delivery.

The characteristics of adoptive parents in our study were similar, although not identical, to those reported by Feigelman and Silverman (1983). No significant differences existed in the age of traditional ($M = 42.3$ years, $sd = 5.0$ years) and preferential parents ($M = 42.9$ years, $sd = 5.1$ years). Similarly, no large differences in educational attainment were noted (traditional: college degree = 40.6%, graduate education = 48.4%; preferential: college degree = 37.5%, graduate education = 51.9%). But like in Feigelman and Silverman, differences did exist in family composition. Almost half of the preferential adopters in our study ($n = 74$, 46.0%) had one or more children in their home at the time of adoption, compared with three-fourths of parents in Feigelman and Silverman's investigation. Approximately one-quarter ($n = 43$, 27.7%) of infertile couples reported having other children in their homes at the time of their adoption.

A difference also existed in the age when children from China were adopted. The average age of children adopted by infertile couples was 11.4 months ($sd = 10.3$), while children adopted by preferential families averaged 14.1 months ($sd = 10.0$). This difference is most likely a reflection of the criteria used by CCAA officials when matching adoptive families and children.

The biggest difference between traditional and preferential adoptive families in Feigelman and Silverman's (1983) study was the reason people gave for adopting a child. Infertile couples emphasized personal reasons, such as the desire for a certain family size, companionship for other family members, or pressure from family members to have children. Parents in preferential adoptive families were more likely to emphasize social and humanitarian reasons for their choice to adopt. Examples included a desire to provide a child with a loving home, religious connections, and the promotion of racial and international harmony. Preferential adopters were also more likely to make a conscious effort to control the composition of their family. They were four times more likely than traditional parents (22% versus 5%) to adopt because of the desire for a girl.[1]

Several parallels exist between Feigelman and Silverman's (1983) findings and the results we obtained from parents with children adopted from China. All respondents were classified according to their reason for deciding to adopt. All traditional families ($n = 156$) indicated infertility as the primary reason for adopting a child (per our criteria). Preferential adoptive families ($n = 161$) cited humanitarian and social reasons for deciding to adopt a child. One-quarter of the adoptive parents ($n = 46$, 28.6%) cited a desire to help children in need of homes. When asked why they specifically chose to adopt a child from China, infertile couples were almost two times more likely to respond that their choice was based on the perceived problems with U.S. adoption law than preferential adopters (17.6% versus 9.4%). In addition, traditional adopters were almost three times more likely than preferential adopters to have chosen China because there was no possibility of parental claims on the child at some later date (15.0% versus 6.3%). Conversely, preferential couples were three times more likely than infertile couples (18.1% versus 5.9%) to indicate that their desire for a girl was the primary reason for selecting to adopt from China.

One other issue of particular interest in our study was the views and practices of parents of intercountry adoptees toward their adopted child's birth culture and heritage. Feigelman and Silverman (1983) found that preferential adoptive parents were slightly more likely to express interest in the cultural heritage of their adopted child and live in an integrated community than traditional adoptive parents. Surprisingly, however, when adoptees' interest and pride (or shame) in their birth culture was later investigated, "children of preferential adopters were described as no more interested in their birth cultures, no more proud of their group affiliations, not possessing any greater sense of shame or discomfort about their appearance than children of infertile adopters" (p. 78). This finding led to the conclusion that "it appears that parents' interests and integrated community living arrangements have a minimal effect in engendering a sense of interest and positive feeling for a transculturally adopted child's ethnic identity" (p. 78).

We examined the degree of importance that parents attached to their child's Chinese heritage and the level of integration (contact) with Chinese adults and children (see Table 7.1). Responses to the survey items that represented perceived importance of cultural heritage and integration with members of the Chinese community revealed that preferential adopters attributed slightly greater importance to cultural heritage and provided more opportunities for contact between their adopted children and Chinese American adults and children than traditional parents. Even so, differences between the two groups were relatively small. To determine whether these differences are replicable or of any practical importance will require further investigation. However, these initial findings suggest that infertility does play a role, albeit minor, in decisions regarding adoption and parenting.

Table 7.1
Perceptions of Traditional and Preferential Adoptive Families toward Acknowledging Chinese Heritage and Integrating Adoptees into Chinese American Communities

Items	Traditional		Preferential	
	M	sd	M	sd
It is *beneficial* to expose our adopted child to Chinese culture.[a]	3.51	0.57	3.64	0.58
It is *important* to expose our adopted child to Chinese culture.	3.52	0.59	3.62	0.59
It is *important* for adopted child to identify with both American and Chinese cultures.	3.38	0.70	3.50	0.72
How knowledgeable are you and your family about Chinese culture?	2.70	0.69	2.78	0.66
Recognition of Chinese culture is/will be relevant to our adopted child's personal adjustment.	3.25	0.63	3.35	0.65
Recognition of Chinese culture is/will be relevant to our adopted child's development of personal identity.	3.34	0.62	3.38	0.71
Contact with Chinese adults[b]				
. . . socially	2.99	1.03	3.20	0.98
. . . at school	2.77	1.62	3.17	1.57
. . . in the neighborhood	3.01	1.37	3.18	1.40
Contact with Chinese children				
. . . socially	2.93	1.12	3.18	1.01
. . . at school	2.77	1.62	2.93	1.62
. . . in the neighborhood	3.04	1.41	3.04	1.35

[a]A four-point Likert-type scale was used to indicate level of agreement: 1 = Strongly disagree, 2 = Disagree, 3 = Agree, and 4 = Strongly agree.
[b]A five-point Likert-type scale was used to determine frequency of contact with Chinese adults and children: 1 = Never, 2 = Seldom, 3 = Occasionally, 4 = Frequently, and 5 = Quite often.

ADOPTING WHEN OTHER CHILDREN ARE IN THE FAMILY

Why do parents with children decide to adopt a child? Why do they choose China? Our understanding is quite limited. In fact, the literature is almost nonexistent on issues related to multiple adoptions by one family and the interaction of adopted siblings. In many respects, adoptive parents face the same concerns—whether they have sufficient money, time, or emotional resources for another child—and rely on the same answers as parents of biological children. Howard (2000) reminds us that the decision to add a second child to a family is momentous for many families, "but these concerns are often amplified by the adoption process" (p. 1). At present, there is practically no reliable data to inform us on issues related to family size and decisions about adoption. Results from our investigation offer preliminary understanding about the perspectives of adoptive parents toward adoption and family size.

Over one-third of adoptive parents in our study ($n = 117$, 37%) reported having multiple children in their household. Table 7.2 provides frequency data on these additional children by gender and adoption status. Several interesting observations can be made. For example, while the number of biological ($n = 93$) and adopted ($n = 87$) children were comparable, 61.7 percent of all adoptees were female ($n = 111$). When considering the gender–adoptive status composition of households with additional children, adopted females ($n = 76$, 42.2%) were the single largest group of additional children, followed, in turn, by male birth children ($n = 58$, 32.2%), female birth children ($n = 35$, 19.4%), and adopted male children ($n = 11$, 6.1%). Seven of every ten female children ($n = 76$) were adopted, either from China or elsewhere, while approximately eight of every ten male children were biological.[2]

Parents who have adopted more than one child from China, or elsewhere for that matter, experience the adoption process very differently the second time. Krueger (n.d.) noted that anxieties and stress typically associated with a first adoption are much less intense the second time because of parents' earlier experiences and the presence of a child in the home: "I felt confident because I knew the [adoption] process and knew how to navigate the paperwork maze. I also had a busy two-year old to fill my time during the wait." A participant in our investigation who was a mother of two adopted daughters from China felt similarly: "The second adoption was different in that the wait was easier. Yes, you get anxious when the time is coming, but you know that in the end it will all happen—the first time it is hard to see the light at the end."

Table 7.2
Siblings of Children Adopted from China by Gender and Adoption Status

	Gender						Total	
	Male			Female				
	n	Row	Column	*n*	Row	Column	*n*	%
By birth	58	62.4	84.1	35	37.6	31.5	93	51.7
By adoption	11	12.6	15.9	76	87.4	68.5	87	48.3

Note: Totals may not equal 100 percent due to missing data and rounding error; *n* = 180. Three children were not categorized due to lack of data. Figures represent row and column percentages based on gender by adoption status frequencies.

Why do parents with children decide to adopt a child from China? Infertility was a primary reason for one-third of couples with other children in the home (*n* = 43) and one-half of childless couples (*n* = 112). Humanitarianism—helping a child in need of a home—was a greater factor in the decision to adopt for parents with children (*n* = 27, 23.1%) than for childless parents (*n* = 19, 9.5%). Finally, about one-third of each group identified reasons other than ones listed on the survey as the primary motivations for their decisions to adopt. For example, Karen, a mother of two adopted daughters from China, explained, "We are in the process of our third adoption. We decided on a second child because we wanted our first child to have a sibling. We have decided on a third adoption as we want our children's race to be the majority in our house—and the fact we love children and parenting." Two common responses in the "Other" category were (1) an inability to identify a single reason (e.g., "A combination of reasons for choosing Chinese adoption, no one reason [was] more important than another"), and (2) the speed and dependability of the adoption process in China.

More childless parents were likely to experience difficulty pinpointing their primary reason for adopting a child from China. Many indicated that an intertwined combination of factors led to their decision: "Even as a young child, I was fascinated by international adoption and knew that one day I would pursue [the] same. [I] never considered domestic adoption because of the inherent problems with the system. Chose China over other countries because my interest in and appreciation of the country and culture . . . [was] important for me since I knew I was establishing permanent connections."

Other parents appeared somewhat overwhelmed by the prospect of prioritizing all the influences that resulted in a decision to adopt, as reflected in this mother's response: "Why did we decide to adopt from China? All the reasons [listed] except not exactly sure. I always visualized a child with black hair and brown eyes. China seemed like a good place to find her!" One childless mother cut through much of the uncertainty evidenced in other responses. Her frank and somewhat abrupt explanation caught our attention: "I adopted a child because I wanted a family—not to save a child or the world!"

Parents with children were more likely to mention specific reasons for adopting a child from China. Their responses often seemed more pragmatic and straightforward. For example, a parent of two Chinese daughters told us there were "many different answers to why we wanted to adopt from China including [a] good chance of a healthy child." For parents who pursued a second (or third) adoption, the intangible "pull" or attraction of China and its millennia-old existence, tradition, and culture was a frequently cited source of motivation. "Having one child from China, it can feel very natural and logical to try for a second from China" (Krueger, n.d.). The most commonly cited factor considered by parents was that adopted siblings would share the same cultural heritage, similar circumstances surrounding their adoptions, and some general physical characteristics.

An older mother of five children, two biological and three adopted, acknowledged that "most important to us was the fact that we fit the requirements, and that the program seemed to be open and above-board with no corruption involved." A mother of one biological son, age thirteen, recalled that several specific issues contributed to her decision to adopt: "We adopted because we wanted to enrich our lives, and if we could, to enrich someone else's life. We chose China first because it was a relatively sure thing (there was a child at the end of this road), and second because we were reading very sad accounts of Chinese orphanages." Finally, a father of two adopted daughters, one from Korea and the other from China, framed the decision factors in this manner: "The simple fact was that we might have adopted from Korea again (from where we adopted our second daughter), but we simply did not fit the allowed criteria for that program and those of others. A Chinese adoption was the most viable because of that. We simply fit the profile of acceptable prospective parents."

SINGLE PARENT BY CHOICE

Exact figures on the number of adoptions by single parents, domestic and intercountry, are not available, since the federal government discontinued collection of adoption statistics in the mid-1970s (Shireman, 1996). However, less comprehensive sources suggest that a considerable increase has occurred in the number of adoptions by single parents over the past thirty years or so. For example, Groze (1991) reported single-parent adoptive placement figures ranging from 5 percent in a 1970 study to 34 percent in 1984. Estimates are that approximately 25 percent of all domestic adoptions of children with special needs and 5 percent of all other adoptions are by single women and men (National Adoption Information Clearinghouse, 1999c). Current estimates place adoptions by single parents at 12 to 15 percent of all adoptions in the United States.

While some disagreement exists about the exact causes for increasing numbers of single-parent adoptions, several reasons appear to contribute to this trend. The ever-growing number of one-parent households in the United States, due to divorce and to unmarried women having and parenting their children, has lessened the social stigma once attached to single-parent families. The substantial number of older and special-needs children available for adoption has also had an impact. As adoption agencies have struggled with finding acceptable placements for these children, many single parents have been willing to adopt difficult-to-place children. Thus, single parents have been more readily recognized as a potential and viable placement option. Finally, the adoption requirements of some foreign governments, including the People's Republic of China, do not distinguish between one- and two-parent families (Adopt.org, n.d.; Mannis, 1999).

Fully one-quarter of respondents in our survey were single parents either by choice ($n = 69$, 21.6%) or through divorce ($n = 13$, 4.1%).[3] Interested, we examined the literature about single adoptive parents but found little to help understand this phenomenon better (one notable exception is the longitudinal work of Joan Shireman, 1995, 1996).

Characteristics of Single Parents Who Adopt

Practically all single adoptive parents are women, similar to single-parent families in the general U.S. population.[4] While the data are sketchy, Shireman (1995, 1996) reports that single parents, primarily women, are usually in their mid- to late thirties when they adopt, are likely to have received some graduate education, and hold stable jobs, usually in the helping professions (e.g., education and social work). Single adoptive parents have also been found to be emotionally mature, possess a high capacity for tolerating frustration, and are not overly influenced by the opinions of others. Single parents report lower incomes than two-parent families, which is attributed to (1) a single source of income as compared to dual income and (2) lower wages that are often received by women, the majority of parents in single-parent families, for completing jobs considered equal in responsibility to those held by men (Groze, 1991).

Several of the descriptors found in the literature applied equally to the single parents in our study. All single parents were women (n = 82) and highly educated (see Table 7.3). As a group, almost two-thirds of single parents reported some graduate education, compared to less than half for respondents in two-parent families. In addition, survey participants from two-parent families were more likely to have less than a four-year college degree.

Reasons for Adopting a Child from China

While the attitude of adoption professionals and society in general is beginning to slowly change, single parents are often still seen as a second-best alternative for adoption placement. As a result, many single adults wishing to adopt are asked to accept an older child or one with special physical or psychological needs. For those persons who want to adopt an infant or small child without serious health or psychological problems, intercountry adoption offers a viable alternative.

Most single parents first consider adoption from China because "China is one of the few countries that will adopt [a child] to 'single' parents." One survey participant, a single mother who had already adopted one child, indicated her decision to adopt a child from China was tied to several specific issues: "I wanted a girl. As a single mom, I felt it would be better to have 2 girls, and I found out there were a lot of little girls in China. I also found out the process was relatively easy." Another single mom agreed: "I think it's very significant that China does not place additional obstacles in the way of single parents who wish to adopt."

Responses to two of the questions we asked on our survey—primary reason for decision to adopt and primary reason for selecting China—revealed differences between single- and two-parent families (see Table 7.3). First, two-parent families were six times more likely to indicate that infertility was the primary reason for their decision to adopt than were single parents. Single parents, on the other hand, were twice as likely to list the desire to help a child in need of a home as their motivating factor for adopting. Many single parents in our study listed other reasons to explain their choice to adopt a child. The most prevalent alternative reason was the desire to nurture and raise a family. Mannis (1999) reported this same

Table 7.3
Select Characteristics and Responses of Single- and Two-Parent Adoptive Families

	Single-parent families		Two-parent families	
	n	%	*n*	%
Education level				
Less than high school	—	—	—	—
High school diploma or GED	—	—	6	2.7
Technical school or some college	3	3.7	24	10.9
College degree	28	34.1	92	41.8
Graduate or professional degree	51	62.2	98	44.5
Primary reason for adopting				
Infertility	11	13.6	142	64.3
Children in need of homes	17	21.0	27	12.2
Concern for population growth	—	—	4	1.8
Promotion of racial tolerance	—	—	1	0.5
Not sure	—	—	2	0.9
Other reasons, not listed	53	65.4	45	20.4
Reasons for selecting China				
Adoption laws in U.S.	8	9.8	34	15.6
Children in need of homes	19	23.2	53	24.3
No possibility of parental claims	6	7.3	26	11.9
Wanted a girl	19	23.2	16	7.3
Respect for Chinese culture	8	9.8	22	10.1
Not sure	2	2.4	3	1.4
Other reasons, not listed	20	24.4	64	29.4

Note: Totals may not equal 100 percent due to missing data and rounding error. A majority of respondents from two-parent families were female (*n* = 182, 82.4%), while only thirty-nine respondents (17.6%) were male. All responses from two-parent families have been included. Figures represent column percentages.

explanation as the most common cited explanation of ten single mothers of birth children. Reasons for selecting China were, in most respects, comparable between single- and dual-parent respondents. One notable difference existed. Single parents were three times more likely than two-parent families to select China because they wanted a girl.

New American Families: Chinese Daughters and Their Single Mothers (Liedtke & Brasseur, 1997) provides a unique view of how single mothers perceive and experience the process of adopting a child from China. The written reflections of twenty-three single mothers discuss various aspects of intercountry adoption: reasons for adopting, experiences during the adoption application process, travel to the People's Republic of China to receive their adopted child, and the adjustments to home life after their return.

Several common themes emerge from the qualitative reflections of the single mothers included in Liedtke and Brasseur's (1997) text. These themes, in no particular order of importance or frequency, are as follows: (1) Each woman had always assumed she would be a parent in adulthood, (2) most mothers had actively pursued and were successful in their chosen careers—lawyer, physician, entrepreneur, university professor—earlier in their lives, and (3) most realized, at some point in their late thirties or early forties, that time was beginning to run out on their prospects of marriage and/or more traditional methods of conceiving and bearing children, including artificial insemination. These findings closely mirror the themes reported by Mannis (1999) for a group of single birth mothers.

We offer several quotes from Liedtke and Brasseur's (1997) book that seem to characterize the experience of single mothers adopting from China. For example, the experience of one woman, Mary Jo, was fairly typical: "There was never a question in my mind about parenting as a single mom. . . . Years ago I told myself I would have a baby on my own if I weren't married by 30. Relationships came and went. Thirty came and went. . . . [After ever more complicated and expensive methods of trying to conceive] my doctor told me I should take some time to think over my options and consider adoption. I was 39" (pp. 152–153). Jean, a woman in her early forties, simply explained that "I never met Mr. Right and as I entered my forties as a single woman, my yearning for motherhood increased" (p. 119). Nancy provides a similar perspective about why she chose to adopt a child from the People's Republic of China:

Many people have asked me how and why I decided to adopt a child from China. Needless to say, there were many factors influencing that decision. I always wanted children. In fact, when I was a child my family thought I would marry young and have lots and lots of children. I thought so too— interesting how differently your life can turn out. I'm 41 years old, have never been married, and had no children until I adopted my daughter. (p. 58)

Finally, Barbara described the thoughts that ultimately led to her decision that adopting a child from China was the best alternative for her:

My dream had always been to get married, have several children of our own and further increase family size through adoption. But somehow the marriage but never happened. So answering the question of how I would grow a family was not hard. Adoption was the option I would choose. . . . The social worker told me that the agency had just established a relationship with China. China was looking for parents who were over 35, single or married, and childless. They were placing girls. China wanted me! And I wanted a girl! (p. 34)

Outcomes of Single-Parent Adoptions

Only a few empirical investigations exist that study single adoptive parents and their children. However, results of those few studies clearly show that single-parent adoptive families can and do provide stable family environments for their children. Feigelman and Silverman (1983) reported on their findings from an initial investigation they conducted in 1975 ($n = 58$) and a follow-up study in 1981 ($n = 35$) of single-parent adoptive families, and concluded that no significant differences in physical or emotional health and development existed between children raised in single-parent families compared to children raised in two-parent families. Some slight and consistent adjustment problems were observed for adoptees in single-parent families, although when compared with the adjustment of adoptees in two-parent families differences were not statistically significant. Feigelman and Silverman admitted they had originally expected that "single parents might have more role conflicts and regrets about having adopted than was true for couples. Yet the data showed substantially similar degrees of agreement. . . . Apparently, being a single adoptive parent is no more likely to inspire role distress and conflict than being half of an adoptive couple" (p. 190). The authors concluded, "With few exceptions, both male and female single parents report experiences substantially similar to those of adoptive couples in raising their children" (p. 191).

Shireman (1995, 1996) has conducted a longitudinal study of single adoptive parents, comparing adoptive and birth families. The study, initiated in 1976, has been an ambitious one, as interviews with adoptive parents and adoptees have occurred every four years. The original sample contained thirty-one single parents, mostly African American women ($n = 25$), well educated, with a median age of thirty-four years. Despite considerable effort, sample attrition reduced the original number to only fifteen by the early 1980s. Even with the limitations imposed by attrition and small sample size, Shireman's efforts provide an intriguing glimpse into the lives of single adoptive parents and their children.

Initially, Shireman and Johnson (1976) expressed concern about the isolation of many single parents and the intensity of the relationship between parent and child. These factors, along with anxiety and lack of support networks, seemed to compound adjustment problems for both parent and child. In a follow-up, Shireman and Johnson (1985) found that most adoptees were doing well and accomplishing tasks considered age appropriate, although 20 percent of the children experienced some adjustment difficulties. While concerned about sexual and racial identity, the investigators found no indication of problems in these areas.

Shireman (1988) conducted a final interview sequence when adoptees where adolescents. She explored five areas, including family relatedness, peer relations, gender identity, school performance, and self-esteem. When adoptees in single-parent families were compared with adoptees in two-parent families, she found no significant differences. Based on her longitudinal findings, Shireman (1996) declared that adoption by single parents was an appropriate placement strategy and, in fact, single parents actually hold particular strengths: "What, then, are the strengths of single parent adoptive families? Commitment to the child and the adoption, strength and capacity to handle crisis, a relatively simple family structure, self-confidence, independence, and ability to develop and use supportive networks. Surely these are qualities to be valued in an adoptive home" (p. 31).

While any statement is speculative at this point, we have no reason to believe that single parents adopting children from China would reflect outcomes significantly different from those reported here. Still, future study is warranted, especially considering that the number of single parents adopting children from China continues to grow.

SUMMARY

Chinese adoptees are growing up in a wide variety of family situations, including those with single parents and the presence of other children (either biological or adopted). Differences in family composition and reasons for adoption among adoptive families reflects, to a small degree, some of the diversity inherent throughout our society. No doubt, the types of families who adopt children from China and elsewhere in the future will continue to reflect this diversity.

While there are a lot of similarities between families who are preferential or traditional adopters and between families with multiple adoptions or children and single parents, it is interesting to consider how the preferential nature of intercountry adoption might affect Chinese children differently than children adopted for traditional reasons like infertility. The ways that parents experience stress and grieve over their infertility and, subsequently, their ability (or inability) to focus on their adopted child's needs warrants investigation. Future research should also consider the impact, if any, of preferential or traditional adoptive relationships on parents' acknowledgment of Chinese cultural heritage. Results of studies like these hold important implications for both preadoption counseling and postadoption support services.

NOTES

1. In his groundbreaking work on domestic adoption, Kirk (1984) devoted an entire chapter to exploring the apparent preference of prospective parents for adopting girls over boys. He provided tentative data to support the following hypothesis: "(a) Men are relatively hesitant in approaching adoption; (b) a hesitancy which is related to kinship sentiments. (c) With the wife as the most obviously deprived party, anxious for adoption, and the husband hesitant, a girl may represent a compromise solution for them" (p. 133).

2. Our data are not complete on the number of additional children who were also adopted from China, since this information was not directly solicited from respondents. However, 27.6 percent of the families with a second adopted female child volunteered that the child was also adopted from China.

3. The literature typically identifies two types of single parents: (1) those who purposively choose to adopt or give birth to a child with the expectation of raising the child as a single parent, and (2) individuals who are single parents due to divorce or death of a spouse (the initial expectation of being a single parent is absent). Groze (1991) explained it this way: "A single parent is one who adopts as a single mother or father; those parents who adopt as a couple and later divorce are not characterized as single parents. The former made a conscious decision to be a parent as a single adult while the latter became single parents as a result of life circumstances" (p. 322).

4. It is difficult for single men to adopt children domestically. Unfounded, but deeply ingrained, suspicions often exist that portray a single man who wants to adopt a child as either gay or sexually attracted to young children or both (Shireman, 1996).

Chapter 8

Who Am I?
Racial, Ethnic, and Cultural
Identity Development

Throughout this book we have mentioned the potential influence that race and cultural heritage have on the development of a strong, positive self-identity for intercountry adoptees (viz., including children adopted from China). In Chapter 6, for example, we examined issues of racism and discrimination—both obvious and concealed, blatant and subtle—toward Chinese adoptees (and family members) as a result of racial background and ethnicity, as well as multicultural family composition. Cultural heritage, ethnicity, and race can be especially prominent issues during adolescence, as young people begin to form adult identities.

Identity formation is a major developmental task for all adolescents as they define who they are and what they are in relation to a variety of life activities: career, family, friendships, religion, moral values, and behavior (Wilkinson, 1995). Erikson (1968) believed that adult identity emerges as alternatives (crises) are explored and, eventually, resolved through decisions about identity that reflect personal investment and commitment. These decisions also reflect attempts to attain individuality and autonomy, both essential to a well-delineated identity. "Mature identity implies an acceptance of and comfort with one's physical self, a sense of direction, and consequently an ability to make decisions" (Hoopes, 1990, p. 145).

The process of answering the question, "Who am I?" is often initiated in response to the rather dramatic physical and psychological changes experienced by adolescents that cause feelings of confusion and disconnectedness (Brodzinsky, 1987). However, the foundations for successful resolution of the identity versus role diffusion crisis are actually established in the successful resolution of Erikson's (1968) earlier psychosocial crises (Hoopes, 1990). While adolescence is the period when issues related to identity formation are most acute, the process of determining an identity of "self" is actually viewed as a lifetime activity characterized by cycles of exploration and commitment or consolidation (Grotevant, 1997b).

Resolving the identity crisis, a concept popularized by Erikson in the 1960s, is difficult enough for most adolescents as they try to answer questions about their existence and their role in the world and try to find out who they are. From the perspective of adoptees from China, as well as other intercountry adoptees, the task of identity formation may be more complicated and require extra attention. Not only are the identity issues common to all adolescents experienced, intercountry adoptees must also resolve issues related to two domains beyond their individual choice: their adoption status and their ethnicity and cultural heritage.

In this chapter we examine the issue of identity formation for intercountry adoptees from the perspective of (1) knowledge about being adopted, and (2) the influence of race–ethnicity on adolescent identity development. Since most children adopted from China are still in childhood, much of our discussion relies on empirical investigations conducted with other groups, most notably Korean adoptees, for whom a large adult population now exists. This information can help to establish an understanding and basis for investigations of identity development of children from China in the years to come.

EGO IDENTITY DEVELOPMENT

Erikson's (1968) theory of ego identity provides a useful starting point for studying the influences of adoption and ethnicity on identity formation. According to Erikson, an individual's overall sense of identity is not represented by a single, uniform entity. Rather, identity refers to the collection and integration of different identities an individual develops for different contexts. Religious, gender, occupational, sexual, physical characteristics, abilities, and personality identities each contribute to an individual's overall sense of identity (Melina, 1998).

Ideally, resolution of the identity crisis occurs when an adolescent confronts the issue "Who am I?" explores alternative solutions to this crisis, and eventually commits to a particular set of values (Brodzinsky, Schechter, & Henig, 1992). In reality, however, adolescents and young adults often encounter difficulties that challenge their abilities to cope with and successfully resolve the identity crisis. Marcia (1980) and others have proposed distinct coping patterns to describe an individual's progress in identity formation based on (1) the degree of active exploration concerning alternative roles and perspectives and (2) the level of commitment made to specific roles and perspectives. Individuals who are not committed and have not engaged in exploration have "diffused" identity. They fail to see the importance of making choices about their identity. In contrast, "committed" adolescents who explore the meaning of ethnicity in their lives and personal identity achieve a clear sense of their ethnicity, feelings of belonging and emotional identification, and confidence in themselves and their ethnic backgrounds. Two other coping patterns reveal problems with either a lack of commitment or exploration. "Foreclosure" represents individuals who adopt the values and perspectives of their parents without question. They are committed but do not personally explore alternative life options. Adolescents stuck in a "moratorium" actively explore the meaning of ethnicity and other identity-related factors but cannot commit to specific values or lifestyles. These individuals can become frozen, in a sense, over the momentous decisions they face and are unable to commit to a particular set of values for fear of making the wrong choices.

Phinney (1990) proposed a three-stage model that maintained Marcia's (1980) four coping patterns but also emphasized a developmental progression from unexamined identity through a period of exploration to an achieved or committed identity.[1] The first stage, unexamined identity, is typical of early adolescence, where exposure to identity issues is minimal. Individuals at this stage are characterized by a lack of identity awareness, exploration, or commitment. This initial stage consists of two distinct coping patterns: foreclosed and diffuse. Adolescents reflecting a foreclosed pattern often appear to have a stable sense of identity because they have committed to a particular life role. In fact, these individuals possess a fragile ego identity and are susceptible to disruption by future life crises. This is because their commitment is made prematurely and without an exploration of alternatives. Adolescents adopt the values, standards, perspectives, and so on of people around them, thus avoiding the struggle of identifying their own personal beliefs. Individuals experiencing identity diffusion, the second identity status, avoid exploring alternatives altogether and, in fact, are unable to commit to a particular identity. The inability to commit to values, lifestyle, and perspectives is fueled by a perceived lack of appealing options. Individuals who exhibit this pattern are floundering with no clear path. "[They are] unsure of what [they] want, unwilling to confront the options, unable to identify with a nurturing figure because none is available" (Brodzinsky et al., 1992, p. 103).

Adolescents in the identity search stage, or moratorium, are actively engaged in the exploration of alternatives but are often confused about the meaning of their ethnicity and, as a result, have not committed to any particular option. This stage is not a long-term solution, since being in moratorium is inherently destabilizing and uncomfortable. Adolescents with identity diffusion and those actively searching for meaning to their lives and the role of race–ethnicity are most commonly seen in clinical practice.

The final stage of identity formation, achieved identity, describes individuals who have actively taken on the challenge of determining their basic beliefs and decided on a particular identity and set of life roles. Commitments reflect clear, secure understanding and acceptance of one's own ethnicity. Decisions are personal choices rather than conformity to the desires or ideas of others (Brodzinsky, 1987). Figure 8.1 portrays the three-stage approach described by Phinney (1989, 1990).

Phinney (1989) conducted a study to determine whether these three stages of ethnic identity development could be reliably applied to adolescents from diverse ethnic backgrounds. Although the small group of Asian American participants ($n = 14$) in her study precludes generalization to a broader group, the results are interesting and may give us a tentative indication of how Chinese adoptees may perceive their adjustment and identity development as adolescents and point the direction for future investigations on adolescent Chinese adoptees. In Phinney's results, just over one-half of the Asian American adolescents ($n = 8$) were not actively involved in identity exploration, reflecting the first stage of identity development, unexamined identity. Slightly less than one-quarter ($n = 3$, 21.4%) reported active involvement in an identity search, while the remainder had achieved a clear sense of personal and ethnic identity. These findings were similar for other ethnic groups in the study. Interestingly, half of the Asian American adolescents reported neutral or slightly negative attitudes toward their own racial group, stating a preference to be white. "Their attitudes tended more toward assimilation that toward ethnic pride and pluralism" (p. 47). This proportion was significantly higher than black and Hispanic adolescent groups. Phinney attributed this finding to a combination of factors, including the pressure to succeed academically, a

Figure 8.1
Stages of Identity Development: Generic Model Incorporating Adopted Status and Ethnicity

Unexamined Identity 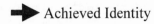 Identity Search 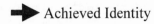 Achieved Identity

Unexamined Identity	Identity Search	Achieved Identity
Characterized by a lack of exploration of either ethnicity or adoption	Engaged in exploration that seeks understanding of meanings attached to adopted status and ethnicity	Clear, confident sense of personal identity and ethnicity
Foreclosed: Avoids crisis, lack of exploration of adoption or ethnicity ⊙ Unquestioning commitment to values, standards, points of view, etc. of parents and significant others ⊙ May appear to have a firm, stable sense of self, but actually ego identity is fragile ⊙ Vulnerable to disruption by life crises	Moratorium: Willingly explores life alternatives but hasn't made definitive decisions or commitment to any particular point of view	Willingly determines basic life beliefs and is able to commit to particular points of view, morals, and standards based on personal choice rather than conformity to others

Diffusion: Lack of interest with or commitment to ethnicity or adoption issues

⊙ Avoids exploration of alternative roles and perspectives and has not found other roles, values, or standards with which to identify
⊙ Vulnerable to psychological maladjustment

Note: Adapted from "Identity in Adolescence," by J. Marcia, 1980, in *Handbook for Adolescent Psychology*, edited by J. Adelson, New York: Wiley; "Stages of Ethnic Identity Development in Minority Group Adolescents," by J. S. Phinney, 1989, *Journal of Early Adolescence, 9*, 34–49; "Ethnic Identity in Adolescents and Adults: Review of Research," by J. S. Phinney, 1990, *Psychological Bulletin, 108*, 499–514.

desire to distinguish themselves from recent Asian immigrants, and the absence of a social movement that stressed ethnic pride.[2]

Although Phinney's (1989) investigation provides useful descriptive information, we still know very little about the identity development of intercountry adoptees. Friedlander (1999) observed, "Although we may conclude that, at least in childhood and adolescence, most children in cross-ethnic adoptive families are at Stage 1 (diffusion or foreclosure) in Phinney's ethnic identity model, we do not know if, when, or how they proceed to Stages 2 (moratorium) and 3 (achieved identity), or if arrival at Stage 3 is important for adjustment in adulthood" (p. 53).

What we do know is that identity formation is an ongoing, dynamic process that includes forming, clarifying, and reclarifying identity issues (Wilkinson, 1995). Likewise, some of the "problems related to identity formation cut across all adolescent populations, as identity formation is recognized as the critical development task of adolescence" (deAnda & Riddel, 1991, p. 84). In addition to these common problems, adolescents adopted from China are faced with two additional tasks: addressing issues resulting from their adoption status and ethnicity. These tasks add several layers of complexity to the identity-formation process that require attention.

HOW ADOPTION STATUS INFLUENCES IDENTITY DEVELOPMENT

A commonly held belief is that being adopted can complicate the identity-formation process, although little is known about how adopted children develop a sense of personal identity (Grotevant, 1992). No consensus currently exists as to whether problems are actually more severe for adolescents who are preoccupied with their adoption, as opposed to those with less concern about being adopted. Those who believe that adoption status imposes unique challenges to resolving identity issues assert that adopted adolescents are often disadvantaged in their struggle to develop secure identities (Brodzinsky, 1987). Hoopes (1990) is quick to remind us, however, that not all adopted adolescents are inherently prone to greater or more sustained difficulty with their identity development. "Adoptive status, in and of itself, need not be predictive of heightened stress among adolescents" (p. 160).

Benson, Sharma, and Roehlkepartain's (1995) findings contradict the notion that identity formation is more difficult for adoptees. They found little evidence to suggest that adopted adolescents are particularly vulnerable to problems with identity development. In their four-year study of over 700 adopted adolescents and their families, Benson and colleagues found adopted adolescents' identity and self-esteem comparable to nonadopted peers. Most adoptees viewed their adoption as a fact of life that they accepted with relative ease. However, for one-quarter of adoptees (27%), adoption had a substantial presence in their lives and was a big part of how they thought about themselves. Girls were more likely to think about their adoption and have their adoption status influence their identity than boys. While adoption was not an obsession or key defining element for most adoptees, it does appear to be an important undercurrent relating to defining one's identity.

Many of the psychosocial tasks and stresses that accompany identity development are common to both biological and adoptive adolescents. However, it is clear that some stresses are unique to adoptive families (Hoopes, 1990). According to Grotevant (1992, 1997a), the identity development of adoptees occurs in a three-stage process (very similar to the model depicted in Figure 8.1). Adoption status does not influence adoptees' perceptions of reality or self-identity during the first stage of development. However, at some point during adolescence, adoptees are likely to experience a crisis that requires confrontation with the full meaning of adoption (i.e., the second stage). In the third stage of identity development, adoptees are likely to arrive at an integrated identity that acknowledges and incorporates their adoptive status into their sense of self.

One potential complication of adoptee identity formation is that of "genealogical bewilderment," a term that denotes a sense of confusion or uncertainty about identity caused by a lack of knowledge about birth parents, origins, and reasons for being relinquished or abandoned. The struggle for self-identity may be further complicated for adoptees because of guilt or feelings of disloyalty to adoptive parents because of the curiosity and desire for such information. Differences in physical appearance, intellectual skills, or talents further hamper an adoptee's capacity to identify with adoptive parents. The difficulty for adoptees, then, is "to achieve a healthy balance between individuation and autonomy, on the one hand, and continuing connectedness to the family, on the other" (Brodzinsky, 1987, p. 38).

The conflicts found in the literature require additional study before a definitive answer is available on the influence of adoption status on identity formation. Some (e.g., Hollingsworth, 1998; Hoopes, 1990) suggest that the influence of adoptive status on identity might actually be moderated, to some degree, by one or more of the following factors: age when adopted, preadoptive factors (experiences), quality of family relationships, degree of communication about being adopted, and parents' attitudes toward adoption. Others, like Brodzinsky (1987), speculate that the answer has to do with the availability of information about birth parents and background, as well as with the attitudes and emotional support of adoptive parents and others regarding the "search for self."

RACIAL–ETHNIC IDENTITY DEVELOPMENT

The time will come in the not-too-distant future when children adopted from China during the mid- to late 1990s will enter adolescence and begin the psychosocial task of identity formation. As a part of answering the question, "Who am I?" these adolescents may wrestle with their origins by questioning the meaning of race, ethnicity, and cultural heritage in their lives. The added layer of determining racial–ethnic identity complicates the identity-development process for intercountry adoptees. Not only are intercountry adoptees faced with resolution of the identity crises experienced by all adolescents and the added layer of resolving adoption status, they must also integrate an identity that includes acceptance of physical appearance, birth heritage, and their heritage of upbringing (Tizard, 1991; Vonk, Simms, & Nackerud, 1999). de Anda and Riddel (1991) described the situation confronted by multiethnic adolescents in this manner: "It is during adolescence that individuals integrate a sense of uniqueness, develop a sense of self-esteem, establish a sense of autonomy and independence, and attain a sense of their relationship to peers, family and society. . . . This process is made all the more difficult by the fact that there are dual family, societal, and reference groups which they must either choose between or struggle to integrate" (p. 85).

It is important to consider the influence that race, ethnicity, and culture may have on identity development, especially since American society is likely to label Chinese adoptees as members of a minority group regardless of how the children were raised and socialized (Kim, 1978). Friedlander (1999) captures the difficulty encountered by many intercountry adoptees and illustrates the importance of developing a strong, positive identity: "As young adults leaving the security of their families for college or the workforce, they may find themselves unprepared to cope with racism, on the one hand, and a lack of acceptance by immigrants from their countries of origin, on the other. This stressful experience of double-consciousness arises when one identifies with two cultures simultaneously but feels alienated from both" (p. 45).

In this section some of the basic issues that surface when discussing identity—as an individual, an adoptees, and a member of a racial and ethnic minority group—are presented. Models of ethnic identity development will explain the process of identity development and the potential impact of race and ethnicity. We also draw from previous studies that have examined the identity development of other intercountry adoptees, particularly those from Korea.

A Generic Ethnic Identity Model

Phinney (1990) views ethnic identity as the way that individuals relate (e.g., feelings, attitudes, involvement) to themselves and their socially ascribed ethnic group versus the dominant or majority group.[3] A number of different ethnic identity models and theories exist (e.g., Cross, 1994; Helms, 1984, 1995; Parham & Helms, 1985), although Park and Park (1999) claimed that much of American race theory either dismisses the significance of Asian Americans altogether or subsumes them into traditional biracial (white–black) models. We identified several models that accounted for Asian American identity development, but no models exist that account for both Asian American and adopted status. Likewise, the models available to explain the role of adoption status on identity do not typically include race–ethnicity as a factor. Despite these limitations, racial–ethnic identity models are still useful to help us conceptualize how race might influence the development of identity for adolescent Chinese adoptees, particularly when a model that offers a more generic view of racial–ethnic influences is used.

Typically, theories explaining ethnic identity development suggest that minority individuals progress through a series of stages characterized by (1) rejection of their own culture in favor of the dominant culture, (2) rejection of the dominant culture in favor of the minority culture, and (3) finding a sense of balance between ethnicity and the dominant or mainstream society. All three of these stages represent an individual's relationship to ethnic heritage and the dominant culture.

Two distinct models exist to explain the relationship between ethnic background and dominant culture. The first model is a linear or bipolar model that views ethnic identity on a continuum from "strong ethnic connections" on one end to "strong mainstream connections" on the other. This model assumes that "a strengthening of one requires a weakening of the other: that is, a strong ethnic identity is not possible among those who become involved in the mainstream society, and acculturation is inevitably accompanied by a weakening of ethnic identity" (Phinney, 1990, p. 501).

The second model describes ethnic identity as a two-dimensional process by which simultaneous (rather than exclusive) relationships between traditional (ethnic) group and dominant group are possible (Berry, 1980).[4] From this perspective, "minority group members can have either strong or weak identifications with both their own and mainstream cultures, and a strong ethnic identity does not necessarily imply a weak relationship or low involvement with the dominant culture" (Phinney, 1990, pp. 501–502). The two-dimensional view offers four different ways to explain how individuals might cope with ethnic-group membership. Individuals who hold positive views of and value their birth culture and the dominant (mainstream) culture, together, are described as "integrated." Terms such as "acculturated" and "bicultural" have also been used to describe members of this group. Most major theories view this approach to ethnic-group membership as the ideal outcome.

Individuals who have a positive, perhaps even exclusive, view of the dominant culture but harbor weak, perhaps negative, feelings toward their birth culture are "assimilated." Most children adopted from China will eventually reflect this particular position rather than a bicultural one (Bagley, 1992; Kim, 1977).[5] While their views toward their Chinese heritage may not be negative, they are likely to be weak because of the constant presence of American cultural values and influences in their homes, schools, neighborhoods, and so forth. Friedlander (1999) wrote, "Research indicates that internationally adopted children tend to be assimilated into the mainstream culture and fare very well if their parents (a) provide a nurturing environment, (b) acknowledge their physical differences but emphasize their psychological similarities, and (c) expose them to affirmative role models from their countries of origin" (p. 53).

A third approach toward ethnic identity is "separation," characterized by a high, perhaps even exclusive, level of identification with the ethnic group. Separated individuals hold negative views toward the dominant culture but view their ethnic culture positively. The final possibility for dealing with ethnic identity, according to Berry (1980), is referred to as "marginality." Marginal individuals hold negative views toward both dominant and ethnic cultures and do not identify with either of them. Figure 8.2 illustrates this particular ethnic identity model and includes terms used to denote the four approaches used to resolve ethnic identity issues.

Past Studies on Racial and Ethnic Identity

Almost all the investigations examining the racial and ethnic identity development of transracial and intercountry adoptees have reported extremely positive outcomes (Hollingsworth, 1997). There is no evidence to suggest that these adoptees are more likely to suffer from insecure or confused identities than other children, although some evidence suggests that adoptees' views toward self and race tend to be different. Bartholet (1993a) indicated that studies "reveal that blacks adopted by whites appear more positive than blacks raised by blacks about relationships with whites, more comfortable in those relationships, and more interested in a racially integrated lifestyle. They think race is not the most important factor in defining who they are or who their friends should be" (p. 103). Transracial adoptees can and do establish strong racial or ethnic identities, contrary to critics' claims. There is absolutely no evidence that the task of identity development is any more difficult or leads to serious psychological problems for this group (Kim, 1995; Silverman, 1993; Tizard, 1991).

Compared to the impressive literature that has accumulated on racial and ethnic identity development for African American youth, only a handful of empirical studies address this topic from an intercountry-adoption perspective. Even so, results of these stud-

Figure 8.2
Integration of Select Racial–Ethnic Identity Models: Possible Orientations toward Ethnic- and Majority-Group Membership

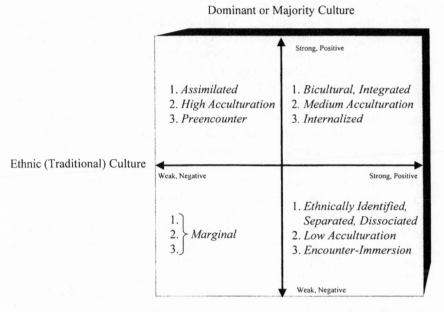

Dominant or Majority Culture

Strong, Positive

1. *Assimilated*
2. *High Acculturation*
3. *Preencounter*

1. *Bicultural, Integrated*
2. *Medium Acculturation*
3. *Internalized*

Ethnic (Traditional) Culture

Weak, Negative   Strong, Positive

1.⎫
2. ⎬ *Marginal*
3.⎭

1. *Ethnically Identified,*
   Separated, Dissociated
2. *Low Acculturation*
3. *Encounter-Immersion*

Weak, Negative

Note: 1. Phinney (1989, 1990); 2. Suinn, Rickard-Figueria, Lew, and Vigil (1987); 3. Cross (1991). Adapted from "The Role of Ethnic Identity and Acculturation in the Vocational Behavior of Asian Americans: An Integrative Review," by F.T.L. Leong and E. L. Chou, 1994, *Journal of Vocational Behavior, 44*, 155–172; "Stages of Ethnic Identity Development in Minority Group Adolescents," by J. S. Phinney, 1989, *Journal of Early Adolescence, 9*, 34–49; "Ethnic Identity in Adolescents and Adults: Review of Research," by J. S. Phinney, 1990, *Psychological Bulletin, 108*, 499–514.

ies generally reflect the overwhelmingly positive findings for transracial adoption. One such study was conducted by Feigelman and Silverman (1983), who found that Korean adoptees were well adjusted, although some espoused negative perceptions about various aspects of their identity. Twenty-six percent of these adoptees were sometimes uncomfortable about their physical appearance, while 20 percent felt ashamed of their Korean origins. Not surprising, the investigators found that adoptees who reported greater pride and less shame in their cultural (ethnic) heritage were also better adjusted psychologically and socially than those who were less enthusiastic. The adoptees' sense of ethnicity appeared to decline with age as peer group and group acceptance became important aspects of their lives. Adolescent adoptees wanted to fit in with peers rather than risk alienation. Almost two-third of the adoptees (63%) said they identified with white society rather than Korean or Korean American identities.

Two Canadian researchers, Westhues and Cohen (1998a) studied the long-term adjustment (including identity development) of 155 intercountry adoptees from three provinces in Canada. Half of the adoptees in their study identified themselves, ethnically, as Canadian or "hyphenated Canadians," although a majority still saw race and minority status as defining factors in their identity. The influence of ethnicity and race was considered important or very important by half of the adoptees, while an additional quarter of adoptees reported that race and ethnicity were neither important or unimportant. Three-fourths of the adoptees reported being comfortable or very comfortable with their racial and ethnic backgrounds.

The more than twenty years of study by Rita Simon and Howard Altstein (1972, 1987, 1991, 1995) provide a unique opportunity to examine the identity development of intercountry (and transracial) adoptees. Although space limits our attention to their impressive work, several findings from their longitudinal investigation (1971 to 1991) of 204 families, composed mostly of African American transracial adoptees, and their Korean adoptee investigation (2000) are of particular note.

The most important finding from Simon and Altstein's (1972) first round of data collection was the absence of white racial preference among the adoptees (mostly African American) and siblings. This particular conclusion contradicted much of the accepted belief at the time. Rather than "becoming white" or developing weak racial identity, as opponents of transracial adoption predicted, adoptees generally developed strong racial identities, were comfortable with their race and members of the black community, but also flourished in their family's predominantly white world. Not surprisingly, this idea about the meaning of race was considered deviant by black separatists such as the NABSW. However, no evidence has even suggested that this type of pluralistic or bicultural perspective and identity is confusing or harmful to adoptees. Writing about their first-round results, Simon and Alstein (1987) recollected that "transracial adoption appeared to provide the opportunity for children to develop awareness of race, respect for physical differences imposed by race, and ease with their own racial characteristics, whatever they may be" (p. 28). The foundation for positive racial identity development were in place as adoptees were preparing to enter adolescence.

In 1991, Simon and Altstein posed the question, "How would you describe your own racial background?" to the longitudinal group of transracial adoptees. Among African American adoptees, 32 percent perceived themselves as black, while the remainder indicated mixed (hyphenated) background. Most non-black adoptees (including intercountry adoptees) labeled themselves by racial designation (e.g., Native American, Korean, or Hispanic). This same question was posed to adoptees in the investigators' Korean study (Simon & Altstein, 2000), and produced the following replies: Korean, 30 percent, Korean or Asian American, 32 percent, Asian, 5 percent, American, 20 percent, white, 7 percent, and Other, 6 percent. Simon and Altstein commented that "for some 73 percent of the respondents, their Korean-American heritage is very much part of their current identity" (p. 105). While speculative, we anticipate the likelihood of similar results for Chinese adoptees as they enter adolescence and into young adulthood.[6]

In 1978, D. S. Kim reported results from one of the first nationwide studies of the long-term adjustment of intercountry adoptees. The investigation focused on the identity and socialization patterns of 406 Korean adolescents who were adopted as young children by white families in the United States. Kim's results were generally quite encouraging. He found adoptees were well adjusted in important areas of life, such as health, interpersonal relationships, academic and cultural adjustment, and maturity and socialization. The self-concept of these individuals was positive, healthy, and "remarkably similar to that of other Americans" (p. 5). Openness and interaction between adoptive parents and children emerged as the single most important factor in the success of these adolescents. Adoptees reported having very little Korean identity, identifying themselves primarily as American or Korean American rather than Korean. This last finding was especially worrisome to Kim, who, one year after publishing his findings, considered the implications of his results:

Although making a good initial adjustment, these adopted foreign children, during the long-term socialization process, are forced to face an inferior status consistently ascribed to ethnic minority group members. Empirical data seem to confirm the impression that the so-called good adjustment of these children is being accomplished at the cost of their unique ethnic cultural heritage and identity, partially reinforced by parents' innocent, yet inept, expectations. (p. 485)

Huh and Reid (2000) found two significant influences on ethnic identity development in their study of forty Korean adoptees, ages nine to fourteen: involvement in culturally related activities and ease of communication with parents about their adoption. Degree of participation in Korean cultural activities had the greatest amount of influence on identity. Specifically, adoptees who were high participators in Korean cultural activities scored higher on Korean identity than adoptees identified as low participators. Adoptees with an integrated Korean identity also had parents who encouraged and participated with them in cultural events and activities. A second influence was the ease with which adoptees and parents could discuss various aspects of the adoption. Huh and Reid acknowledged that while adolescents with high participation in Korean cultural activities were not necessarily better adjusted than others, they possessed certain attributes—"integrated" identities and greater ease in discussing adoption with parents—that were highly desirable.

In a follow-up study of Chinese girls who had been adopted by English parents living in Hong Kong, Bagley and Young (1981) found that most of the adoptees identified themselves as English, although 40 percent maintained strong emotional or intellectual interest in Chinese culture and institutions. The authors concluded, "The successful resolution of identity problems and dilemmas earlier in life; the fulfillment in Maslow's terms of various basic needs; strong bonding; and relationships based on love, affection, and concerned tolerance . . . created ego-strengths in these girls and young women" (p. 106).

SUMMARY

Despite critics' claims of the potential harm associated with adolescent identity development, the vast majority of intercountry adoptees grow up to be happy, well-adjusted adults. Will this situation hold true for children adopted from China? The literature offers no reason to think otherwise. Yet as we speculate on the identity-development process of children adopted from China, race and adoptive status will almost certainly have some role, although not necessarily negative. Important questions about the influence of these factors remain to be answered: For example, How is identity development influenced by parents' who nurture a sense of cultural heritage throughout their adopted child's lifetime? Is identity development significantly harmed if parents' minimize focus on cultural heritage?

The issue of racial difference and adoptees' sense of belonging to dominant and/or minority groups is another issue that will require study. We anticipate that the results of these proposed future studies will only serve to confirm, extend, and refine the results of past investigations. Will Chinese adoptees feel as if they are in a psychological no-man's land, as suggested by Dalen and Saetersdal (1987): not accepted by members of the dominant culture because of their minority status, yet not accepted by members of the minority group because they possess cultural values of the dominant culture? How do adolescents successfully negotiate the potential pitfalls? What factors allow adolescents to successfully integrate themselves into both worlds?

NOTES

1. Tse (1999) described a four-stage ethnic identity-formation model—ethnic unawareness, ethnic ambivalence–evasion, ethnic emergence, and ethnic identity formation—that she applied to understanding ethnic identity development in Asian Americans. Although Tse's approach is organized differently than the one proposed by Phinney (1989), both models describe the same process of ethnic identity development, including a lack of awareness about one's ethnicity and feelings of being ambivalent about ethnic origins (Phinney combined these steps), an increasing awareness of ethnicity and searching for an identity that incorporates ethnicity, and attainment of a mature ethnic identity.

2. Meier (1999) reported a similar developmental trajectory for cultural identity development, with Korean adoptees, of denial, self-awareness, and emerging cultural consciousness about Korean heritage.

3. The terms "race," "ethnicity," and "culture" are often used interchangeably, but actually refer to three distinct concepts. These terms, like adoption, are aspects of an individual's identity that are assigned by society (Grotevant, 1992). While race is often assumed to refer to biological differences between people, Helms (1995) noted that race is a sociopolitical concept that classifies people according to social, political, and economic categories. Several Asian authors (e.g., Dhooper, 1991; Park & Park, 1999) have posited that most discussion involving race theory in the United States assumes a bipolar perspective between white and African American groups, thus dismissing the role or importance of Asian Americans and other minority groups in the United States. Although a number of different definitions have been proposed for the term ethnicity, the essential elements of most definitions focus on social and cultural forms of self- and group identity. Ethnicity commonly refers to a number of characteristics that are shared by a group of people including national origin, religion, symbols and artifacts, common histories, family structure, and culture (Kwan & Sodowsky, 1997). Melina (1998) adds that "ethnicity is a matter of biological and historical fact and is not changed by the culture in which a person grows up" (p. 213). Ethnic identity, on the other hand, is defined as a person's sense of attachment or belonging to a particular group (internal identity) and sharing the perceptions, feelings, and behaviors attributable to the group (called "external identity" by Kwan & Sodowsky). Ethnicity refers to group patterns while ethnic identity refers to individual acquisi-

tion of group patterns (Rotheram & Phinney, 1987). Huh and Reid (2000) asserted that "ethnic identity of transracially and internationally adopted children may be thought of as a feeling of connection with both one's cultural past and one's present adoptive heritage" (p. 75). As Chinese adoptees grow up, they will maintain their ethnicity regardless of their upbringing. However, even if these children know a great deal about their cultural heritage—Chinese language, customs and rituals, values, social interactions, music, and so on—their ethnic identity will reflect that of their adoptive family. Without a reinforcing culture in the United States, it is highly unlikely that Chinese culture will be regularly used as the basis for looking at and interpreting the world (Tessler, Gamache, & Liu, 1999). "If [she] is raised in a white, middle-class, Midwestern, Protestant family, [her] cultural identity is likely to be similar to other white, middle-class, Midwestern, Protestant people, while [her] ethnic identity is likely to be similar to that of other [Chinese] children adopted by white Americans" (Melina, 1998, p. 214).

4. Leong and Chou (1994) note that study of the ethnic identity of Asian Americans has been haphazard in scope (i.e., very little cohesion or linear progression can be found in the literature). However, two notable exceptions—Sue and Sue (1973), and Suinn, Rickard-Figueria, Lew, and Vigil (1987)—contain concepts and ideas similar to the two-dimensional approach discussed here.

5. What is Asian American ethnic identity? Oyserman and Sakamoto (1997) believe that Asian American ethnic identity builds on the interdependence and group connectedness that are said to be cultural hallmarks of Asian cultures of origin. They proposed a multidimensional model focused on four content domains: feelings of interdependence with family; a sense of pride and connectedness to heritage and tradition; awareness of structural barriers, discrimination, and racism; and belief that achievement reflects well on family and is integral to group membership. Oyserman and Sakamoto's (1997) model is not particularly applicable to the majority of Chinese adoptees who will grow up in white (non-Asian) families with predominantly mainstream values, beliefs, and experiences. Even so, throughout adolescence and adulthood Chinese adoptees will have to come to terms with the meaning of being an Asian American along with the meaning attached to their adoptive status. Lack of a reference group, little or no recollection of the birth country and culture, and daily interactions with mainstream family members mean that it is highly probable they will identity with their families more than their own ethnic group (Friedlander, 1999; Kim, 1978). From their study of 168 Korean adults who were adopted by white families, Simon and Altstein (2000) concluded that "Korean transracial adoptees are aware of their backgrounds but are not particularly interested in making them the center of their lives. They feel good about having grown up with the families they did" (p. 106).

6. Simon and Altstein (2000) reported that only 5 percent of parents of Korean adoptees believed their children experienced difficulties with identity issues during adolescence.

Chapter 9

Final Thoughts:
Where Do We Go from Here?

I believe very firmly that being entrusted with the love and care
of children born to someone else in another part of the world carries an obligation of stewardship. In becoming an internationally adoptive family, we claim a place in the global family.
                                                   Register, 1991, p. 210

While completing this book we have been struck by the unique and
interesting yet simultaneously ordinary findings that describe children and parents involved in intercountry adoption from China.
From our vantage point this is good news. With few exceptions, it
appears that adoptive parents need not possess extraordinary skills
and knowledge in order to raise their children with positive self-
identities and bright futures. We do not, however, prematurely dis-
miss the importance of adoption status, race–ethnicity, and cultural
heritage from the lives of children adopted from China. These three
issues, along with myriad others—transracial adoption, national
and international politics, identity development, attachment, single
parenting, racism and discrimination, and cultural acknowledgment
and celebration—each represent complex issues that have the potential to affect the lives of children adopted from China, their families and friends, and society at large.

A STUDY IN CONTRASTS

In many respects, the process of adopting a child from China reflects our personal impressions of Chinese society (viz., a study in
contrasts). During our brief travel in China it was not uncommon
to see the best of Chinese architecture, tradition, and modernity
existing adjacent to dilapidated dingy buildings and antiquated
methods of production, commerce, and transportation: cell phones
versus pushcarts, BMWs versus bicycles, vast expanses of rural
farmland versus densely populated urban centers. And so it is with
intercountry adoption from China, a phenomenon that results from
centuries-old traditions and beliefs intertwined with efforts to eliminate the threat of uncontrolled population growth and a profound
love of children but a dire need to limit childbirth to ensure life for
those already born.

The types of contrasts we observed were not lost on Cheri Register (1991), who, a decade earlier, discussed the paradox of intercountry adoption and called for action to change existing inequities
in the world that made it a reality: "Adoption is paradoxical through
and through, a mix of grievous losses and joyous gains, tragic separation and firm belonging. We who live with the paradox day by
day can manage yet another one: To be advocates for international
adoption while simultaneously working to make it unnecessary"
(p. 212).

Register's point extends the contrasts even further. The good fortune of adoptive families results from the misfortune of birth families half a world away. It is not uncommon for adoptive parents to
acknowledge this paradox and be aware of its implications. Some
even advocate for its end. "International adoption is an undeserved
benefit that has fallen largely to [us] primarily because of the ineq-
uitable socioeconomic circumstances in which we live. In the long
run, we ought to be changing those circumstances" (Winston, 1995).
Bartholet (1996) noted that events such as "the current tendency
to glorify group identity and to emphasize the importance of ethnic
and cultural roots has made transracial and international adoption newly suspect" (pp. 271–272). Undoubtely, the controversy over
transracial and intercountry adoption is assured of a continued
presence into the foreseeable future.

Several respondents in our survey related stories that epitomize
the explosion of intercountry adoptions from China as merely a
passing fad, a decision seen by some as trendy and chic. Just like
owning a big SUV, wearing designer clothes, or being seen at the
right restaurants, Chinese adoption is equated to the selection of
an exotic breed of dog that happens to be the current rage, a ploy

for attaining some measure of status and attention. While this scenario is certainly within the realm of possibility, the perspective does a grave injustice to people involved in international adoption. To reduce a family's decision to adopt a child from China to such a mindless effort is an insult to both families and adoption professionals. It seems highly unlikely that a majority of prospective parents choose a difficult, expensive, and extended process or submit themselves to intrusion into their personal and professional lives merely for the sake of appearance and status.

The families we have had the good fortune to interact with have not struck us as people overly concerned with personal image. There is no doubt, of course, that adopting a child from China brings immediate public attention to the family, mostly positive but always present. People are curious. Some ask questions. Others merely stare. Many encounters are motivated by a stranger's familiarity with intercountry adoption from China through friends or family members. In fact, adoptive parents say they often feel like ambassadors of sorts for intercountry adoption and for U.S.–China relations. These interactions, however, are the result of having adopted a child from China, rather than a motivator for adopting in the first place. True, intercountry adoption from China has experienced a tremendous increase from the early 1990s to the present. And while it is possible that the upward trend could signal some type of fad, we feel the reasons voiced by our survey participants are much more likely: humanitarian concerns, infertility, wanting to adopt a girl, and the combination of current U.S. adoption law and the relatively straightforward adoption process in China.

FUNDAMENTAL DIFFERENCES: A SOCIAL MOVEMENT?

Issues associated with intercountry adoption from China have parallel, often identical, themes in other literatures that have informed our inquiry (e.g., topics and arguments related to domestic adoption, transracial adoption, and intercountry adoption from other countries, particularly South Korea). Based on the accumulated evidence of these resources, we were almost ready to conclude that there is relatively little new or unique in the practice and study of adopting children from China. And yet, something does strike us as being fundamentally different about the phenomenon of Chinese adoption when compared with past waves of intercountry adoption (e.g., from Europe after World War II or from South Korea following the Korean War).

We were first alerted to the possibility of this difference by Tessler, Gamache, and Liu (1999). They observed adoptive parents' firm belief that offering opportunities for Chinese socialization will prove to be a positive force in their child's life: "In the past, parents who adopted internationally did not attach much importance to social-izing their children in their birth cultures. . . . In fact, there [is] evidence of a *genuine social movement* surrounding the preference for Chinese socialization in that parents have formed organizations and joined community activities to achieve their goals" (p. 58, em-phasis added).

A social movement? In hindsight, we were rather quick to dis-miss this assertion at first. Granted, parents with children from China that we have met and talked with seemed involved, knowl-edgeable, and proactive about issues related to acknowledging Chi-nese cultural heritage. But to call the efforts of these people a social movement seemed a bit of a stretch. However, through our work over the past year we have gradually changed our thinking. A com-munity of families with children adopted from China has clearly emerged at the grassroots level over the past decade and continues to grow. Whether an informal playgroup organized by local par-ents, Internet-based e-mail lists and chat rooms, or national orga-nizations like Families with Children from China or Our Chinese Daughters Foundation (OCDF) representing thousands of families, parents of children from China are actively involved in seeking out other families who have had similar experiences to provide their adopted children with experiences that place value on and promote positive aspects of Chinese cultural heritage and provide support for both prospective and actual adoptive parents.[1]

It appears that families of Chinese adoptees are more likely to be involved in a parent support group than other intercountry adop-tive families. In fact, K. Evans (2000) estimates that approximately 20 percent of all families with children from China belong to a local (or state) FCC chapter. "This East–West group of parents and chil-dren has become its own global village [and] is an unprecedented attempt by thousands of parents to honor their children's origins" (pp. 178–180).

No doubt, much of the impetus for an adoptive parents' move-ment can be attributed to the sustained advocacy, support, and leadership efforts of FCC. But the movement, whatever that may be, is not dependent on FCC. We are convinced that even without the guidance of a group like FCC there would be local, individual efforts at developing networks of people who share similar concerns and in-terests. Evidence of the vast network of support and advocacy that is available can easily be witnessed on the Internet, which contains lit-erally thousands of Web sites describing personal adoption journeys, offering up-to-date information about the adoption process, and even giving advice on how to pack for travel to China. Equally important, local playgroups that offer adoptive parents and their children the time to socialize and share with one another are common.

What is the source of adoptive parents' desire to provide socialization opportunities for their children to learn about Chinese cultural heritage? And why don't we find the same scope and intensity of postadoption efforts and concerns with past waves of intercountry adoption (e.g., for those children adopted in the aftermath of World War II and from Korea starting in the late 1950s)? For one thing, the world is a much smaller place today than in years past. Global news organizations, the Internet, satellite communications, a reliance on quick and efficient air travel, international business conglomerates, and the like bring us breaking news and human interest features instantly, as well as reflect the sense of a shrinking global community. Situations and experiences that might once have appeared to be isolated or out of the ordinary, like adopting a child from a different country, are more likely to seem commonplace today as we encounter stories about the plight of abandoned children in China and people who made the decision to adopt these children.

Contrary to past professional practice that urged parents to minimize the influence of a child's birth culture and support the assimilation of intercountry adoptees into American culture, adoptive parents today are actively encouraged by adoption-agency personnel to affirm their adopted child's Chinese cultural heritage. Many agencies even provide social and educational opportunities for their clients, such as periodic reunions of adoptive parents and their families, pre- and postadoption workshops that focus on various aspects of intercountry adoption from China, and summer culture camps that provide a means of teaching children (and parents) about their Chinese cultural heritage. Required travel to China in order to complete the adoption process may also heighten interest in and respect for Chinese culture and traditions. Plus, as part of the formal adoption process, Chinese adoption officials typically ask parents about their intentions to teach their child about China and Chinese heritage. While seen as a simple formality by some, these questions underscore the importance of maintaining a connection to Chinese heritage.

Perhaps an awareness of these and other issues forces parents to address cultural heritage today, while these issues may have been overlooked in the past.[2] Replication of longitudinal investigations like the over-twenty-year study of Rita Simon and Howard Altstein (1972–2000) are needed to determine the long-term development

of Chinese adoptees. We believe it is realistic, however, to understand that philosophy and political ideology and rhetoric are not
easily swayed, regardless of empirical evidence.

The centuries-old traditions of China's past, as well as China's
current political status and emerging economic status in the world
may place a different perspective on the process of intercountry
adoption from China. In the past, intercountry adoption has most
likely been associated with the casualties of war, famine, or natural disaster. Today, parents are just as likely to decide on pursuing
intercountry adoption because of infertility problems. Future studies that contrast past intercountry adoption efforts with adoption
from China would greatly add to our understanding.

Times are different in other ways, most notably societal views
about race and the demographic composition of the United States.
Although a small but often vocal opposition exists, current social
views tend to reinforce and advance the celebration of cultural diversity rather than cultural assimilation (i.e., being absorbed into
the great melting pot that was the norm in the first half of the
twentieth century). Many parents adopting children from China
grew up in the 1950s and 1960s, a time when individual rights and
freedoms were championed. Early experiences may have sensitized
adoptive parents to issues of human rights in the United States
and abroad. Other factors—emotional maturity, high levels of formal education, and greater than average income—may also contribute to a higher level of sensitivity to cultural origin and
differences, and the ability to engage in direct action.

Time will tell what mainstream U.S. attitudes toward adopted
children from China will become. Adoptive parents told us that for
the most part the types of interactions they have had with other
people have been positive experiences. However, it is important to
remember that most adoptees are still young children and afforded
protection against most forms of bias and discrimination by their
families. In the not-too-distant future the potential for bias and
discrimination will likely increase as adoptees gradually become
independent and are no longer protected by family members. When
experienced, racial discrimination may be especially difficult for
Chinese adoptees who possess a visible status of racial minority
but have had a lifetime of experience as part of the cultural mainstream. Will children from China find ways to bridge this type of
no-man's land? Will the support and encouragement of Chinese
adoption support groups minimize the likelihood of this experience?
The phenomenon—feelings of being alienated from both dominant
and minority cultural groups—requires critical examination in the
years ahead.

The notion of all Asian Americans being a "model minority" is a possible indicator of how the general public may perceive the growing cohort of children adopted from China. Stereotypical expectations of high academic performance and a strong work ethic may ultimately limit career alternatives or social interactions. As adults, Chinese adoptees will often be seen as foreigners and treated as such. Although members of this select group will be every bit as American as their white peers, their physical appearance guarantees that first impressions will be of their racial differences to the mainstream. This recognition increases the likelihood that adoptees may be marginalized by society; that is, caught between two worlds—not wholly accepted as American because of physical differences and not accepted as Chinese because of cultural background and upbringing.

While the likelihood of this scenario exists, another possibility may also emerge in the years to come. Joe Kelly (1999), an adoptive father of a daughter from China, asserts that society's reaction to minority groups is relative and continually being redefined:

We will be part of this process of redefinition and so, of course, will our daughters. Inevitably, as members of a nonwhite race in a white dominated society, they will experience the racism and cultural discrimination that is as American as apple pie. But my bet is that they will have plenty to say about it. And if they are even one-tenth as organized and assertive as their parents, they will play an active role in doing something about it, adding a distinct and completely unpredictable dimension to their generation of Chinese-Americans. Personally, I can hardly wait.

Indeed, it will be interesting to watch the progress of children from China, particularly to see if the collective efforts of individuals and groups forming the social movement can make a difference in how society perceives and reacts to Chinese adoptees as adults.

THE IMPORTANCE OF ACKNOWLEDGING CULTURAL HERITAGE

We began our investigation with an interest in knowing if and how parents with children from China acknowledged their child's cultural heritage. Do parents need to be attentive to this particular issue? Is the acknowledgement of Chinese cultural heritage important to the psychological and social well-being of adopted children? Information from a variety of sources indicates that, indeed, this aspect of parenting intercountry adoptees does have some importance. Yet a variety of opinions still exist about the extent of parents' efforts to expose their children to Chinese cultural heritage.

Should parents adopt a Chinese perspective in raising their children, presenting to them all things Chinese and totally immersing family members in Chinese ways? Or should parents minimize the differences between themselves and their adopted children, only touching on those aspects of cultural heritage that simply acknowledge the existence of adoptive and racial status differences? Kelly (1999) reflects on the implications these questions have for himself and his family:

Our goal is ostensibly to help our daughters to have it both ways—to embrace their Chinese heritage *and* feel secure in their status as full-fledged Americans.... Events and activities that bring us together with others going through the same experiences help create safe places. As simplistic as they may seem, the mooncakes, the Mandarin classes, the Chinese Lantern-making have as much to do with the interior dynamics of our adoptive families as they do with generating a conscious Chinese-American identity.

A fairly large window exists that will likely accommodate many different approaches by adoptive parents to help their children "have it both ways." Perhaps an equally important issue is the consideration of whether the absence of cultural socialization affects adult adjustment to an equal degree. The complexity of the tasks parents must grapple with associated with acknowledging and nurturing a sense of cultural heritage is apparent. Regardless of if and how parents choose to acknowledge their children's cultural background, the issue must be addressed.

While we can easily describe the challenges facing adoptive parents, it is often difficult in practice. There is still much to be learned. In this vein, Kirk's (1984) words regarding the importance of biological, genetic, and constitutional factors in adoptive situations are directly relevant to children adopted from China:

This heritage we can perhaps come to understand; certainly we must accept it. What we can not do is change it. Even acknowledging differences ourselves to their communications will at best bring them, *with their heritage,* into the community of our family. . . . By admitting our children's genetic and constitutional heritage we admit also their ancestors. Without doing so we shut off a part of our children's lives, not only against them but against ourselves. (pp. 176, 184)

FUTURE ISSUES

Where do we go from here? As we consider the future of research on intercountry adoption, any number of theoretical and practical issues emerge. Will Chinese adoptees want to search for their birth families? Will this even be possible? Will we see a trend toward more openness in intercountry adoption, similar to domestic adoption (Freivalds, 2000)? What are the areas in greatest need of future investigation? Examining current and future directions for research in the field of intercountry adoption is an important but exceedingly difficult task. We recognize the folly in trying to map out a relevant research agenda for a field of study and declare it representative of the field. Alone, we can't. However, by offering suggestions about future research directions we might initiate dialogue on important issues in the field and establish a base of understanding about critical issues inherent in the adjustment and development of intercountry adoptees from China.

Perhaps the most important reason to consider future research issues is that without research, targeted on relevant issues and problems, social workers and adoption professionals may resort to unsystematic trial-and-error (hit-or-miss) methods of resolving problems, governed more by what makes sense as opposed to relying on knowledge about adoptive parents and children that has been systematically collected and using techniques and strategies that have been demonstrated effective. Reitz (1999) posited that high-quality guidelines for practice in intercountry adoption "come from high quality research done with people whose life experience can inform about outcomes" (p. 328). Serbin (1997) stated a similar position, noting that researchers are increasingly "being approached to provide answers and guidelines for policy regarding the *who, when, where,* and *how* of international adoption" (p. 86). The interplay of theoretical and practical domains is an important element that can steer research efforts clear of charges of being esoteric or having little to do with day-to-day concerns.

Brodzinsky, Smith, and Brodzinsky (1998) reviewed much of the empirical literature available on adoption and offered their observations on the current and future states of adoption research. To date, most published investigations have been atheoretical in nature, causing the authors to argue for a great emphasis on theory-based investigations. Many studies reflect simplistic research questions and designs, resulting in a recommendation that future studies be designed in ways that acknowledge the complexity and variability that exists in adoptive situations. Brodzinsky and colleagues recommended that the current focus on risks and problems associated with transracial adoption be changed to examine factors that support the healthy psychological adjustment of children in transracial family environments. They called for more interdisciplinary research on adoption and listed a number of areas for future study: "Particular attention needs to be paid to the influence of children's biological and prenatal histories, pre-placement rearing experiences, family transition experiences, and post-adoption developmental, family, and social experiences on patterns of adjustment" (p. 114).

Adoption is a lifetime process that represents changing issues and concerns throughout the lifecycle. To some degree we can anticipate that research on the early life experiences of intercountry adoptees is likely to focus on issues of attachment, adjustment, health, and development. As adoptees enter adolescence and young adulthood, the focus will predictably shift toward adoptee perspectives on being adopted from China, encounters and reactions to racism and discrimination, and the development of racial identity and a sense of belonging. Investigation focusing on adoptees as adults has been particularly neglected in the past and is in need of attention (Feigelman, 2000).

With this understanding, we constructed a matrix that used major topics covered in this book—attachment, cultural heritage, racial discrimination and bias, preferential adoption, and racial (self) identity development—and considered possible questions based on three major research paradigms: empirical–analytic (quantitative), interpretive (qualitative), and critical perspectives. Each of these paradigms represents a differing view and understanding of the world, and hence reflects important questions from different viewpoints. The cumulative result of studies conducted from all three perspectives should provide a more comprehensive picture of intercountry adoption and the people involved in the process.

The empirical–analytic or quantitative research paradigm assumes that behavior can be studied from an objective perspective and that observations can be reduced to numbers that are analyzed using probability theory and inferential statistics. Empirical–analytic research attempts to determine cause-and-effect relationships based on the belief that, under certain conditions, research findings can be generalized. This knowledge can then be used to predict and, ultimately, control future behavior or situations (Gall, Borg, & Gall, 1996; Huck, 2000).

Examples of future directions for research on intercountry adoption from China using empirical–analytic methods are numerous (see Table 9.1). One major research strand might seek answers to a question about the relative contribution of various factors either known or suspected of influencing adoption success for children from China. The results of investigations on this issue would be of both theoretical and practical importance. Issues related to improving the adoption process might also be considered, such as What is the best method of reducing adoptee anxiety and enhancing attachment during the early weeks following adoption? Quantitative inquiry might also take a longitudinal approach, similar to the seminal work of Simon and Altstein (1972), to determine the psychological developmental patterns experienced by Chinese adoptees. Factors such as age at adoption, degree of acknowledging or rejecting Chinese heritage, and family geographic location are examples of issues that could be examined from either cross-sectional or longitudinal perspectives to determine their influence on adoptee identity development.

Interpretive (qualitative) research is characterized by a belief that behavior, indeed all phenomena, must be experienced and explained in context to be understood. Contrary to the quantified research approach of the empirical–analytic paradigm, qualitative inquiry would view intercountry adoption as a series of subjectively experienced events. Here, data would be represented by the dialogue of people involved in intercountry adoption that is then analyzed for the meaning, perceptions, and experience of individuals involved. Interpretive researchers do not rely on predefined constructs, definitions, or hypotheses, but would develop these throughout the research process (Gall et al., 1996).

Qualitative investigations are made to uncover the meanings and emotions that people ascribe to a particular event or experience: How do adoptive parents view the criticisms from opponents of intercountry and transracial adoption? What meanings do adolescent and young-adult Chinese adoptees attach to being adopted? What are the personal experiences of adoptive parents during the preadoption phase of the process? How do parents explain their feelings and experiences during this time? As these questions illustrate, a major concern is with individual perceptions and feelings (see Table 9.1).

A third viewpoint that can be used to define research is the critical perspective. Like the interpretive paradigm, the critical perspective is also concerned with issues of meaning and understanding from an individual view. However, critical inquiry goes beyond description and actively questions the underlying assumptions of a situation and examines how these assumptions affect both the individual and society. Typically, critical research is concerned with problems about what ought to be done and how people should act or live. Investigators often become actively involved in seeking ways to bring about change for those being exploited or dominated. In fact, a major focus of critical inquiry is on examining the beliefs, values, and ideologies of major stakeholders. An underlying tenet of critical theory holds that long-held assumptions are not taken for granted but are directly challenged (see Table 9.1). Examples of

Table 9.1
Examples of Future Research Questions on Intercountry Adoption of Children from China

Major areas of inquiry	Empirical–analytic paradigm
Philosophical issues	• What are similarities and differences in U.S. and PRC adoption policies? • Are the perceptions of U.S. and PRC citizens toward ICA similar or different?
Intercountry adoption process	• How will the Hague Convention affect ICA? • What are the most effective methods of facilitating ICA? • How do U.S. and PRC government officials view ICA and their roles in facilitating ICA? • How do social workers view ICA and their role in the process?
Adjustment and development	• What are the long-term development patterns of children adopted from China? • What are the differences in adjustment of adoptees in foster care versus those institutionalized until adoption? • What are the best methods for supporting adoptees' personal growth and development?
Attachment	• What are short- and long-term affects of adoptees receiving institutionalization versus foster care prior to adoption on attachment? • What is the prevalence of attachment disorder-difficulties in Chinese adoptees? • Do theories of attachment apply to Chinese adoptees? • How does age at adoption affect attachment?

research questions reflecting a critical perspective might include the following: Who benefits from the ongoing practice of intercountry adoption from China? What types of bias and discrimination do families with children adopted from China face? What can be done to minimize the possibilities for problems with identity development in Chinese adoptees?

Interpretive paradigm	Critical perspective
• What meanings do officials and citizens attach to the principles outlined in the Hague Convention? • What do U.S. and PRC citizens feel toward the process of ICA and adoptees?	• How does ICA affect the interaction of the U.S. and PRC governments? • Who benefits from the continued practice of ICA? Who benefits if practices are changed? • What are the underlying assumptions about the continued practice of ICA?
• What types of experiences do adoptive parents have during the ICA process? • What meaning is attached to ICA by adoptees? Adoptive family members? Others?	• How are children's rights protected under current or future ICA procedures? • How would changes in the ICA process effect adoptees and prospective families?
• How do Chinese children perceive their lives at different stages of life (e.g., in childhood, adolescence, adulthood)? • How are siblings affected when a child is adopted from China? • How do parents relate the story of adoption to child and other? Is myth used to portray the experience? What meanings do parents attach to the initial postadoption adjustment period?	• How does the addition of a Chinese adoptee affect the balance of power and attention in families with and without other children? Are findings different for other adoptees?
• How do adoptive parents describe the problems experienced with attachment? • What methods do parents use to enhance attachment between adoptees and family members? • How are siblings affected by difficulties with attachment?	• Why do some adoptees have difficulty in making attachments to their adoptive parents and family members? • Do racial differences influence attachment of Chinese adoptees? • How do Chinese and Chinese Americans view ICA from China?

Increasingly, researchers are being asked to provide answers to policy and practice questions connected to intercountry adoption (Serbin, 1997). The use of systematic inquiry reflecting different investigative perspectives provides the best approach to gaining a comprehensive understanding of relevant issues, as well as identifying useful alternatives to address problems and concerns. Fu-

Table 9.1 (*continued*)

Major areas of inquiry	Empirical–analytic paradigm
Acknowledging Chinese cultural heritage	• When are optimal times for families to initiate or reduce focus on Chinese heritage? • How do parents acknowledge their child's Chinese cultural heritage? • What influence do different approaches to acknowledging Chinese cultural heritage have on later development? • What patterns of acknowledging and rejecting physical or cultural differences are present in adoptive families?
Racism-discrimination and transracial adoption	• How do people in the U.S. and PRC view ICA from China? • What factors influence people's reaction to ICA? Is race an important factor? • Do incidents of racial discrimination increase with adoptees' age? What types of incidents are reported?
Preferential adoption	• What are the most effective methods of preparing siblings for arrival of a sister or brother from China? • Do preferential families experience more or less stress than other adopters? • Do coping styles and degree of acknowledging adoption differ between traditional and preferential adopters?
Identity development	• Does a developmental process based on racial identity exist for Chinese adoptees • What is the impact of early and sustained involvement in Chinese socialization activities on adoptees' identity development? • Does frequent interaction with Chinese Americans in social, school, and neighborhood settings influence adoptee identity development? • Does a strong sense of ethnic identity promote psychological well-being? Is it necessary?

ture investigations of intercountry adoption from China should first articulate current and emerging levels of understanding in a given area of study, and then outline the types of information still needed to address pressing issues and concerns.

Interpretive paradigm	Critical perspective
• What meanings do adoptive families and others place on adoptees' Chinese cultural heritage? • How do relatives and nonadoptive families react to a family's acknowledgment of Chinese cultural heritage? • Why do adoptive families join support groups like Families with Children from China?	• Do adoptees benefit socially or emotionally from having an emphasis placed on their Chinese origins? • Will acknowledgment of cultural heritage reduce potential for isolation from mainstream and Chinese social groups?
• How do Chinese adoptees and their families react to incidents of racism or discrimination? • How do parents explain racism and discrimination to their adopted child?	• Why do people react negatively to transracial adoption? • What can adoption professionals and families do to decrease negative reactions toward ICA? • Can adoptive parents adequately prepare their adoptees to successfully cope with racial bias and discrimination?
• How do single adoptive parents view their decision to adopt a child from China? • What types of problems do single parents face when adopting from China?	• How do adoption agencies influence prospective parents' decisions to adopt from China?
• How do adoptees' describe their sense of identity? What meanings do they attach to their Chinese origins? • What are the feelings of adoptees when interacting with Chinese or Caucasian groups of peers at school? In community?	• What is the influence of external pressures on identity development? • Does race influence adolescent adoptees' choices of friends? Dating? Career? • What meanings do Chinese adoptees attribute to searching for their birth families?

SUMMARY

Despite the sensitivity of the Chinese government to outside scrutiny and criticism of their internal affairs, CCAA officials have placed substantial attention and importance on receiving postplacement reports about Chinese children placed in the United States and elsewhere.[3] Guo Sijin (1999), director general of the CCAA, commented on his hope that "adoption organizations will attach importance to post-placement report[s] on the life and upbringing of the children in the adoptive families. . . . To a certain extent, to serve the post-placement well appears to be more important than serving the preadoption. It is also a measurement by which we judge the quality of work done by the adoption organization."

In a sense, our investigation serves as a postplacement report, and contributes to an emerging body of literature on the life experience of children adopted from China and their adoptive families. For the most part the report is extremely positive and reveals the variety of perspectives and approaches taken by families toward issues of cultural heritage and adoption. In years to come we will be eager to learn about various aspects of the long-term development of Chinese adoptees. Based on the cumulative knowledge of intercountry adoption, we are optimistic that development will be a relatively normal one.

We are hopeful that, armed with an ever-greater understanding of intercountry adoption and the experiences of children adopted from China and their families, society will begin to acknowledge and celebrate the racial and cultural diversity that exists in growing numbers of families throughout North America. That through this recognition and celebration we gain a deepening understanding and appreciation of the meaning of family and community. And, equally important, that we, as a global community, come to recognize the common bonds we all share as part of humanity.

NOTES

1. Families with Children from China is composed of a network of not-for-profit, volunteer parent-support groups located throughout the United States, Canada, and the United Kingdom. FCC chapters vary in their structure, from formal organizations guided with by-laws and a board of directors to loose-knit groups that provide support and opportunities for interaction. The organization promotes three goals: (1) to support families who have adopted a child from China through postadoption and Chinese cultural programs, (2) to encourage and support families waiting to adopt a child from China, and (3) to advocate for and support children remaining in Chinese orphanages. Examples of the types of activities offered by various FCC chapters include newsletters, family picnics and potluck suppers, celebrations of Chinese festivals and holidays, preadoption information meetings, Chinese language and culture classes for children, and parent speakers (FCC, 1999b). Our Chinese Daughters Foundation was founded by Dr. Jane Liedtke, herself an adoptive mother of a daughter from China,

in 1995 as a nonprofit private foundation designed to be both a funding agency and a support group for single parents and their children adopted from China. OCDF provides funding to single parents, primarily women, for a variety of endeavors, including adoption travel, developing parent support groups, Chinese cultural programs such as summer culture camp, and educational scholarships for adoptive mothers and their daughters (Liedtke & Brasseur, 1997).

2. We feel, as many do, that incountry alternatives for child placement should be vigorously pursued. However, if suitable options for placement are not available, then intercountry adoption can have distinct advantages (Bagley, 1993b; Bartholet, 1991, 1993a, 1996). We cannot justify, under any circumstances, the sacrificing of abandoned children in China or anywhere else in the world to force the development of incountry services and alternatives for orphaned and abandoned children. Unfortunately, children are often seen as evidence for failed government policy or national resources, rather than as children with fundamental needs and rights to shelter, food, family, and love.

3. As with most issues pertaining to the internal affairs of China, the U.S. Department of State (1999) advises people adopting a child from China to "act with discretion and decorum," and warns that "high profile attention to adoption in China could curtail or eliminate altogether adoption of Chinese children by persons from countries causing adoption to become the subject of public attention" (p. 2).

Select Studies Examining the Behavior and Adjustment Patterns of International Adoptees

Note: This table does not represent an exhaustive list of all research studies in the literature that examine behavioral or psychological adjustment and/or developmental issues of intercountry adoptees.

Appendix A
Select Studies Examining the Behavior and Adjustment Patterns of International Adoptees

Research study	Purpose of study	Participants
Rojewski, Shapiro, & Shapiro (2000)	Parental assessment of Chinese adoptee behavior in early childhood	Chinese adoptees (n = 45; 39 females, 6 males; $\underline{M}$ age = 46.9 months)
Aronson (1999)	Reviews medical issues most common in children adopted from China.	Not a single study, per se, but summary of results from adoption centers across the U.S. and over 650 children
Evan B. Donaldson Adoption Institute	Descriptive study of Korean adoptees as adults to gain insight into experiences and adjustment of Korean adoptees	167 Korean adult adoptees (82.0% female; $\underline{M}$ = 31 years; 70% were college graduates; age at time of adoption, $\underline{Mdn}$ = 2 years old
Hendrie (n.d.)	Determine *overall health, behavioral adjustment* and *development* of Chinese adoptees	263 children adopted from China from 9/91–6/96 (females, n=248) from 28 orphanages in 8 provinces
Kim, Shin, & Carey (1999)	Compared psychosocial adjustment of Korean adoptees with biological children of adoptive parents	15 families representing 18 Korean adoptees (female, n = 14; $\underline{M}$ = 5.2 years) and 9 biological children (female, n = 4; $\underline{M}$ = 11.3 years)

Measurement(s)	Findings
Parent Rating Scale of Behavior Assessment System for Children (BASC)	• Means on all 9 BASC subscales fell within normal range • Variability on 4 scales (hyperactivity, aggression, conduct, attention) indicated elevated risk of problems, albeit small • Child's age at time of adoption was not a significant factor
Medical examinations and observations	• Adoptees have limited long-term medical problems. Medical issues are generally resolved with proper diagnosis and treatment • Many health issues of adoptees are health issues for all children in China • Top five medical issues in children living in China: rickets, malnutrition, anemia, lead poisoning, and asthma • About three-fourths of all adoptees exhibit developmental delay in at least one area
Self-developed questionnaires (sent to adults adopted through Holt International Services)	• One-third viewed selves as white when adolescents, but two-thirds viewed ethnicity as Korean American as adults. • Over half explored Korean heritage while growing up. • While growing up, three-fourths of adoptees involved in Korean adoptee organizations • 70% reported experience with some discrimination • Three-fourths had no knowledge of Korean language
Medical examinations; health, speech–language, mobility, behavior	• 96% of group tested negative for Hepatitis B • 12% had abnormally high levels of lead or internal parasites • No adoptee tested positive for syphilis or AIDS • Normal childhood infections fewer than expected • 8 children experienced attachment difficulties • 40% reported to be superior in intelligence • Overall, adoptees were extraordinary healthy, and have done well adjusting to new families
• Structured demographic, medical, and clinical survey • Child Behavior Checklist–Parent Report (CBCL–P; Achenbach & Edelbrock, 1983)	• Behavior/emotional: ANCOVA used to adjust for age differences; biological children significantly higher on internalizing behavior; no differences on total or externalizing problem subscales • Competence: Adoptees less competent on social subscale but no significant difference on others (activities, school) • Overall, considered well adjusted

Appendix A (*continued*)

Research study	Purpose of study	Participants
Westhues & Cohen (1998a)	Perceptions of adult adoptees on adjustment and integration issues; belonging, acceptance, self-esteem, comfort with race-ethnicity, and racism	A total of 155 adult adoptees in Canada; representing many countries (40% of sample from South Korea, only 1 person from China)
Wickes & Slate (1997)	Explored psychological issues of self-concept and acculturation for adult Korean adoptees	Sample of 174 adult Korean adoptees (females, $n = 138$; M age = 23.9 years)
Simon & Altstein (1991)	Assessed the interactive effects of intercountry adoption on the psychosocial adjustment of adoptees and adoptive parents and siblings.	2 samples: (1) 59 families (94 adoptees) in Star of David (50% of adoptees were Korean or other Asian); (2) 21 families (42 adoptees) in Families Adopting Children Everywhere (75% of adoptees were Korean or other Asian).
Saetersdal & Dalen (1991); Dalen & Saetersdal (1987)	Investigated Indian and Vietnamese adoptees and their Norwegian parents (families)	182 Norwegian parents with Indian or Vietnamese children under age 17 years of age (81% of population); 98 Vietnamese adoptees aged 17 to 22 years old and their parents

Measurement(s)	Findings
• Qualitative interviews • Family Integration scale (Gill & Jackson, 1983) • Index of Peer Relations (Hudson, 1982) • Self-concept scale (Rosenberg, 1965) • Ethnic Identity Index– modified (Isajiw, 1981)	• Strong sense of family belonging; no differences based on gender, age at placement, or country of origin • No significant differences in proportions having difficulty with peer relations by gender, age at placement, or origin • Self-esteem of adoptees was higher than general population • Adoptees had weaker sense of ethnic-racial identity than adoptees in families of similar background • Over half had experienced some form of racism or discrimination
• Demographic data sheet • Self-description questionnaire– III (Marsh, 1987) • Suinn-Lew Asian Self-Identity Acculturation scale (Suinn, Rickard-Figueroa, Lew, & Vigil, 1987) • Asian American Cultural Identity scale (Lee, 1988)	• Korean adoptees exhibited higher mean scores than norms on religion, physical appearance, honesty, relations with opposite sex, and general self-concept • Korean adoptees exhibited lower mean scores than norms on math, emotional stability, and relations with parents self-concept • The older adoptees were at time of adoption, the higher math and honesty, but the lower verbal self-concept scores • Adoptees perceived themselves as acculturated into the mainstream or dominant culture • Conclusion: acculturation, cultural identity, and placement had limited influence on self-concept
Personal interviews in homes with parents and children.	• Adoptee academic performance was average or above • Self-esteem was fairly equivalent to birth children • Adoptees had comparable feelings of family integration to birth children (siblings) • Looking different than parents was not a problem for two-thirds of adoptees • Concluded that older children present greater risks for adoptive parents
• Researcher-developed questionnaire • In-depth interviews with adoptees	• 73% of children (India) had satisfactory physical condition • Over ½ of adoptees showed initial adjustment problems (e.g., sleeping, eating). One-third had serious adjustment problems, substantial progress between 3 and 12 months • Majority of Vietnamese adoptees were psychologically and socially well adjusted • Social development in school considered very good • Language problems (comprehension) for older adoptees • Lack of academic attainment limited future career goals • Psychological paradox; "Norwegian soul in Vietnamese body"

Appendix A *(continued)*

Research study	Purpose of study	Participants
Feigelman & Silverman (1983)	Interested in changing trends of adoption in late 1970s and early 1980s including intercountry adoption, examined how preferential parents responded to adoption	Subgroup of larger study of families with children adopted from Korea ($n =$ 298; M age $= 17.4$ years old)
Kim, Hong, & Kim (1979)	Explored the adjustment patterns and behavioral development of Korean adoptees in the U.S.	15 white families in New York who adopted 21 Korean children (females, $n = 12$)
Kim (1977)	First nationwide (U.S.) study on the self-concept of Korean adolescent adopted as children	406 Korean children adopted by U.S. families; age ranged from 12 to 17 years old (M age $= 14$ years, 1 month old)

Measurement(s)	Findings
Researcher-developed questionnaire	• Between 50 and 67% of adoptees had pride in birth culture. • 26% of adoptees expressed discomfort with physical appearance • 74% of Korean adoptees felt well adjusted; 65% were free of serious emotional problems; 9% received professional help • 55% of adoptees were above average in school work; 46% had above average interest in school activities • Age of placement influenced adjustment. The older at placement, the more frequent and serious adjustment problems
Self-developed questionnaire looking at 8 areas of development	• Primary reason for adopting was desire to have a child; varying degrees of interest in helping adoptees learn about Korean cultural–heritage, uncertain about how to proceed • Nine couples reported behavioral symptoms in 16 (of 21) adoptees in which they sought or thought about seeking professional help • Temper tantrums, excessive or frequent crying were common when adopted before age 3; for those adopted after age 3, learning difficulty and shyness–withdrawal were common • Behavior was transient reaction or adjustment to new environment
• Researcher-developed questionnaires • Supplemental interviews and observations	• Most parents were very satisfied with health, development, interpersonal relationships, academic and cultural adjustment, maturity, and socialization • Adoptees had little Korean identity; lost cultural patterns rapidly; self-concept was similar to native born adolescents • Adoptees placed at older ages fared almost as well as those placed earlier • Supportive family climate and open communication positively affected self-concept

Select Studies Examining How Adoptive Families Acknowledge and Nurture the Cultural Heritage of Intercountry Adoptees

Note: This table does not represent an exhaustive list of all research studies in the literature that examine acknowledgment of intercountry adoptees' cultural heritage.

Appendix B
Select Studies Examining How Adoptive Families Acknowledge and Nurture the Cultural Heritage of Intercountry Adoptees

Research study	Purpose of study	Participants
Tessler, Gamache, & Liu (1999)	Examined the attitudes and experiences of parents with children adopted from China about bicultural socialization issues. Focused on importance parents attach to nurturing or reinforcing child's birth culture	Total of 526 parents representing 361 families and 391 children adopted from China (97% female; M age = 2.1 years)
Westhues & Cohen (1998b)	Sought answers to a series of questions dealing with identity development of adoptees, particularly bicultural (ethnic-racial) identity	155 adolescents and young adults living in Canada; representing many countries (73% female; 40% of sample from South Korea, only 1 person from China)
Trolley, Wallin, & Hansen (1995)	Families' perceptions toward the relevance, frequency, and means of acknowledging adoption and birth culture	34 families from western New York state who adopted internationally (54.4% of adoptees were Asian, M age = 6 years)
Altstein et al. (1994)	Examined the psychosocial adjustment of intercountry adoptees and their families. Was particularly interested in religious and ethnic practices of respondents	A total of 29 adoptees and 23 sets of parents participated (females, n = 26; M = 22 years; all Asian-born with 90% from Korea)
Simon & Altstein (1991)	Assessed the interactive effects of intercountry adoption on the psychosocial adjustment of adoptees and adoptive parents and siblings	Two samples: (1) 59 families (94 adoptees) in Star of David (50% of adoptees were Korean or other Asian); (2) 21 families (42 adoptees) in Families Adopting Children Everywhere (75% were Korean or other Asian).
Feigelman & Silverman (1983)	Interested in changing trends of adoption in late 1970s and early 1980s including intercountry adoption; examined how preferential parents responded to adoption	Subgroup of a larger study consisting of families with children adopted from Korea (n = 298; M age = 17.4 years)

Measurement(s)	Findings
• 16-page paper and pencil questionnaire • First-person stories • Historical accounts • Key informant perspective	• Some importance attached to most measures of Chinese socialization • Parents did not agree about the importance of specific facets of Chinese socialization • Parents mostly agreed with importance of their child being proud of Chinese heritage, exposed to Chinese culture, learning about China and the area where they were born • One-third of parents had as much opportunity to learn about Chinese heritage as desired (often linked to residence); culture camps and language classes often used • Over one-half of parents indicated no negative reactions from others to adoption of child from China (few problems)
Qualitative interviews containing research questions about adoptees' view on ethnicity and race (e.g., identity, importance, comfort level, parents' activities to promote racial-ethnic identity, etc.)	• 51% of males and 40% of females thought of themselves as Canadian. One-quarter of males and one-third of females identified ethnically with country of origin • Almost half said ethnicity and race are important or very important • Over three-fourths were comfortable or very comfortable with their ethnicity and race • Books (62.4%) and cultural events (36.0%) were most common activities provided by parents to promote ethnicity-race • One-half of parents had friends of same ethnicity-race as child • One-half of families had neighbors of same ethnicity-race as child
• Attitudes Toward Adoption questionnaire (Kirk, 1988) • Culture Form (Trolley, 1995)	• Majority of parents discussed adoption with children and others on occasional or frequent basis • Most parents felt exposure to birth culture was beneficial, but may not be a priority • Majority of parents believed that awareness of birth culture is related to adoptee's self-identity • Books were a primary means of exposure to birth culture • Half of the sample noted seldom making contact with people of the adoptee's racial background
Face-to-face interviews composed of 40 closed-ended questions	• 24 of 29 said their teenage best friend was Caucasian • 20 of 29 dated mostly Caucasian people during high school • 72% characterized neighbors as all or mostly white • 79% had artifacts in home representing native cultural heritage • Adoption made little difference in family dynamics • Adoptees reported heightened interest in birth culture during adolescence as identity formation occurred
Personal interviews in homes with parents and children.	• 75% reported engaging in ceremonies and rituals derived from adoptee's birth culture (books, artifacts, friends, organizations)
Researcher-developed questionnaire	• Substantial minority of parents actively encouraged children to learn about birth culture: 40% read or provided reading material on Korean culture; 87% occasionally talked about Korean background; 37% of families attended events associated with culture

References

Achenbach, T. M., & Edelbrock, C. (1983). *Manual for the child behavior checklist and revised child behavior profile*. Burlington: University of Vermont, Department of Psychiatry.

Adomavicius, J. (n.d.). *Adoption issues*. Retrieved December 28, 1999, from the World Wide Web: http://www.rainbowkids.com

Adopt.org (n.d.). *What you need to know about single parent adoption*. Retrieved May 21, 2000, from the World Wide Web: http://www.adopt. org/datacenter/bin/AQ_single1.htm

Ainsworth, M.D.S. (1973). The development of infant–mother attachment. In B. M. Caldwell & H. N. Riccuitti (Eds.), *Review of child development research* (Vol. 3, pp. 1–94). Chicago: University of Chicago Press.

Ainsworth, M.D.S. (1979). Infant–mother attachment. *American Psychologist, 34,* 932–937.

Alexander, R., Jr., & Curtis, C. M. (1996). A review of empirical research involving the transracial adoption of African American children. *Journal of Black Psychology, 22,* 223–235.

Alperson, M. (1997). *The international adoption handbook: How to make an overseas adoption work for you*. New York: Holt.

Altstein, H., Coster, M., First-Hartling, L., Ford, C., Glasoe, B., Hairston, S., Kasoff, J., & Grier, A. (1994). Clinical observations of adult intercountry adoptees and their adoptive parents. *Child Welfare, 73,* 261–269.

Altstein, H., & Simon, R. J. (1991). Introduction. In H. Alstein & R. J. Simon (Eds.), *Intercountry adoption: A multinational perspective* (pp. 1–20). New York: Praeger.

Aronson, J. (1999, May 17). *An update on health issues in children adopted from China.* Retrieved February 29, 2000, from the World Wide Web: http://members.aol.com/Jaronmink/upchina.htm

Aronson, J. (n.d.). *Overview of health issues and alcohol-related disorders in children adopted from abroad.* Retrieved February 29, 2000, from the World Wide Web: http://members.aol.com/Jaronmink/overview.htm

Bagley, C. (1992). The psychology of adoption: Case studies of national and international adoptions. *Bulletin of Hong Kong Psychological Society, 28/29,* 95–115.

Bagley, C. (1993a). Chinese adoptees in Britain: A twenty year follow-up of adjustment and social identity. *International Social Work, 36,* 143–157.

Bagley, C. (1993b). *International and transracial adoptions: A mental health perspective.* Brookfield, VT: Ashgate.

Bagley, C., & Young, L. (1981). The long-term adjustment of a sample of intercountry adopted children. *International Social Work, 23,* 16–22.

Bartholet, E. (1991). Where do black children belong? The politics of race matching in adoption. *University of Pennsylvania Law Review, 139,* 1163–1256.

Bartholet, E. (1993a). *Family bonds: Adoption and the politics of parenting.* New York: Houghton Mifflin.

Bartholet, E. (1993b). International adoption: Current status and future prospects. *The Future of Children: Adoption, 3* (1), 89–103.

Bartholet, E. (1996). What's wrong with adoption law? *International Journal of Children's Rights, 4,* 263–272.

Bartholet, E. (1998). *Adoption and race.* Retrieved March 17, 2000, from the World Wide Web: http://www.pactadopt.org/press/articles/adopt-race.html

Bausch, R. S., & Serpe, R. T. (1997). Negative outcomes of interethnic adoption of Mexican American children. *Social Work, 42,* 136–143.

Benson, P. L., Sharma, A. R., & Roehlkepartain, E. C. (1995). New study identified strengths of adoptive families. *Search Institute: Growing up adopted.* Retrieved December 30, 1999, from the World Wide Web: http://www.search-institute.org/archives/gua.htm

Berry, J. W. (1980). Acculturation as varieties of adaptation. In A. M. Padilla (Ed.), *Acculturation: Theory, model, and some new findings* (pp. 9–25). Boulder, CO: Westview.

Boeree, C. G. (n.d.). *Erik Erikson: Personality theories.* Retrieved January 7, 2000, from the World Wide Web: http://www.ship.edu/~cgboeree/erikson.html

Borchers, D. A. (1999). *An open letter to pediatricians on Chinese adoption medical issues.* Retrieved May 1, 2000, from the World Wide Web: http://catalog.com/fwfc/pediatricianletter.html

Bowlby, J. (1969). *Attachment and loss: Vol. 1. Attachment.* New York: Basic Books.

Bradley, N. (n.d.). *Sampling for Internet surveys: An examination of respondents selection for Internet research*. Retrieved June 26, 2000, from the World Wide Web: http://www.wmin.ac.uk/~bradlen/papers/sam06.html

Brodzinsky, D. M. (1987). Adjustment to adoption: A psychosocial perspective. *Clinical Psychology Review, 7*, 24–47.

Brodzinsky, D. M. (1993). Long-term outcomes in adoption. *The Future of Children: Adoption, 3* (1), 153–166.

Brodzinsky, D. M., Schechter, M. D., & Henig, R. M. (1992). *Being adopted: The lifelong search for self*. New York: Anchor Books.

Brodzinsky, D. M., Smith, D. W., & Brodzinsky, A. B. (1998). *Children's adjustment to adoption*. Thousand Oaks, CA: Sage.

Brooks, D., Barth, R. P., Bussiere, A., & Patterson, G. (1999). Adoption and race: Implementing the Multiethnic Placement Act and the Interethnic Adoption Provisions. *Social Work, 44*, 167–178.

Buck, P. S. (1972). *The good earth*. New York: Pocket Books.

Carstens, C., & Julia, M. (1995). Legal, policy and practice issues for intercountry adoptions in the United States. *Adoption & Fostering, 19* (4), 26–33.

Carstens, C., & Julia, M. (2000). Ethnoracial awareness in intercountry adoption: U.S. experiences. *International Social Work, 43*, 61–73.

Cecere, L. A. (1999). *October 1998 amendment of China's adoption law*. Retrieved July 18, 2000, from the World Wide Web: http://www.autocyt.com/China_Seas/chinaslaw.html

Coomber, R. (1997). Using the Internet for survey research. *Sociological Research Online, 2* (2). Retrieved June 26, 2000, from the World Wide Web: http://www.socresonline.org.uk/socresonline/2/2/2.html

Courtney, M. E. (1997). The politics and realities of transracial adoption. *Child Welfare, 76*, 749–779.

Crawford, B. (1998). Need to support Chinese identity. *China Connection*. Retrieved November 9, 1999, from the World Wide Web: http://mh106.infi.net/~bcrawf/needsupp.htm

Creswell, J. W. (1998). *Qualitative inquiry and research design: Choosing among five traditions*. Thousand Oaks, CA: Sage.

Crnic, L. S., Reite, M. L., & Shucard, D. W. (1982). Animal models of human behavior: Their application to the study of attachment. In R. N. Emde & R. J. Harmon (Eds.), *The development of attachment and affiliative systems* (pp. 31–42). New York: Plenum.

Cross, W. E. (1994). Nigrescence theory: Historical and explanatory notes. *Journal of Vocational Behavior, 44*, 119–123.

Culp, T. (1996, March). How much Chinese culture? E-mail message to listserve. Retrieved December 7, 1999, from the World Wide Web: http://www.pshrink.com/chinadopt/How_Much_Culture.html

Dalen, M., & Saetersdal, B. (1987). Transracial adoption in Norway. *Adoption & Fostering, 11* (4), 41–46.

Deacon, S. A. (1997). Intercountry adoption and the family life cycle. *American Journal of Family Therapy, 25*, 245–260.

de Anda, D., & Riddel, V. A. (1991). Ethnic identity, self-esteem, and interpersonal relationships among multiethnic adolescents. *Journal of Multicultural Social Work, 1,* 83–98.

Dhooper, S. S. (1991). Toward an effective response to the needs of Asian-Americans. *Journal of Multicultural Social Work, 1,* 65–81.

Dodds, P. (1999). *International adoption: Opening Pandora's box.* Retrieved December 1, 1999, from the World Wide Web: http://www.adopting.org/dodds.html

Ebrey, P. (1981). *Chinese civilization and society: A sourcebook.* New York: Free Press.

Erikson, E. H. (1963). *Childhood and society* (2nd ed.). New York: W. W. Norton.

Erikson, E. H. (1968). *Identity: Youth and crisis.* New York: W. W. Norton.

Evan B. Donaldson Adoption Institute. (n.d.). *Survey of Korean adoptees* (Report of findings). Retrieved September 23, 1999, from the World Wide Web: http://www.adoptioninstitute.org/proed/korfindings.html

Evans, K. (2000). *The lost daughters of China.* New York: Tarcher/Putnam.

Evans, M. (1997). International adoption: Changes and challenges. *Adoptive Families.* Retrieved September 23, 1999, from the World Wide Web: http://www.jcics.org/afa.html

Evans, M. (2000). *The Hague Convention on Intercountry Adoption.* Retrieved on March 29, 2000, from the World Wide Web: http://www.jcics.org/hagueinfo.html

Fancott, H. (n.d.). *Attachment: What is it and why is it important?* Retrieved February 29, 2000, from the World Wide Web: http://www.bcadoption.com/Info/Articles/attachment.htm

FCC (Families with Children from China). (2001). *Statistical information on adoptions from China.* Retrieved January 15, 2000, from the World Wide Web: http://www.fwcc.org/statistics.html

FCC. (1999a, October). *Frequently asked questions about adoption in China.* Retrieved April 4, 2000, from the World Wide Web: http://www.fwcc.org/faq.htm

FCC. (1999b, February). *Information about Families with Children from China.* Retrieved July 29, 2000, from the World Wide Web: http://www.catalog.com/cgibin/var/fwcfc/facinfo.htm

Feigelman, W. (2000). Adjustments of transracially and inracially adopted young adults. *Child and Adolescent Social Work Journal, 17,* 165–183.

Feigelman, W., & Silverman, A. R. (1983). *Chosen children: New patterns of adoptive relationships.* New York: Praeger.

Fieweger, M. E. (1991). Stolen children and international adoptions. *Child Welfare, 70,* 285–291.

Fisher, B., Margolis, M., & Resnick, D. (1996). Surveying the Internet: Democratic theory and civic life in cyberspace. *Southeastern Political Review, 24* (3).

Freivalds, S. (2000). The Hague Convention on intercountry adoption: An international treaty that recognizes the right of every child to a permanent family. *Adoptive Families, 33* (2), 24–26.

Friedlander, M. L. (1999). Ethnic identity development of internationally adopted children and adolescents: Implications for family therapists. *Journal of Marital and Family Therapy, 25* (1), 43–60.

Gall, M. D., Borg, W. R., & Gall, J. P. (1996). *Educational research: An introduction* (6th ed.). White Plains, NY: Longman.

Gill, O., & Jackson, B. (1983). *Adoption and race: Asian and mixed race children in white families.* New York: St. Martin's Press.

Gindis, B. (n.d.). *Navigating uncharted waters: School psychologists working with internationally adopted post-institutionalized children* (copy of article originally published in *COMMUNIQUE, 27*). Retrieved on October 12, 1999, from the World Wide Web: http://j51.com/~tatyana/communique-article.htm

Goddard, L. L. (1996). Transracial adoption: Unanswered theoretical and conceptual issues. *Journal of Black Psychology, 22,* 273–281.

Gorman, P. (1999, November). *The Korean adoption experience: A look into our future?* Retrieved on March 9, 2000, from the World Wide Web: http://222.catalog.com/fwcfc/kopreanadoption.html

Grotevant, H. D. (1992). Assigned and chosen identity components: A process perspective on their integration. In G. Adams, T. Gullotta, & R. Montemayor (Eds.), *Adolescent identity formation* (pp. 73–90). Newbury Park, CA: Sage.

Grotevant, H. D. (1997a). Coming to terms with adoption: The construction of identity from adolescence into adulthood. *Adoption Quarterly, 1,* 3–27.

Grotevant, H. D. (1997b). Family processes, identity development, and behavioral outcomes for adopted adolescents. *Journal of Adolescent Research, 12,* 139–161.

Grotevant, H. D., & McRoy, R. G. (1990). Adopted adolescents in residential treatment: The role of the family. In D. M. Brodzinsky & M. D. Schechter (Eds.), *The psychology of adoption* (pp. 167–186). New York: Oxford University Press.

Grow, L., & Shapiro, D. (1974). *Black children, white parents: A study of transracial adoption.* New York: Child Welfare League of America.

Groze, V. (1991). Adoption and single parents: A review. *Child Welfare, 70,* 321–332.

Groze, V., & Rosenthal, J. A. (1993). Attachment theory and adoption of children with special needs. *Social Work Research and Abstracts, 29* (2), 5–12.

Guo, S. (1999, October). *Speech at the seminar of the adoption organizations of the four Scandinavian countries (excerpts).* Retrieved April 4, 2000, from the World Wide Web: http://www.chinaccaa.org/amjhe.htm

GVU's (Graphic, Visualization, and Usability Center) WWW Surveying Team. (n.d.). *GVU's 10th WWW survey results* [Research report]. Retrieved January 10, 2000, from the World Wide Web: http://www.gvu.gatech.edu/user_surveys/survey-1998-10/

Halsall, P. (1995). *Chinese cultural studies: Understanding culture* [Course handout]. Retrieved January 31, 2000, from the World Wide Web: http://academic.Brooklyn.cuny.edu/core9/phalsall/texts/culture.html

Harnott, C., & Robertson, R. (1999). Intercountry adoption: Implications for adoption agencies and medical advisers. *Adoption & Fostering, 23* (4), 26–34.

Harrison, A. O. (1996). Comments on transracial adoption. *Journal of Black Psychology, 22,* 236–239.

Hartman, A., & Laird, J. (1990). Family treatment after adoption: Common themes. In D. M. Brodzinsky & M. D. Schechter (Eds.), *The psychology of adoption* (pp. 221–239). New York: Oxford University Press.

Helms, J. E. (1984). Toward a theoretical explanation of the effects of race on counseling: A black and white model. *Counseling Psychologist, 12,* 153–165.

Helms, J. E. (1995). An update of Helms' white and people of color racial identity models. In J. G. Ponterotto, J. M. Casas, L. A. Suzuki, & C. M. Alexander (Eds.), *Handbook of multicultural counseling* (pp. 181–198). Thousand Oaks, CA: Sage.

Hendrie, N. W. (n.d.). *Follow up medical study of 263 Chinese babies and children adopted by American families* (Summary of findings). Retrieved November 20, 1999, from the World Wide Web: http://www.ultranet.com/~emd92/hendrie.html

Herbert, M. (1988). *Working with children and their families.* Chicago: Lyceum.

Hoksbergen, R.A.C. (1997). Turmoil for adoptees during adolescence? *International Journal of Behavioral Development, 20,* 33–46.

Hollingsworth, L. D. (1997). Effect of transracial/transethnic adoption on children's racial and ethnic identity and self-esteem: A meta-analytic review. *Families and Adoption,* 99–130.

Hollingsworth, L. D. (1998). Adoptee dissimilarity from the adoptive family: Clinical practice and research implications. *Child and Adolescent Social Work Journal, 15,* 303–319.

Holt International. (2000, July). *An explanation of Holt's services and fees.* Retrieved July 18, 2000, from the World Wide Web: http://www.holtintl.org/fees.html

Hoopes, J. L. (1990). Adoption and identity formation. In D. M. Brodzinsky & M. D. Schechter (Eds.), *The psychology of adoption* (pp. 144–166). New York: Oxford University Press.

Howard, C. (2000). Deciding on a second child. *Adoptive Families, 22* (2), 28–31.

Huang, B. (2000). *Scholars report on their visits with adoptive parents.* Retrieved May 15, 2000, from the World Wide Web: http://www.night.net/rosie/9805-scholar.html

Huck, S. W. (2000). *Reading statistics and research* (3d ed.). New York: Addison Wesley Longman.

Hudson, W. (1982). *The clinical measurement package: A field manual.* Homewood, IL: Dorsey.

Huh, N. S., & Reid, W. J. (2000). Intercountry, transracial adoption and ethnic identity. *International Social Work, 43,* 75–87.

INS (Immigration and Naturalization Service). (1999, July). *International adoptions—1989–1998.* Retrieved July 25, 1999, from the World Wide Web: http://www.hopeforchildren.org/adoptionsgraph.html

Isajiw, W. (1981). *Ethnic identity retention.* Canada: University of Toronto, Department of Sociology.

Jaisingani, S., & Jain, A. (1998). Using the World Wide Web as a survey tool. Retrieved on January 7, 2000, from the World Wide Web: http://www.usfca.edu/~huxleys/UsingWWW.html

Jenista, J. A., & Chapman, D. (1987). Medical problems of foreign-born adopted children. *American Journal of Diseases of Children, 141,* 293–302.

Johnson, D. (n.d.). *Adopting an institutionalized child: What are the risks?* Retrieved on October 15, 1999, from the World Wide Web: http://www.adoption-research.org/risks.html

Johnson, D., & Fein, E. (1991). The concept of attachment: Applications to adoption. *Children and Youth Services Review, 13,* 397–412.

Johnson, D., & Traister, M. (n.d.). *Health status of adopted Chinese orphans on arrival in the U.S.* (Summary of research findings). Retrieved on February 29, 2000, from the World Wide Web: http://www.fwcc.org/healthdanajohnson.html

Johnson, K. (1996). The politics of the revival of infant abandonment in China, with special reference to Hunan. *Population and Development Review, 22,* 77–98.

Johnson, K., Huang, B., & Wang, L. (1998). Infant abandonment and adoption in China. *Population and Development Review, 24,* 469–510.

Joint Council on International Children's Services. (1999). *The Adopted Orphaned Citizenship Act.* Retrieved July 27, 2000, from the World Wide Web: http://www.jcics.org/s1485.html

Joint Council on International Children's Services. (2000). *Hague Convention* (Web announcement). Retrieved March 29, 2000, from the World Wide Web: http://www.jcics.org/

Joint Council on International Children's Services. (n.d.). *The need for citizenship.* Retrieved July 27, 2000, from the World Wide Web: http://www.jcics.org/citizenship.html

Kane, S. (1993). The movement of children for international adoption: An epidemiologic perspective. *Social Science Journal, 30,* 323–339.

Keck, G. C., & Kupecky, R. M. (n.d.). What is reactive attachment disorder? Retrieved on February 29, 2000, from the World Wide Web: http://members.aol.com/RADchina/RADpg2.html

Kelly, J. (1999). Ethnic identity: Yours, mine, and ours (reprint of article appearing in the Fall 1999 issue of the *FCC–NY Newsletter*). Retrieved October 11, 2000, from the World Wide Web: http//www.lightlink.com/nyscc/T-Rarts/ethnicident.html

Kim, D. S. (1977). How they fared in American homes: A follow-up study of adopted Korean children. *Children Today, 6* (2), 2–6.

Kim, D. S. (1978). Issues in transracial and transcultural adoption. *Social Casework, 59,* 477–486.

Kim, S. P., Hong, S., & Kim, B. S. (1979). Adoption of Korean children by New York area couples: A preliminary study. *Child Welfare, 63,* 419–428.

Kim, W. J. (1995). International adoption: A case review of Korean children. *Child Psychiatry and Human Development, 25,* 141–154.

Kim, W. J., Shin, Y., & Carey, M. P. (1999). Comparison of Korean-American adoptees and biological children of their adoptive parents: A pilot study. *Child Psychiatry and Human Development, 29,* 221–228.

Kirk, H. D. (1964). *Shared fate.* New York: Free Press.

Kirk, H. D. (1984). *Shared fate* (rev. ed.). WA: Ben-Simon.

Kirk, H. D. (1985). *Adoptive kinship: A modern institution in need of reform* (rev. ed.). WA: Ben-Simon.

Kirk, H. D. (1988). *Exploring adoptive family life.* WA: Ben-Simon.

Kirk, H. D. (1997). Search and rescue: A belated critique of "Growing up adopted." *Families and Adoption, 25,* 225–249.

Klatzkin, A. (1999). *An overview of adoption in China in the 1990s.* Retrieved July 30, 1999, from the World Wide Web: http://www.bcadoption.com/fcc/NewsletterArticles/AnOverviewOfAdoptionInChina.htm

Krueger, C. (n.d.). *As your family grows . . . Things to think about when pursuing a second adoption.* Retrieved May 21, 2000, from the World Wide Web: http://www.fwcc.org/secondtime.html

Kwan, K. K., & Sodowsky, G. R. (1997). Internal and external ethnic identity and their correlates: A study of Chinese American immigrants. *Journal of Multicultural Counseling and Development, 25,* 51–67.

LaFromboise, T., Coleman, H.L.K., & Gerton, J. (1993). Psychological impact of biculturalism: Evidence and theory. *Psychological Bulletin, 114,* 395–412.

Lee, S. R. (1988). Self-concept correlates of Asian American cultural identity attitudes. *Dissertation Abstracts International, 49* (University Microfilms No. AAC8827090).

Leong, F.T.L., & Chou, E. L. (1994). The role of ethnic identity and acculturation in the vocational behavior of Asian Americans: An integrative review. *Journal of Vocational Behavior, 44,* 155–172.

Leung, B. (1987). *Cultural considerations in working with Asian parents.* Los Angeles: National Center for Clinical Infant Program (ERIC Document Reproduction Service No. ED 285 359).

Levy-Shiff, R., Zoran, N., & Shulman, S. (1997). International and domestic adoption: Child, parents, and family adjustment. *International Journal of Behavioral Development, 20,* 109–129.

Liedtke, J. A., & Brasseur, L. E. (Eds.). (1997). *New American families: Chinese daughters and their single mothers.* Bloomington, IL: StarNet Digital.

Mainemer, H., Gilman, L. C., & Ames, E. W. (1998). Parenting stress in families adopting children from Romanian orphanages. *Journal of Family Issues, 19,* 164–180.

Mannis, V. S. (1999). Single mothers by choice. *Family Relations, 48,* 121–128.

Marcia, J. (1980). Identity in adolescence. In J. Adelson (Ed.), *Handbook of adolescent psychology* (pp. 159–187). New York: Wiley.

Marsh, H. W. (1987). The big-fish–little-pond effect on academic self-concept. *Journal of Educational Psychology, 79,* 280–295.

McRoy, R., & Zurcher, L. (1983). *Transracial and inracial adoptees.* Springfield, IL: Thomas.

Meier, D. I. (1999). Cultural identity and place in adult Korean-American intercountry adoptees. *Adoption Quarterly, 3* (1), 15–48.

Melina, L. R. (1998). *Raising adopted children: Practical reassuring advice for every adoptive parent* (rev. ed.). New York: HarperPerennial.

Michalak, E. E., & Szabo, A. (1998). Guildines for Internet research: An update. *European Psychologist, 3* (1), 70–75.

Miller, L. C. (1999). Caring for internationally adopted children. *New England Journal of Medicine, 341* (20). Retrieved May 1, 2000, from the World Wide Web: http://www.nejm.org/content/1999/0341/0020/1539.asp

Miller, L. C., & Hendrie, N. W. (2000). Health of children adopted from China. *Pediatrics, 105* (6), E76.

National Adoption Information Clearinghouse. (1998, September). *Intercountry adoption.* Retrieved January 7, 2000, from the World Wide Web: http://www.calib.com/naic/factsheets/foreign.html

National Adoption Information Clearinghouse. (1999a, June). *The adoption home study process.* Retrieved February 1, 2000, from the World Wide Web: http://www.calib.com/naic/factsheets/homstudy.htm

National Adoption Information Clearinghouse. (1999b, December). *Adoption research and statistics: Intercountry adoption.* Retrieved January 25, 2000, from the World Wide Web: http://www.calib.com/naic/adptsear/adoption/research/stats/intercountry.htm

National Adoption Information Clearinghouse. (1999c, March). *Adoption statistics—A brief overview of the data.* Retrieved January 12, 2000, from the World Wide Web: http://www.calib.com/naic/adptsear/adoption/research/stats/overview.htm

National Adoption Information Clearinghouse. (1999d, March). *Explaining adoption to your child.* Retrieved July 21, 2000, from the World Wide Web: http://www.calib.com/naic/factsheets/explain.htm

National Adoption Information Clearinghouse. (1999e, April). *Transracial adoption.* Retrieved March 20, 2000, from the World Wide Web: http://www.calib.com/naic/adptsear/adoption/research/stats/transracial.htm

Neal, L. (1996). *Focal point: The case against transracial adoption* (Report from the Regional Research Institute for Human Services). Retrieved January 18, 2000, from the World Wide Web: http://www.rtc.pdx.edu/fp/spring96/transrac.htm

Oyserman, D., & Sakamoto, I. (1997). Being Asian American: Identity, cultural constructs, and stereotype perception. *Journal of Applied Behavioral Science, 33,* 435–453.

Parent Network for the Post-Institutionalized Child. (1995). *PNPC news* (Portions of parent newsletter). Retrieved on December 8, 1999, from the World Wide Web: http://www.pnpic.org/news3.html

Parham, T., & Helms, J. (1985). Attitudes of racial identity and self-esteem of black students: An exploratory investigation. *Journal of College Student Personnel, 26,* 143–147.

Park, E.J.W., & Park, J.S.W. (1999). A new American dilemma? Asian Americans and Latinos in race theorizing. *Journal of Asian American Studies, 2,* 289–309.

Pendry, P. (n.d.). *Ethological attachment theory: A great idea in personality?* Retrieved March 13, 2000, from the World Wide Web: http://galton.psych.nwu.edu/greatideas/papers/pendry.html

Perry, T. L. (1996). Thinking and teaching about transracial adoption. *FOCUS, 12* (1). Retrieved March 23, 2000, from the World Wide Web: http://www.abanet.org/publiced/focus/f96adop2.html

Petertyl, M. (1996, April 8). How much Chinese culture? (e-mail message to listserv). Retrieved December 7, 1999, from the World Wide Web: http://www.pshrink.com/chinadopt/How_Much_Culture.html

Pfund, P. H. (1996). *1993 Hague convention on intercountry adoption (rev.)* (Briefing paper). Retrieved January 20, 2000, from the World Wide Web: http://www.webcom.com/kmc/adoption/law/un/ica-briefing.html

Phinney, J. S. (1989). Stages of ethnic identity development in minority group adolescents. *Journal of Early Adolescence, 9,* 34–49.

Phinney, J. S. (1990). Ethnic identity in adolescents and adults: Review of research. *Psychological Bulletin, 108,* 499–514.

Portello, J. Y. (1993). The mother–infant attachment process in adoptive families. *Canadian Journal of Counselling, 27,* 177–190.

Power, M. B., & Eheart, B. K. (1995). Adoption, myth, and emotion work: Paths to disillusionment. In M. G. Flaherty & C. Ellis (Eds.), *Social perspectives on emotion* (pp. 97–120). Greenwich, CT: JAI Press.

Register, C. (1991). *Are those kids yours? American families with children adopted from other countries.* New York: Free Press.

Reitz, M. (1999). Groundswell change in adoption requires anchoring by research. *Child and Adolescent Social Work Journal, 16,* 327–354.

Richters, J. E., & Waters, E. (1991). Attachment and socialization: The positive side of social influence. In M. Lewis & S. Feinman (Eds.), *Social influences and socialization in infancy* (Genesis of Behavior Series, Vol. 6). New York: Plenum. Retrieved March 14, 2000, from the World Wide Web: http://www.psychology.sunysb.edu/ewaters/reprints/socializ/soc1.htm

Riley, N. E. (1997). American adoptions of Chinese girls: The sociopolitical matrices of individual decisions. *Women's Studies International Forum, 20,* 87–102.

Rivera, R. (2000). *The Hague treaty on intercountry adoptions.* Retrieved January 15, 2000, from the World Wide Web: http://r-rivera.com/haguearticle.html

Rojewski, J. W., Shapiro, M. S., & Shapiro, M. (2000). Parental assessment of behavior in Chinese adoptees during early childhood. *Child Psychiatry and Human Development, 31* (1), 79–96.

Rosenberg, K. F., & Groze, V. (1997). The impact of secrecy and denial in adoption: Practice and treatment issues. *Families in Society: The Journal of Contemporary Human Services, 78,* 522–530.

Rosenberg, M. (1965). *Society and the adolescent self-image.* Princeton, NJ: Princeton University Press.

Rotheram, M. J., & Phinney, J. S. (1987). Introduction: Definitions and perspectives in the study of children's ethnic socialization. In J. S. Phinney & M. J. Rotheram (Eds.), *Children's ethnic socialization: Pluralism and development* (pp. 10–28). Newbury Park, CA: Sage.

Rushton, A., & Minnis, H. (1997). Annotation: Transracial placements. *Journal of Child Psychology and Psychiatry, 38,* 157–159.

Rushton, A., & Minnis, H. (2000). Review research: Transracial placements. *Adoption & Fostering, 24* (1), 53–58.

Ryan, A. S. (1983). Intercountry adoption and policy issues. *Journal of Children in Contemporary Society, 15* (3), 49–60.

Saclier, C. (1999). Children and adoption: Which rights and whose? *Innocenti Digest, 4,* 12–13. Retrieved January 7, 2000, from the World Wide Web: http://www.unicef-icdc.org

Saetersdal, B., & Dalen, M. (1991). Norway: Intercountry adoptions in a homogeneous country. In H. Altstein & R. J. Simon (Eds.), *Intercountry adoption: A multinational perspective* (pp. 83–107). Westport, CT: Praeger.

Sarri, R. C., Baik, Y., & Bombyk, M. (1998). Goal displacement and dependency in South Korean–United States intercountry adoption. *Children and Youth Services Review, 20,* 87–114.

Schmidt, W. C. (1997). World-Wide Web survey research: Benefits, potential problems, and solutions. *Behavior Research Methods, Instruments, and Computers, 29,* 274–279.

Segall, M. M. (1986). Culture and behavior: Psychology in global perspective. *Annual Review of Psychology, 37,* 523–564.

Serbin, L. A. (1997). Research on international adoption: Implications for developmental theory and social policy. *International Journal of Behavioral Development, 20,* 83–92.

Sharma, A. R., McGue, M. K., & Benson, P. L. (1996). The emotional and behavioral adjustment of United States adopted adolescents: Part I. An overview. *Children and Youth Services Review, 18,* 83–100.

Shireman, J. F. (1988). *Growing up adopted: An examination of some major issues.* Chicago: Chicago Child Care Society.

Shireman, J. F. (1995). Adoptions by single parents. *Marriage & Family Review, 20,* 367–388.

Shireman, J. F. (1996). Single parent adoptive homes. *Children and Youth Services Review, 18,* 23–36.

Shireman, J. F., & Johnson, P. (1976). Single persons as adoptive parents. *Social Service Review, 50,* 103–116.

Shireman, J. F., & Johnson, P. (1985). Single parent adoptions: A longitudinal study. *Children and Youth Services Review, 7,* 321–334.

Silverman, A. R. (1993). Outcomes of transracial adoption. *The Future of Children: Adoption, 3* (1), 104–118.

Silverman, A. R., & Feigelman, W. (1990). Some factors affecting the adoption of minority children. *Social Casework, 58,* 554–561.

Simon, R. J., & Altstein, H. (1972). *Transracial adoption.* New York: Wiley.

Simon, R. J., & Altstein, H. (1987). *Transracial adoptees and their families: A study of identity and commitment.* New York: Praeger.

Simon, R. J., & Altstein, H. (1991). Intercountry adoptions: Experiences of families in the United States. In H. Altstein & R. J. Simon (Eds.), *Intercountry adoption: A multinational perspective* (pp. 24–54). New York: Praeger.

Simon, R. J., & Altstein, H. (1995). The case for transracial adoption. *Children and Youth Services Review, 18,* 5–22.

Simon, R. J., & Altstein, H. (2000). *Adoption across borders: Serving the children in transracial and intercountry adoption.* Lanham, MD: Rowman & Littlefield.

Singer, L. M., Brodzinsky, D. M., Ramsay, D., Steir, M., & Waters, E. (1985). Mother–infant attachment in adoptive families. *Child Development, 56,* 1543–1551.

Smith, C. B. (1997). Casting the nest: Surveying an Internet population. *Journal of Computer Mediated Communication, 3* (1).

Stirling, R. (2000). *Referral and age graphs.* Retrieved June 14, 2000, from the World Wide Web: http://homepages.wwc.edu/staff/stirra/waiting.htm

Stolley, K. S. (1993). Statistics on adoption in the United States. *The Future of Children: Adoption, 3* (1), 26–42.

Sue, S., & Sue, D. W. (1973). Chinese-American personality and mental health. In S. Sue & N. N. Wagner (Eds.), *Asian-Americans: Psychological perspectives* (pp. 111–124). Palo Alto, CA: Science and Behavior Books.

Suinn, R. M., Rickard-Figueria, K., Lew, S., & Vigil, P. (1987). The Suinn–Lew Asian self-identity acculturation scale: An initial report. *Educational and Psychological Measurement, 47,* 401–407.

Tessler, R., Gamache, G., & Liu, L. (1999). *West meets East: Americans adopt Chinese children.* Westport, CT: Bergin & Garvey.

Tizard, B. (1991). Intercountry adoption: A review of the evidence. *Journal of Child Psychology and Psychiatry and Allied Disciplines, 32,* 743–756.

Triseliotis, J., Shireman, J., & Hundleby, M. (1997). *Adoption theory, policy, and practice.* London: Cassell.

Trolley, B. C. (1995). Grief issues and positive aspects associated with international adoption. *Omega: Journal of Death and Dying, 30,* 257–268.

Trolley, B. C., Wallin, J., & Hansen, J. (1995). International adoption: Issues of acknowledgement of adoption and birth culture. *Child and Adolescent Social Work Journal, 12,* 465–479.

Tse, L. (1999). Finding a place to be: Ethnic identity exploration of Asian Americans. *Adolescence, 34,* 121–138.

UNICEF International Child Development Centre. (1999). Intercountry adoption. *Innocenti Digest, 4.* Retrieved January 7, 2000, from the World Wide Web: http://www.unicef-icdc.org

University of California, Irvine. (n.d.). *Psychosocial and moral growth and the learning process* (Online lecture notes). Retrieved January 7, 2000, from the World Wide Web: http://www.gse.uci.edu/ed173/resources/lectures/unit3_lectures.html

U.S. Department of State. (1999). *International adoption–China* (Government circular). Retrieved May 23, 2000, from the World Wide Web: http://www.usembassy-china.org.cn/english/us-citizen/adopt_acs.html

Verhulst, F. C., Althaus, M., & Versluis-den Bieman, H.J.M. (1990). Problem behavior in international adoptees: I. An epidemiological study. *Journal of the American Academy of Child and Adolescent Psychiatry, 29,* 94–103.

Verhulst, F. C., & Versluis-den Bieman, H.J.M. (1995). Developmental course of problem behaviors in adolescent adoptees. *Journal of the American Academy of Child and Adolescent Psychiatry, 34,* 151–159.

Versluis-den Bieman, H.J.M., & Verhulst, F. C. (1995). Self-reported and parent reported problems in adolescent international adoptees. *Journal of Child Psychology and Psychiatry and Allied Disciplines, 36,* 1411–1428.

Vonk, M. E., Simms, P. J., & Nackerud, L. (1999). Political and personal aspects of intercountry adoption of Chinese children in the United States. *Families in Society: The Journal of Contemporary Human Services, 80,* 496–505.

Watson, K. W. (1997). Bonding and attachment in adoption: Towards better understanding and useful definitions. *Marriage and Family Review, 25,* 159–173.

Wei, L. (1999). Amended law to improve adoption. *Beijing Review, 42* (8), 13–14.

Westhues, A., & Cohen, J. S. (1997). A comparison of the adjustment of adolescent and young adult intercountry adoptees and their siblings. *International Journal of Behavioral Development, 20,* 47–65.

Westhues, A., & Cohen, J. S. (1998a). The adjustment of intercountry adoptees in Canada. *Children and Youth Services Review, 20,* 115–134.

Westhues, A., & Cohen, J. S. (1998b). Ethnic and racial identity of internationally adopted adolescents and young adults: Some issues in relation to children's rights. *Adoption Quarterly, 1* (4), 33–55.

Wickes, K. L., & Slate, J. R. (1997). Transracial adoption of Koreans: A preliminary study of adjustment. *International Journal for the Advancement of Counselling, 19,* 187–195.

Wilkinson, H. S. (1995). Psycholegal process and issues in international adoption. *American Journal of Family Therapy, 23,* 173–183.

Winston, C. (1995). Building bridges to your child's ethnic community. *Roots and Wings Adoption Magazine.* Retrieved March 9, 2000, from the World Wide Web: http://www.adopting.org/fwbridge.htm

Zuniga, M. E. (1991). Transracial adoption: Educating the parents. *Journal of Multicultural Social Work, 1,* 17–31.

Author Index

Subject Index

ABOUT THE AUTHORS

Jay W. Rojewski is a professor in the Department of Occupational Studies, University of Georgia. He has published widely in scholarly journals primarily on his work with career behavior, career development, and occupational choice of adolescents and young adults. He is the past editor of the *Journal for Vocational Special Needs Education* and the *Journal of Vocational Education Research*. With his wife, Jacy, he is the proud parent of a four-year-old daughter, Emily, who was adopted from Fuzhou, China, in 1997, and baby Claire, who is waiting for the family in China.

Jacy L. Rojewski is a special education teacher at Morgan Country Middle School in Madison, Georgia, a state-recognized School of Excellence, where she is responsible for teaching students with mild learning and behavioral disabilities.